CW00905481

HITLER'S DEATH'S
HEAD DIVISION

PEN & SWORD MILITARY CLASSICS

We hope you enjoy your Pen and Sword Military Classic. The series is designed to give readers quality military history at affordable prices. Pen and Sword Classics are available from all good bookshops. If you would like to keep in touch with further developments in the series, telephone: 01226 734555, email: enquiries@pen-and-sword.co.uk, or visit our website at www.pen-and-sword.co.uk.

Published Classics Titles

Forthcoming Titles

HITLER'S DEATH'S HEAD DIVISION

SS-Totenkopf Division

Rupert Butler

PEN & SWORD MILITARY CLASSICS

First published in Great Britain in 1985 by by Arrow Books Limited
Published in 2004, in this format, by
PEN & SWORD MILITARY CLASSICS
an imprint of
Pen & Sword Books Limited
47 Church Street
Barnsley
S. Yorkshire
S70 2AS

ISBN 1 84415 205 7

A CIP record for this book
is available from the British Library.

Printed and bound in Great Britain by
CPI UK

Pen & Sword Books Ltd incorporates the imprints of
Pen & Sword Aviation, Pen & Sword Maritime, Pen & Sword Military,
Wharncliffe Local History, Pen & Sword Select,
Pen & Sword Military Classics and Leo Cooper

For a complete list of Pen & Sword titles please contact:
PEN & SWORD BOOKS LIMITED
47 Church Street, Barnsley, South Yorkshire, S70 2AS, England.
E-mail: enquiries@pen-and-sword.co.uk
Website: www.pen-and-sword.co.uk

TO JOE AND REGINA ROSE

The survivors

ACKNOWLEDGEMENTS

In the preparation of this book I have, as always, been assisted most ably by various members of the staff of the Imperial War Museum, London, notably Terry Charman and George Clout, who were tireless in answering questions and searching out relevant books and documents. I am also grateful for background on Josef ('Sepp') Dietrich and Max Simon supplied by James Lucas, co-author of *Hitler's Elite*: *Leibstandarte-SS* (Macdonald & Jane's). Many other invaluable details were provided with unlimited patience by the Institute of Contemporary History and Wiener Library, London. The staffs of the London Library and Wandsworth Library also supplied much material. No one writing on SS-Panzer Division Totenkopf can fail to be indebted to *Soldiers of Destruction: The Death's Head Division 1933–1945* by Charles W. Sydnor, Jr (Princeton University Press). I salute the cheerful courage of my good friend Joe Rose who, with complete absence of bitterness, talked of his appalling sufferings in Buchenwald at the hands of the Totenkopfverbaende, and also supplied many details about the camp. I also wish to acknowledge suggestions, information and editorial assistance from Andrew Mollo, Paul Watkins, Joyce Rackham and Vicky Clayton.

SELECTED BIBLIOGRAPHY

Barker, A.J., *Waffen SS at War*, (Ian Allan, 1982)

Berben, Paul, *Dachau 1933–45: The Official History*. (Privately published in London for the Comité International de Dachau, 1975)

Brown Book of the Hitler Terror: Prepared for the World Committee for the Victims of German Fascism. (Gollancz, 1933)

Carrell, Paul, *Hitler's War on Russia: The Story of the German Defeat in the East*. (Harrap, 1964)

Carrell, Paul, *Scorched Earth: Hitler's War on Russia, Volume 2*. (Harrap, 1970)

Clark, Alan, *Barbarossa: The Russian-German Conflict 1941–45*. (Hutchinson, 1965)

Deschner, Gunther, *Reinhard Heydrich: Statthalter der Totalen Macht*. (Bechtle Verlag, 1977)

Erickson, John, *The Road to Berlin*. (Weidenfeld & Nicolson, 1983)

Foley, Charles, *Commando Extraordinary*. (Longman, 1954)

Gallo, Max, *The Night of the Long Knives*. (Souvenir Press, 1972)

Graber, G.S., *History of the SS*. (Robert Hale, 1978)

Guderian, Heinz, *Panzer Leader*. (Michael Joseph, 1952)

Hoess, Rudolf, *Kommandant in Auschwitz*. (Deutsche Verlags-Anstalt, 1958)

Horne, Alistair, *To Lose a Battle: France, 1940*. (Macmillan, 1969)

Infield, Glenn, *Skorzeny — Hitler's Commando*. (St Martin's Press, 1981)

Jolly, Cyril, *The Vengeance of Private Pooley*. (Heinemann, 1956)

Kogon, Eugen, *Der SS Staat*. (Farrar, Strauss and Cudahy, 1950)

Krausnick, Helmut & Martin Broszat, *Anatomie des SS-Staates*. (Walter-Verlag AG, 1965)

Le Chene, Evelyn, *Mauthausen: the History of a Death Camp*. (Methuen, 1971)

Lucas, James and Matthew Cooper, *Hitler's Elite: Leibstandarte-SS.* (Macdonald & Jane's, 1975)

Manstein, Erich von, *Lost Victories.* (Arms and Armour, 1982)

Manvell, Roger & Fraenkel, Heinrich, *The July Plot.* (Bodley Head, 1964)

Mollo, Andrew, *To the Death's Head True: The Story of the SS.* (Thames-Methuen, 1982)

Mollo, Andrew, *Uniforms of the SS: Volumes 4 & 7.* (Historical Research Unit, 1976)

Musmanno, Michael A., *The Eichmann Commandos.* (Peter Davies, 1961)

Quarrie, Bruce, *Hitler's Samurai: The Waffen-SS in Action.* (Patrick Stephens, 1983)

Reitlinger, Gerald, *SS: The Alibi of a Nation 1922–45.* (Arms & Armour, 1981)

Schneider, Jost W., *Verleihung Genehmigt: An illustrated and documentary history of the Knight's Cross holders of the Waffen-SS and police, 1940–1945.* (Bender Publishing Co., 1977)

Shirer, William, *The Rise and Fall of the Third Reich.* (Secker & Warburg, 1960)

Stein, George H., *The Waffen SS, 1939–1945.* (Cornell University Press, 1966)

Sydnor, Charles W., Jr, *Soldiers of Destruction, The SS Death's Head Division, 1933–1945.* (Princeton University Press, 1977)

Vincent, Adrian, *The· Long Road Home.* (Allen & Unwin, 1956)

Ziemke, Earl F., *Stalingrad to Berlin: The German Defeat in the East.* (Office of the Chief of Military History, United States Army, 1968)

'The sight of a large number of men, both mentally and physically disciplined and co-ordinated, with an obvious or latent will to fight, makes an enormous impression on all Germans...'

Pfeffer von Salomon, head of the SA in the 1920s.

1

Opochka, northern Russia, 1941. It was July, but not summer as the Germans understood it. At one moment, the sun would smile, then the mood would switch and the storms come.

The waves of two gigantic armies churned up the cloying, suffocating dust; the soldiers' flame-throwers intensified the already appalling heat. Out of the sulphurous darkness bayonets were thrust deep into German and Russian bellies.

The prize that the Germans were to snatch was the town of Opochka on the vital Stalin Line, and the Russians had flung in all they had.

Right in the thick of it were very special men of the Waffen-SS, fighters whose division could be identified because they wore on their collar patches the distinctive Death's Head insignia which was also their title — SS-Totenkopf, most brutal and most feared of the baleful black legions of Heinrich Himmler's sinister Schutz-staffel.

The Russians, in the seventy-two hours of fighting before Opochka was wrenched away, learnt graphically what sort of fighting men they were.

At one point, a Totenkopf radio truck, detached from the general mêlée, rumbled to the edge of a forest. To the driver, the scene in the clearing ahead recalled one of those stark museum dioramas of battle.

There were four Russians in the clearing and they were indisputably dead. But it was not this which held the driver's attention, nor the fact that the Russians had obviously been shot at close range because of the wide powder burns on their field jackets.

Attention was rooted because they lay in a semi-circle in the middle of which was another corpse. This man had been an SS-Obersturmfuehrer of Totenkopf Division. He had stood his ground and shot them all.

After that he had suspected that there must still be stragglers against whom he would be powerless. Even after he surrendered, they would make him into a human torch and hack his body to pieces. So the young Obersturmfuehrer had turned his machine-pistol on himself. There was to be none of the dishonour of surrender.

Here, to the radio truck crew, was displayed the stark reality of waging war in the dreadful nightmare of Stalin's Russia. The SS man's fate and that of thousands of others flung into this vortex of slaughter had been sealed six years before in another country.

Nuremberg, southern Germany, 1935. An atmosphere of feverish tension gripped the ancient city. Throughout the night, crowds numbered in tens of thousands lined the streets and jostled the pavements to witness the highspot of the Nazi party's annual rally.

At just after 4 p.m. Adolf Hitler, Fuehrer and saviour of a reborn Germany, flew to Nuremberg and began his swastika-bedecked procession to the elaborate opening ceremony at the city's town hall.

There was a distinctly operatic air about these occasions; particularly in September 1935, when the rally was graced by the proud new symphony orchestra providing a jaunty musical background to the seemingly endless succession of speeches and parades.

The event was merely a series of magnificently staged set pieces — above all the candlelit scene in the chamber of the town hall where Hitler received a replica of the Imperial Sword, the original of which had for centuries been the pride of Nuremberg.

The eyes of the world were focussed on the still infant Nazi state and no opportunity was wasted in extolling the virtues of the Hitler miracle.

Long before the rally began, foreign visitors were accosted by swarms of hawkers selling postcards with portraits of Frederick the Great, Bismarck, President Hindenburg and Hitler with the embracing caption: *What the King conquered, the Prince formed, the Field Marshal defended, the Soldier saved and unified.*

This, however, was primitive stuff; education designed to impress the visitor became more profound when he was whisked off to a three-day intensive seminar to be acquainted with the recent political changes of the new Germany.

The superficial observer saw only a distinctly carnival occasion. After all, Nazi propagandists made much of the fact that ten thousand workers from all over Germany had been invited to attend the rally as the guests of the party. All their expenses, including transport, had been paid by the government. At special camps sited in fields near the city, guests were treated to elaborate firework displays, which this year had the theme of the four seasons. Representations of blossoming bushes and flowers symbolised the spring, large fruits the summer, sheaves of grain the autumn and, inevitably, there was a fiery swastika which recalled the ancient German heliotrope festivals of winter.

Yet other visitors, perhaps more discerning, saw the 1935 party rally as something decidedly more significant than a piece of consummately staged theatre.

The clues were there to be seen from the moment Hitler's aircraft touched down and he was greeted by the party faithful: devoted acolytes including deputy party leader Rudolf Hess and his subordinate Martin Bormann, Franconian party Gauleiter Julius Streicher — and Heinrich Himmler.

Above all, Heinrich Himmler. Of the leading Nazis other than Hitler, the presence of Himmler that day proved the most significant. The prudish, studious son of a former tutor to the royal Bavarian household had but two years before held the minor office of Bavarian president of police. Since then, Himmler had moved swiftly to consolidate his power. By April 1934, the former air ace and national hero Hermann Goering, creator of the Gestapo, had relinquished control of that organisation to Himmler, along with responsibility for the concentration camps.

In the late 1920s, Himmler, the bespectacled, weedy bureaucrat who firmly believed that the future lay with blond Nordic people reared in pagan simplicity, had assumed the pompous title of Reichsfuehrer-SS. The SS were the black-uniformed élite, the knights of Nazism. About twenty thousand of them were on duty in Nuremberg that day. Thirteen thousand were detailed as honour guards along the route that Hitler followed and they formed a ring of steel around his hotel.

Aside from the parades, the beery *bonhomie*, the boy-scout camaraderie and the fireworks, the presence of the SS represented the true face of Nazism. Heinrich Himmler literally controlled Nuremberg that day.

The Sunday of the rally belonged to the SS and its rival organisation in terror, the brown-shirted street thugs of the Sturmabteilung (SA). A year before Hitler had organised the slaughter of more than one thousand members of the SA and of its leader, the scarfaced homosexual Ernst Roehm, all of whom had been accused of a bid to overthrow the new government. But rivalries were laid aside for the moment in favour of an elaborate procession at Nuremberg culminating in a ceremony honouring those who had fallen in the cause.

Hitler addressed the representatives of both organisations. Heinrich Himmler, the racial crank and former chicken-breeder who had proudly called his SS a sworn community of superior men, was in seventh heaven.

Another of Himmler's followers that day was, if possible, even happier. For Theodor Eicke, one-time sub-postmaster and deranged patient of the psychiatric clinic at Wuerzburg, this rally was to be of considerable importance.

For Eicke had the job of administering the SS-Totenkopfverbaende, the SS Death's Head units whose delicate task was to administer the growing number of concentration camps throughout the Reich.

At Reich Party Day in Nuremberg that September,

Eicke heard his Fuehrer Adolf Hitler proclaim publicly for the first time: 'The Totenkopfverbaende consists of party formations in the service of the Third Reich.'

It was a significant move; previously, each region of Germany had been responsible for the guards. Now they came under the full embrace and approval of the party.

The hitherto shadowy arm of Nazi terror which, via many metamorphoses, was to become a military division sporting the Death's Head insignia on its collar patches — and one of the most notorious of the Waffen-SS (armed SS) divisions — had already enjoyed a brief but bloody history.

Now it was getting a most agreeable seal of public approval as a party organisation. Further confirmation from Himmler came the following March when the Totenkopfverbaende was allowed to increase its size from 1,800 to 3,500 men and became indisputably the concentration camp guard organisation of the Third Reich.

Eicke — the man his more fanatical followers called 'Papa' Eicke — scented real power that day in Nuremberg.

However, he had seized his first big chance a full year earlier.

2

'*Der Fuehrer will es! Heil Hitler! Feuer.*' ('It is the will of the Leader. Heil Hitler! Fire.')

In barrack squares in Munich and Berlin and other towns throughout Germany, the words echoed with dread monotonous regularity. The slaughter began in the early hours of that terrible 30 June 1934 and went on for two blood-soaked days. Bullets from the rifles of the SS firing-squad crashed into the bodies of allegedly traitorous members of the Sturmabteilung. Hitler declared of his storm troopers: 'They are planning to overthrow the National Socialist state.'

In Munich, firing-squads were drawn up in the courtyard of Stadelheim prison. Gruppenfuehrer 'Sepp' Dietrich strode rapidly down the prison corridors, pausing only at each cell to shout at its occupants: 'The Fuehrer has condemned you to death for high treason. Heil Hitler!'

The salvos of death followed one another throughout the afternoon, punctuated by shouts and cries, even a 'Heil Hitler!' from a condemned man who had been given no time to discover why he was dying and remained steadfastly loyal to the leader who had spurned him.

What had happened in Hitler's new Germany? Why had the triumphant and united party of January 1933 turned upon itself? Why were the jackals of repressive terror seemingly determined to tear themselves apart?

Away from ranting platform rhetoric and the elaborate stage-managed trappings of the party rallies, the Nazis newly in power now faced the unglamorous responsibilities of government. The movement had to show at least a superficially respectable face to the world; the truth was that, beneath the surface, Nazi Germany seethed with discontent.

There were militants of the left — the men who believed that National Socialism actually had something to do with socialism — and the conservative right, which regarded the Nazis as mere caretakers and their leaders as cut-throat bandits. There were, of course, the bullet and the axe and the concentration camp for such nuisances.

The storm-troopers, however, were another matter.

The arrogance of Ernst Roehm had spread throughout the cohorts of the SA. They drank, swaggered and bullied in every town of Germany. They wrecked the beerhouses when they encountered real or imagined lack of respect. Employers were beaten up if they did not give jobs to SA-approved candidates.

None of this brutality worried Hitler particularly, but Roehm's talk of a 'second revolution' was something else entirely. It was decided to deal with the SA. Hitler was later to claim: 'Roehm was getting ambitious. He was plotting to overthrow the present regime, make himself head of all military and all naval services. Sedition was spreading throughout the SA and a widespread revolt had been planned. I was to be arrested and kept under guard while the rebels took charge.'

The rival SS saw its chance. Hitler and Himmler planned a terrible swift revenge on Ernst Roehm and his SA. There was to be a key role for Theodor Eicke in the schemes of Fuehrer and Reichsfuehrer.

Like most of his generation, Alsace-born Theodor Eicke had been thrust demoralised into the maelstrom of post-World War I Germany. As a youth of seventeen in 1909, he had enlisted in the 23rd Regiment at Landau in the Rhineland Palatinate, endured a singularly un-impressive career as a clerk and a paymaster, and earned in the process the Iron Cross Second Class. It was a shabby distinction, cutting no ice whatever in the bankrupt Weimar Republic, where discontented veterans of the Kaiser's Germany seethed with hatred against the government.

Eicke and his wife Bertha settled in Ilmenau in Thuringia to be near her family. Bertha's father resolutely refused to support his indigent son-in-law. In desperation, Eicke grabbed thankfully at the chance of becoming a paid police informer — spying on members of national groups thought to threaten the security of the new republic.

The trouble was that Eicke himself was steeped in anti-government intrigue and found it impossible to conceal his own deep-seated loathing of his rulers. He was dismissed from a succession of shadowy jobs with police forces in Cottbus, Weimar and Ludwigshafen. The almost obsessive ambition to become a professional policeman had to be laid aside in favour of second best — a job in the I.G. Farben plant in Ludwigshafen as a security officer.

By 1928, the Nazi party with its paramilitary flavour had become a raucous and aggressive influence in the Rhineland Palatinate. Its blatant nationalism, its scream of hatred against the ruling 'traitors' were potent appeals.

17

On 1 December 1920, Theodor Eicke joined the Nationalsozialistische Deutsche Arbeiterpartei (Nazi) with Party Card No. 114-901, at the same time entering the ranks of the SA.

Eicke was to remain in the SA for the next two years and then, wisely as it turned out, transfer to the better disciplined SS. It was plain enough that the SA consisted of perverts and rowdies who would eventually overreach themselves, but there was another more practical reason for Eicke's change of organisation. The SS was smaller and promotion quicker.

And it was to prove speedy indeed. On 27 November 1930, Reichsfuehrer-SS Heinrich Himmler appointed Eicke to the rank of SS-Sturmfuehrer, giving him command of Sturm (platoon) No. 148 at Ludwigshafen am Rhein.

It was at that point that Eicke exhibited his very considerable talent for organisation. So highly did Himmler regard him that within three months Eicke was promoted to Sturmbannfuehrer with orders to create a second SS-Sturmbann (battalion) for the projected 10th SS Standarte (Regiment) of the SS-Palatinate. By the end of 1931, Eicke was a Standartenfuehrer and commander of the 10th SS-Standarte — not a bad record for the assistant paymaster of a decade earlier.

But the depression in Germany hardened. Eicke became a victim with the loss of his job at I.G. Farben. A few years before, he would have viewed the prospect of unemployment with dismay. Now things were different — full time could now be allotted to the SS. Theodor Eicke was on the edge of a new career.

It was inevitable that his cancerous ambition and total ruthlessness should bring him a fair crop of enemies. Easily matching him in brutality was Josef Buerckel, Gauleiter (District Leader) of the Palatinate, whose dream had been to unite all the SA and SS units under his personal command.

Understandably, such a scheme found no favour whatever with Eicke, whose career had been progressing most agreeably in the SS and who now luxuriated in the exalted rank of SS-Oberfuehrer. He had no intention of allowing the tedious Buerckel to interfere with his plans. Such an incubus must be removed.

Eicke gathered a suitable dedicated bunch of his SS cronies. Together the party stormed the headquarters of the Ludwigshafen Gau. Buerckel was seized and promptly locked in a caretaker's cupboard. But Eicke had not been quick enough. The local Schutzpolizei (security police) had been alerted. Eicke and his fellow SS were arrested and Gauleiter Buerckel, seething with indignation and injured pride, was released.

In a tumultous fury, the Gauleiter extracted a grotesque revenge. He stormed: 'Even to contemplate such a thing, the Oberfuehrer must be mentally ill. He is certainly a danger to the community.' Thus it was that Eicke found himself an unwilling patient of the Nervenklinik in Wuerzburg — detained in a strait-jacket for psychiatric observation.

He was shrewd enough to realise that his best chance of release was to become a paragon of sweet reasonableness. He was courteous and accommodating to the puzzled staff, who eventually wondered what he was doing there. Eventually, his personal psychiatrist was able to write Himmler that his patient seemed neither disturbed nor a chronic troublemaker.

On 26 June 1933, a completely rehabilitated Eicke left the Wuerzburg clinic armed with orders, signed by Himmler as chief of the Bavarian police, to take up a new post. He was to become commandant of one of the first Nazi concentration camps, at Dachau.

Nature had always been unkind to that part of Bavaria lying to the north-west of Munich where the town of Dachau lay at the mercy of long bitter winters and the thick snow had a way of persisting well into April.

Before the advent of National Socialism, the region with its peat bogs and grasslands had a melancholy beauty, which gave rise to the so-called 'Dachau School' of painting. The small town had hitherto been known only through the activities of men devoted to art, but all that changed on 21 March 1933 when the newspapers published a communiqué from Heinrich Himmler, 'Kommissarischer Polizeipraesident der Stadt Muenchen'.

It stated that Dachau concentration camp would be opened, that five thousand people could be accommodated there. On 24 March, a local newspaper, *Der Amperbote* announced that the Freiwillige Arbeitsdienst (Voluntary Labour Service) had, in three days, made hasty preparation for the reception of the first prisoners, around sixty.

The camp site consisted originally of a derelict explosives factory, built during World War 1 and abandoned in 1919 to conform with the requirements of the Versailles Treaty which had virtually disarmed Germany. As the buildings crumbled, the local townspeople optimistically appropriated some of the material to build houses. But the Nazis had other ideas for the place and, as soon as Hitler came to power, Himmler's SS pressed the area into service with plans which included a vast complex of barracks, dwellings and industrial buildings.

At first the camp was intended as a handy pool for free labour. Private land was compulsorily seized by the SS; the reasons given were cloaked under the vague term of 'national security'. No one was unwise enough to enquire any further. At first, the prisoners housed there were all opponents of the regime, *politische Haeftlinge* ('politicals'), but before long other categories, 'anti-socials' and 'emigrés' swelled the numbers.

It was early days in Nazi Germany and it was still necessary to present something of a respectable front even in camps like Dachau. Blatant ill-treatment of prisoners that might lead to distressing publicity was therefore frowned upon.

Dachau's first commandant, SS-Oberfuehrer Hilmar Waeckerle suffered from few inhibitions. His prescription for dealing with recalcitrant prisoners was simply to murder them with total lack of discrimination. Waeckerle was dismissed and replaced by Theodor Eicke.

Eicke was aware that his career, even by Nazi standards, was somewhat chequered. If he did not succeed in Dachau, Himmler was perfectly capable of dispensing with his services and he was under no illusions that the SS would not be particularly expert in dealing with one of their own who had fallen from grace. It was vital that he make his mark at Dachau. He was, during his brief tenure in the job, quick to do so.

He soon discovered that Dachau had been used by Waeckerle as a dump for all the SS's unwanted men. The guard unit was drawn largely from the ranks of the 56th SS Foot Regiment, which enjoyed an unsavoury reputation, even by SS standards. The men were regarded, quite literally, as the scum of the earth.

Eicke was soon shooting a disgruntled volley of memos to Himmler. When he had taken over he had found a 'corrupt guard detachment of barely 120 men'. Eicke went on: 'We were generally regarded as a necessary evil which merely cost money; insignificant guards behind barbed wire. At times I was forced literally to beg the treasuries for the meagre wages of my officers and men.'

Things changed rapidly. Eicke, with his consummate ruthlessness and gift for organisation, was to create a model for all future SS concentration camps. A new disciplinary code was drawn up for inmates. Concentration camp staff and guard units were separated. Arbitrary mistreatment by guards was forbidden — not out of humanity, but simply because such action was likely to lead to a series of regrettable scandals such as those which had engulfed the unspeakable Waeckerle. Discipline became steadily harsher; hanging replaced indiscriminate beatings to death.

Eicke was not attracted by the calibre of camp staff, either. The sadists and bullies left over from the early days of the Fuehrer's struggles were edged out. Eicke then set about improving the discipline and morale of those who remained. Between 1934 and 1935, together with newly recruited personnel, they formed SS-Wachsturmbann I Oberbayern. By 1937, the battalion had become a Totenkopf regiment — SS-Totenkopfstandarte Oberbayern.

It was but the first stage of Eicke's sinister empire. SS-Totenkopfstandarte II Brandenburg sprang into existence to take over the Sachsenhausen camp at Oranienburg. By

December 1937, SS-Totenkopfstandarte III Thuringen received responsibility for guarding and running the big camp at Weimar; this was Buchenwald. The Anschluss (union with Austria in 1938) gave Eicke the chance to add yet another regiment to the SS-Totenkopfverbaende — SS-Totenkopfstandarte IV Ostmark. From September 1938 it was to control the camp of Mauthausen near Linz.

Dachau was to serve as a model camp whose example others were expected to follow. Just what a camp guard was expected to do was embodied in regulations.

Eicke saw to it that there were regulations for everything. A member of the guard staff could barely carry out the simplest action without reference to the rule book. And that rule book was very comprehensive indeed. Disciplinary procedures issued in October 1933 laid down to the very last detail how the roll-call of prisoners was to be carried out, how they were to march off to work in military style, the duties of sentries and escorts, even the wording of individual commands.

In addition to a natural brutality, Eicke's other outstanding quality was thoroughness. What distance should guards keep from prisoners? There was a rule about that. What was the form of salute prisoners should throw to the guards? Consult the rule book!

The regulations specified:

'The only duty of the escort is to guard the prisoners. They will watch the prisoners' behaviour at work. Lazy prisoners will be urged to work. But any form of maltreatment or chicanery is strictly prohibited.

'If a prisoner is openly careless and lazy at work or gives impudent answers the guard will take his name. After work he will make a report. . .If the prisoners are to respect the SS guards, the SS man on guard duty cannot be permitted to lounge about, to lean against something, to push his rifle on to his back or to place his hand over the muzzle.

'A guard who shelters from the rain becomes a figure of fun and does not behave like a soldier. . .The SS man must show pride and dignity. . .The use of the familiar

Du [thou] amounts to fraternisation. It is humiliating for a man who wears the Death's Head to allow himself to become an errand boy for Bolsheviks and bosses. . .The SS escort will not engage in private conversation with the prisoners. . .'

As for the Death's Head insignia, Eicke himself had the idea of using it on the right collar-tab as the distinctive insignia for the SS guard units; all insignia worn by the pre-war SS were hand-made by craftsmen in the camp tailors' shops.

The 'men who wore the Death's Head' were of course to become figures of power and terror far beyond the watch-towers and barbed wire. But even in their days as concentration camp guards, these baleful branches of the family of the black knights were feared figures indeed.

They were soon clashing openly with the civil law. In the spring of 1935, when Eicke had left Dachau as concentration camp supremo, two prisoners were shot in Berlin's Columbia-Haus camp.

The investigating public prosecutor took an interest; his inquisitiveness was not encouraged. Those who had taken part in the executions adopted an air of injured pride; they referred the prosecutor to Eicke's regulations.

Such regulations were not merely for the maintenance of discipline. Eicke's hardness was tempered with sadism that went beyond introducing solitary confinement on bread and water, which could drive a prisoner insane.

As might have been expected, cruelty was fuelled to white-heat through Eicke's hatred of the Jews. For them, he invented a special sort of collective punishment. Every time stories of atrocities in the camps appeared in the foreign press, the Jews were forced to lie in bed for anything from one to three months. They were allowed to get up only for meals and roll-call.

Their quarters were not allowed to be ventilated, the windows were kept screwed down. The notorious Rudolf Hoess, later Commandant of Auschwitz, who had been posted to Dachau in 1934, reported in his memoirs:

'This was a cruel punishment, with particularly severe psychological effects. As a result of this compulsory staying in bed for long periods, they became so nervous and overwrought that they could no longer bear the sight of each other, and could not stand one another's company. Many violent brawls broke out . . .'

Corporal punishment was introduced with enthusiasm. Regulations provided for 'twenty-five strokes of the cane' which could be ordered in addition to arrest. Even more sinister were disciplinary regulations stipulating the death penalty in certain cases.

Paragraphs 11 and 12 laid down that a prisoner caught 'talking politics' for the purpose of incitement, or who gathered with others, passed 'atrocity propaganda' and other similar calumnies 'shall be hanged as an agitator according to revolutionary law'. A prisoner who assaulted a guard, refused to obey or indulged in any form of mutiny 'will be shot on the spot. . .or subsequently hanged'.

Eicke was also fond of lecturing his Death's Head lieutenants at length.

Rudolf Hoess has left a distillation of Eicke's sermonising:

'Any trace of pity revealed to the "enemies of the State", was a weakness which they would immediately exploit. Any pity whatsoever for "enemies of the State" was unworthy of an SS man. There was no place in the ranks of the SS for men with soft hearts and any such would do well to retire quickly to a monastery.

'He [Eicke] could only use hard, determined men who ruthlessly obeyed every order. It was not for nothing that their emblem was the Death's Head and that they carried a loaded gun. They were the only soldiers who even in peace time faced the enemy day and night, the enemy behind the wire. . .

'Eicke had drummed the concept of "dangerous enemies of the State" so forcefully and convincingly into his SS men that anyone who knew no better was firmly convinced by it. . .

'The purpose of Eicke's everlasting lectures and orders to the same effect was. . .to turn his SS men completely against the prisoners, to stir up their feelings against the prisoners. . .'

It was recorded, however, that Eicke could be equally merciless against ill-disciplined or dishonest members of his own staff. Hoess related:

'It was discovered that an immense racket had been organised in the butcher's shop by the prisoners and by non-commissioned officers of the SS. Four members of the SS were sentenced by a Munich court — SS courts were not then in existence — to long terms of imprisonment.

'These four men were then paraded in front of the entire guard unit, personally degraded by Eicke, and then discharged with ignominy from the ranks of the SS. Eicke himself tore off their national emblems, their badges of rank and SS insignia, had them marched past each company in turn, and then handed them over to the prison authorities to serve their sentences. Afterward he took this opportunity to deliver a long, admonitory speech. He said that he would dearly have liked to have seen these four men dressed in concentration camp clothes, flogged and put behind the wire with their associates. The Reichsfuehrer of the SS, however, had not allowed him to do so.'

Eicke evolved what he was pleased to call the 'Dachau spirit'. To train his guard staff in the old-fashioned, traditional comradely type of military instruction — sentimental songs and Bavarian beer — was quite inadequate for the special duties of Dachau.

The injunction was: 'Every order is to be carried out, however harsh it may be.'

There were times when the harshness became too much for some individual SS men. Hoess cited the case of a group of senior General-SS (Allgemeine-SS) overheard in the mess expressing the view that 'hangman's work' soiled their black uniforms. Eicke acted swiftly; the men were rounded up, lectured and promptly demoted to the level of Obersturmfuehrer or Hauptsturmfuehrer, ranks they held until the end of the war. From then on, there was the threat of total expulsion, which would have reduced them forthwith to the status of unemployable.

Yet it has to be said that the feared and respected Theodor Eicke was also 'Papa' Eicke who could, for all his toughness, exhibit a rough affection for his men. It was reciprocated. The approach of the 'soldier's soldier' was to stand him in good stead when he came to command a division in war. As Inspector of Concentration Camps, just as commander of SS-Totenkopf Division, he insisted on talking directly to the guards and lower ranks without the inhibiting shadow of their superior officers.

His ultimate object though was the accumulation of still more power. His methods of gaining the confidence of his men were cunning successful exercises in public relations. In every camp he had letter-boxes put up which could only be opened by him, giving every SS man the chance to communicate reports and complaints directly.

Eicke had been merely 'Inspektor der Konzentrationslager' in 1934. By 1938, such a lack-lustre title had given place to 'Fuehrer der SS-Totenkopfverbaende und Konzentrationslager'. Yet — at least on paper — Eicke was subject to certain constraints. His overall governing authority was the SS-Verfuegungstruppe (forerunner of the Waffen-SS) and the Allgemeine-SS. The bureaucracy for the two organisations was in the hands of a certain SS-Gruppenfuehrer August Heissmeyer.

Eicke sensed that Heissmeyer had a nose for power and possibly the ruthlessness to achieve it. Eicke let it be known in no uncertain terms that the only superior he recognised was Himmler.

No matter that the finances of the SS Death's Head formations came under the Reich Minister of the Interior; no matter that Heissmeyer had the authority to issue guidelines for organisation and even the style of uniform. Eicke contemptuously ignored all this, announcing blithely: 'The concentration camps are under my personal control.'

When he wrote to Himmler, Eicke contented himself by forwarding a copy of the letter to the fuming Gruppenfuehrer Heissmeyer.

Such arrogant assertion of independence invariably brought him enemies. Even he could not remain immune from the Byzantine intrigues of the SS, the jockeying for power, the almost unslakeable thirst among its senior officials for still more offices.

The greatest menace to Eicke was, predictably, the Gestapo under its serpentine intriguer, Reinhard Heydrich. The Gestapo could issue protective-custody orders or authorise the release of a prisoner into its care. 'Political sections' within the camps — legalised informers — peddled back required information.

Such a clash of interests was bound to lead to crisis; in August 1936 Eicke was battling to hold on to a power which had suddenly started to look precarious.

The challenge came from SS-Standartenfuehrer Karl Werner Best, the Gestapo's Chief of Bureau at the Ministry of the Interior and (potentially even more serious) deputy to Reinhard Heydrich.

Best had been declaring to influential Gestapo circles: 'Disgusting things are going on in the concentration camps. It's high time they were under Gestapo control.'

This was followed by attempts to withdraw the Death's Head formations from Eicke altogether and hand them over to the Allgemeine-SS.

The Gestapo went even further. It ceased to matter whether the civil courts had abandoned prosecutions for political offences or whether an accused had been acquitted. The Gestapo was still able to step in under the powers of 'protective custody'. The implication was obvious; the Gestapo regarded the civil authority and its verdicts with contempt.

Equally, Eicke, for all his titles, had little say in the prisoners he was likely to be responsible for. Hitler several times personally ordered prisoners in the charge of judicial authorities to be transferred to the Gestapo, who in turn dumped the unfortunate victims on Eicke. Predictably, the Fuehrer found an enthusiastic disciple in

Heinrich Himmler.

On 23 February 1937, the Reichsfuehrer ordered that about 'two thousand professional and habitual criminals or criminals who are a threat to public morality' should be taken into protective police custody and 'arrested with lightning speed everywhere in the Reich' and 'transferred to the concentration camps of Sachsenhausen, Sachsenburg, Lichtenburg and Dachau.'

The shadow of the Gestapo grew ever longer; its say in just who should be sent to the camps was interpreted by Eicke as an implied threat to his authority.

It was no mere neurotic obsession, not simply touchiness that his power was seemingly being undermined. The Gestapo had its knives out and was intriguing with Himmler. On 26 January 1938, Himmler, prompted by Heydrich and Best, announced a 'single comprehensive swoop' on so-called work-shy elements. They were to be the responsibility of the Gestapo 'which is alone responsible in every case for a decision regarding protective custody and transfer to a concentration camp . . .'

Himmler's lieutenants, among them Werner Best, were obviously working to discredit Eicke and possibly remove him. The architect of the Death's Head formations did his utmost to remain on the right side of the Reichsfuehrer-SS and roll with the punches delivered by the Gestapo lieutenants.

It worked; Eicke survived the storms. Up to the start of World War II he remained Inspector of the Concentration Camps and leader of the Death's Head formations.

One man at least was conscious of a long-standing debt to Eicke. Adolf Hitler was notoriously loyal to old friends, the more disreputable the better. The Fuehrer had good reason to be particularly grateful to the former mental home inmate.

Just why can be seen by recalling the muggy June days of 1934. For that was the summer when the smouldering dispute between Hitler and the SA of Ernst Roehm finally ignited.

And, incidentally, it paved the way for the further flowering of the SS-Totenkopfverbaende.

3

Foetid cloying heat had wrapped itself around most of the cities of Germany that eventful June and July of 1934.

But there was another smell abroad which had nothing whatever to do with soaring temperatures and stinking pavements.

It was the smell of fear.

In every town of the Third Reich there were men desperately afraid. In the cells of the Stadelheim prison, at the Lichterfelde Barracks and at the Columbia-Haus of the Gestapo, bewildered members of the SA, many of them of senior rank and of unimpeachable loyalty to their Fuehrer, waited in terror.

Ernst Roehm, their leader, had stormed publicly about the need for 'a second revolution'. This, according to Hitler, and his strident, club-footed propaganda chief Dr Joseph Goebbels — the so-called 'poison dwarf' of Nazism — had amounted to high treason. It had meant a call for armed insurrection against the government.

That was why men such as SA-Gruppenfuehrer Karl Schreyer had been roused from a cell in Columbia-Haus by a grinning SS man and told: 'You will be taken out and shot. Put your head under the tap like the others, so that you look fresh and make a good impression.'

That was why a loyal brownshirt, who until his arrest might well have been a Brigadefuehrer in charge of fifty thousand SA, was apt to find himself being marched across the hot pavement stones of the courtyard of the grim Lichterfelde Barracks, where a platoon of twelve men in two rows of six were lined up, shouldering their weapons.

The Brigadefuehrer would just have had time to take in

a macabre touch: a large Krupp truck, run on diesel, drawn up nearby with the SS driver deliberately revving the engine to drown the sound of what was to come.

Then the condemned man would have been thrust unceremoniously against a wall beneath which fresh sand had been spread that morning — sand with a crimson stain that had been spreading since the executions began the previous day.

The noise of the truck all but drowning his words, an SS-Untersturmfuehrer would read out the sentence. The last protestations of loyalty from the Brigadefuehrer would not be heard.

Then came the volley; the body slumped into the warm, welcoming sand.

Theodor Eicke's role in the Roehm purge — the so-called 'Night of the Long Knives' — began on the early sweltering afternoon of 1 July.

News that the SS was preparing to move in on Ernst Roehm had filtered down to Eicke from the Gestapo, the secret state police over which Himmler had gained control the previous April.

The plot to eliminate Roehm went by the codename 'Colibri', ('humming bird'). Himmler, however, saw no reason for wrapping things up.

The Reichsfuehrer's voice came over the line at the Munich offices of Southern Regional Administrative District: 'The Fuehrer's decision is that Ernst Roehm is to be shot. The one qualification — and the Fuehrer insists on this — is that he is to be first given the chance to commit suicide.'

Eicke's role in the various executions had been to muster members of the Dachau guard detail — Totenkopf men, soon to be publicly acknowledged as such by Hitler — and to assist the district commander, Sepp Dietrich, and two companies of Dietrich's crack SS-Liebstandarte.

But the killing of Roehm was a delicate business to which only a couple of really trusted subordinates could possibly be privy.

Eicke summoned his adjutant, SS-Sturmbannfuehrer

Michael Lippert, and the liaison officer for the SS and army during the purge, SS-Gruppenfuehrer Ernst Heinrich Schmauser.

On arrival, the trio found the fatigued and fearful prison doctor, Robert Koch, who had a merited reputation as a rigid bureaucrat. He stood his ground, telling Eicke firmly: 'I can't deliver Ernst Roehm or anyone else without the necessary signed authorisation from the Minister of Justice.'

Eicke snapped: 'Then get it.'

Koch lifted the telephone and asked to be put through to Bavarian Minister Hans Frank, and diffidently asked for instructions.

It was too much for Eicke, who, with mounting fury, snatched the instrument and screamed at Frank: 'You've no business interfering in this matter. I'm acting under the direct orders of the Fuehrer.'

Koch wisely agreed to keep out of the affair; Eicke, Lippert and Schmauser made their way to Roehm's cell — No. 474.

Roehm, who had been hustled to the prison stripped to the waist, watched almost in a dream as Eicke put a copy of the party newspaper, *Voelkischer Beobachter*, on the table. It reported the dismissal of Roehm and listed the names of the executed SA.

Eicke also placed a revolver on the table, loaded with a single bullet. Then he withdrew. Not a single word was spoken.

Ten minutes passed and there had only been silence from cell No. 474. Lippert and Eicke threw open the door.

Eicke shouted: 'Make yourself ready.'

In spite of himself, Lippert could not stop shaking. It took three bullets to kill Ernst Roehm, who died, like so many of his followers, regretting the parting from Hitler, an old party comrade, and a vision of what might have been.

'Mein Fuehrer, Mein Fuehrer,' he had seemed to murmur.

Eicke, the perpetual cynic, was immune to sentiment. He riposted: 'You ought to have thought of that before!'

With Roehm's death, Eicke had proved to Himmler and, equally important, to Hitler that he was capable of carrying out a delicate mission to prove his unquestioned loyalty. It would surely augur well for the future.

The blood-bespattered, corpse-ridden saga of the Roehm purge undoubtedly had its advantages for the career of Theodor Eicke, but it was nevertheless a diversion from the far more serious business of maintaining discipline within the concentration camps and seeing there were enough guards to enforce it.

The out-and-out thug with a taste for blood and for inflicting pain still had his place, no doubt, but now, with the Totenkopfverbaende turned 'respectable', there could be no more scandals such as those which had preceded Eicke's arrival at Dachau.

Inducements to join the Totenkopf were made especially attractive. Eicke lost no time in reminding recruits that they were part of an élite.

He proclaimed: 'Since the camps are the main repositories for the most dangerous political enemies of the state, and since the Fuehrer has given the Totenkopfverbaende — a racially select group of men — sole responsibility for guarding and running the camps, then the Totenkopfverbaende is an élite structure within the SS.'

It was no longer enough to take a country boy who had joined the SS through a taste for adventure and then to proceed to turn him into an automaton fuelled by hatred. He was expected to become an all-rounder for his Fuehrer; certainly there could be no question of concentration camp guard duties being, for instance, a handy way of dodging military service. That had to be done, either in the SS-Verfuegungstruppe or in the Wehrmacht.

Such pliable young talent was·seen to be of immense value to National Socialism; the business of ideological indoctrination was turned over to the Rasse- und Siedlungs-Amt, the Race and Settlements Office of the Third Reich, under Richard Walter Darre, author of such weighty treatises as *Farming as the Life Source of the Nordic Race*.

Eicke's opinion of Darre and his scheme for mustering eventually two hundred million Nordic farmers around Germany as a bulwark against Bolshevism is not known, but when it came to racial indoctrination few were more energetic than the concentration camp supremo.

His racialism was of the crudest kind; it meant convincing the men of the Totenkopfverbaende that his charges were verminous, sub-human and dangerous. The new recruit to a camp swiftly received an object-lesson in just how verminous inferiors were to be treated. He was marched into the protective-custody compound to witness a flogging.

And there were plenty of those. One survivor of Buchenwald, the German-Jewish painter Joe Rose, now living and working in London, still has good reason to remember the concentration camp guards.

Originally a member of a semi-military republican organisation, Reichsbanner Schwarz-Rot-Geld, Rose was arrested on his honeymoon in 1938 and sent to Buchenwald. He recalled:

'The guards interpreted discipline as making you stand rigidly to attention while attending a public hanging. Milder penalties included being forced to do press-ups for hours on end.

'On marches, each prisoner would be given a stone. Lines were drawn on the roads. If anyone, weighed down by the stone, staggered across the lines, they were shot immediately by the guards.'

In 1933, Rose had spent nine months in another camp, a long-term penal establishment at Sonnenburg near Berlin where most of the guards were 'pure sadists'.

This was borne out by *The Brown Book of the Hitler Terror*, published in the same year by the World Committee for the Victims of German Fascism. It stated:

'Letters and reports from prisoners and even official

33

statements, show beyond doubt that Sonnenburg is a real torture chamber. Working class leaders and intellectuals are subjected to the most disgraceful maltreatment. Throughout Germany the camp is known as the "Sonnenburg hell".'

A letter from a worker who escaped from Sonnenburg gave a graphic description of the conditions:

'The first batches of prisoners were met at Sonnenburg station by storm troop detachments and police. They were compelled to sing and were literally beaten to the camp. The inhabitants at Sonnenburg can testify to this. When they arrived at the camp, the prisoners were compelled to stand in the courtyard in streaming rain. Then the first ones were taken to the rooms. Each had to fetch straw for himself from another floor. Storm troopers were standing on the stairs, and they beat the prisoners mercilessly with their rubber truncheons. Some were made to empty the closet pails of the Nazis, in the course of which they were again brutally mishandled. One storm trooper held a prisoner's head between his legs, while another storm trooper beat him. The comrades were compelled to count the blows in a loud voice. Some of the prisoners received as many as 185 blows. In addition they were kicked and otherwise mishandled. . .

'The first three weeks were the worst. In the single cells we were attacked in the night and terribly beaten. The backs of many comrades were quite black. I don't know whether Litten a fellow prisoner will get through with his life. The wives of several of the Sonnenburg prisoners raised such sharp protests that Mittelbach, of the public prosecutor's department, was sent to Sonnenburg to investigate; Litten begged him to have him shot, as he could no longer bear the brutal mishandling that was being inflicted on him.'

Eventually released from Sonnenburg but re-arrested five years later, Joe Rose was sent to Buchenwald, where although there was brutality enough, discipline curbed some of the sadism.

For the inhabitants of Buchenwald the events of 29 November 1938 were to have a dreadful significance.

The appalling blood-letting saga began three weeks earlier when Herschel Grynszpan, a seventeen-year-old Polish-Jewish refugee, shot and mortally wounded Ernst vom Rath, third secretary of the Germany Embassy in Paris.

Grynszpan's father had been just one of ten thousand Jews who had been herded into a boxcar and deported to Poland.

The teenager burned with revenge; his quarry at the embassy had originally been the ambassador himself, Count Johannes von Welczeck.

The young third secretary was detailed to deal with the overwrought Herschel: he received five bullets in the stomach. It was the supreme irony, for Rath, already under Gestapo surveillance, could scarcely be described as a dedicated Nazi and anti-Semite.

Next day, the Nazi official newspaper the *Voelkischer Beobachter* thundered: 'The German people will draw their own conclusions from the deed.' Nazi Propaganda Minister Joseph Goebbels acted as if he had only been waiting for the shots from Paris as his cue. The day following Herschel's crime, Goebbels travelled to Munich along with other party veterans to hear Hitler speak. That evening, the Fuehrer was handed a telegram announcing that embassy secretary vom Rath had died of his wounds that afternoon. Hitler, according to eyewitnesses, was too stunned to speak.

The ever-ambitious Goebbels took swift advantage. He leapt to his feet, delivering a speech suffused with hatred of the Jews. His message was clear, shot through with cynicism though it was.

Goebbels proclaimed: 'I have reported to the Fuehrer that, in many places, spontaneous action had been taken against the Jews. The Fuehrer has decided that such demonstrations were neither to be prepared nor organised by the party. So far as they rose spontaneously, however, steps were not to be taken to prevent them.'

This was a broad enough hint to the organisers of terror in the Third Reich.

That night has gone down in history as *Kristallnacht* (The Night of the Broken Glass). It was to take the Third Reich down a dark and savage road of no return. Synagogues, Jewish homes and shops went up in flames. Jews, men and women and children, were shot or otherwise murdered trying to escape being burnt to death.

A preliminary confidential report was made by Gestapo chief Reinhard Heydrich to Hermann Goering on the following day, 11 November:

> 'The extent of the destruction of Jewish shops and houses cannot be verified by figures. . .815 shops destroyed, 171 dwelling-houses set on fire or destroyed only indicate a fraction of the actual damage so far as arson is concerned. . .119 synagogues were set on fire, and another 76 completely destroyed. . .20,000 Jews were arrested. Thirty-six deaths were reported and those seriously injured were also numbered at 36. Those killed and injured are Jews.'

As for the concentration camps, Eicke received instructions from Himmler which were to be passed on to the Death's Head guards. Eicke made provisions for ten thousand prisoners to be admitted to Buchenwald alone.

No account was taken of age. Ten-year-old boys were seized along with octogenarians. On the way from Weimar railway station, stragglers were mown down; survivors were forced to drag the bloody bodies into the camp. The main entrance was slammed shut and the prisoners were forced to squeeze their way through a narrow gap in maximum discomfort. Inside stood the block leaders, wielding their iron rods, whips and truncheons.

On the very first night, sixty-eight Jews lost their reason. They were clubbed to death systematically, four at a time at specially arranged public executions.

A mood of hysterical revenge seemed to grip Eicke's men within Buchenwald. There were at least two incidents of slaughter.

A Breslau Jew named Silbermann was forced to stand by as one of the guards beat his brother to death. The sight drove Silbermann mad; later that night he screamed that the barracks were on fire. Hundreds threw themselves out of upper windows and entire tiers of bunks collapsed. Panicking, the guards shot into the crowd.

The security of the camp was plainly threatened. The incident had to be interpreted as a Jewish mutiny. Examples must be made. The officer in charge, Rosl, had seven hostages taken from the building and handcuffed together. Three block leaders then let loose trained dogs; the hostages were torn to pieces.

Joe Rose recalls the other reprisal: 'There were ten thousand Jews in the camp on five tiers of bunks, two thousand to a hut. One thousand at least were machine-gunned by the guards on a single night.'

Conscious of the appalling reputation of the Totenkopfverbaende, post-war apologists for the organisation that eventually became the Waffen-SS were to argue that there was a great deal of difference between it and — inevitably mentioned with a pious shudder — the men for whom Eicke was responsible.

Pre-war it was certainly true. For one thing, Totenkopf personnel wore brown uniforms and not the black of the Allgemeine-SS and the grey of the Verfuegungstruppe.

The Leibstandarte, which regarded itself as an élite and a law unto itself, demanded that a recruit be at least 5 feet 11 inches tall (later 6 feet 0.5 inches) and be between the ages of 17 and 22. But 5 feet 7.5 inches (later reduced to 5 feet 6.7 inches) was reckoned acceptable for the Totenkopfverbaende with its upper age limit of 26.

Still mindful of the threat posed by poachers from the Gestapo, Eicke began to look for ways to extend his power still further. His main complaint to Hitler now was the ubiquitous Sepp Dietrich, who persisted in dumping on the camps a lion's share of undesirables, much addicted to sadism but totally unacquainted with discipline.

In a barrage of complaining correspondence to Himmler, Eicke pleaded that Dietrich was an obstructive menace. Would it not be better to sever all relations and put Dachau directly under the control of the Reichs-fuehrer? Eicke was cunning enough not to press his suit too hard. If the matter was raised at discreet intervals Himmler might actually end up by believing that the idea for a switch in command had originated from him.

Himmler proved sympathetic, but the idea of Eicke having a 'private army' did not appeal to the notoriously touchy Reichsfuehrer-SS. The chance of a major move came in the summer of 1938 with Hitler's impending destruction of Czechoslovakia. Himmler argued to his Fuehrer that, with the increasingly belligerent foreign policy of the Third Reich, it was vital to have an enlarged armed SS giving an additional measure of internal security to the state.

Hitler, contemplating the seemingly mesmerised impotence of the democracies, agreed. Himmler undertook responsibility for boosting adherents to the Totenkopf-verbaende and turned over the job to the SS's chief recruiter, the Swabian Gottlob Berger.

It proved a wise choice. With consummate ruthless-ness, Berger circumvented army recruitment channels and began laying his hands on all the recruits he could. In a top-secret Fuehrer decree of 17 August 1938 it was stipulated that 'for special domestic tasks of a political nature, or for use by the German army in the event of mobilisation, the SS-Verfuegungstruppe, the SS-Junker-schulen (officer cadet school), the SS-Totenkopfver-baende and its reserve units are to be armed, trained and organised as military units.'

The Totenkopfverbaende was to be relieved from the duty of guarding concentration camps and transferred as a skeleton corps to the SS-Verfuegungstruppe.

Section 5, headed 'Regulations in case of Mobilisation', read:

'The SS-Totenkopfverbaende form the skeleton corps for the reinforcement of the SS-Verfuegung-struppe (police reinforcement) and will be replaced in the guarding of the concentration camps by members of the Allgemeine-SS who are over 45 years of age and have had military training.'

Eicke worked feverishly to train, equip and organise the new recruits into additional Totenkopf regiments. The expansion of the SS-Totenkopfverbaende which had been made during the Czech crisis was to be officially recognised and made permanent.

In yet another decree, dealing with the armed SS and dated 18 May 1939, the permanent minimum size of Eicke's Totenkopfverbaende was fixed at fourteen thousand men. Himmler was authorised to increase it to a strength of twenty-five thousand should there be a further mobilisation.

The demands of the army for additional manpower were shrill. To satisfy them, Hitler finally decreed that service in the SS-Totenkopfverbaende would count as army service for all SS officers and men who had joined the Death's Head units on or before 20 September 1938. In addition, the Totenkopfverbaende's role in the event of war was clearly spelt out. It was to serve as combat replacements for the units of SS-Verfuegungstruppe.

The new decree came not a moment too soon; Hitler was pushing ahead with his grand design for the immolation of Europe. By the end of August, all Totenkopf reservists received their emergency call-up.

Now the concentration camps had a new role — launching-pads at Buchenwald, Sachsenhausen and Mauthausen for fully armed Death's Head units with a strength of twenty-four thousand.

Hitler had previously made clear that as party formations the Totenkopfverbaende belonged neither to the Wehrmacht nor to the police. It was a standing force of the SS — an ever-ready force for just about any activity the Fuehrer required.

On the brink of invading Poland, Hitler announced that Totenkopfverbaende would be given a 'secret assignment' in the new war zone. That assignment, as it turned out, was to be to the particular tastes of Theodor Eicke.

4

The entire mechanised juggernaut of *Blitzkrieg* (lightning war) was unleashed on 1 September 1939 with cruel ruthlessness on undefended Poland.

Four days later, the battle for the Polish Corridor ended with the meeting of General Hans Gunther von Kluge's Fourth Army, knifing eastward from Pomerania, with the Third Army of General Georg von Kuechler, which had pressed westward from East Prussia. The decisive battle involved the tanks of General Heinz Guderian and they, perhaps more than anything else, explained the sad and dreadful destruction of the proud Polish Army. At one point, the tanks were attacked by the Pomorska brigade of cavalry — the long lance of the horse against the long cannon of the tank.

And then there was the Polish Air Force, most of its aircraft bombed before they could even leave the ground. On 6 September, Cracow, Poland's second city, fell and that same night the government fled from Warsaw to Lublin.

What of Adolf Hilter? The man who had vowed to destroy Poland and, in a speech to generals on 22 August, had declared he would use his Death's Head formation to annihilate men, women and children before pressing on to the Soviet Union, left Berlin for the battlefront in a steel cocoon of safety. He was aboard *Fuehrersonderzug Amerika*, his armoured special train (later renamed *Brandenburg*) which arrived in Bad Polzin, some one hundred kilometres east of Stettin, at dawn on 4 September. It had been watched over throughout by a squad of aircraft, under the command of SS-Gruppenfuehrer Hans Bauer.

Such protection was doubtlessly welcomed by the

40

Fuehrer's adjutants and aides, the physicians and secretaries, and SS and Foreign Office liaison officials — and, above all, by Theodor Eicke.

To be afforded the protection of the Fuehrer's special train was flattering enough, but now Eicke, the concentration camp supremo and former psychiatric clinic inmate, was dressed with additional authority. He carried the official title of Hoehere-SS und Polizei Fuehrer (higher SS and police leader), a distinction afforded him by the all-powerful decree of Heinrich Himmler.

It meant that Eicke was the direct representative of the Reichsfuehrer-SS. He possessed sweeping authority to deal with the Polish population. No one could gainsay his decisions when it came to measures for 'pacifying' the conquered areas of Poland. From now on, until they were withdrawn to be reformed into the Totenkopf Division in October 1939, three Totenkopf regiments — Oberbayern, Brandenburg and Thuringen — and the units and security police of the SD (Sicherheitsdienst, secret service), were, under Eicke, the supreme police authority of the Reich. Their fief was the provinces of Poznan, Lodz and Warsaw. Furthermore, part of Eicke's sinister remit was that the regiments were to operate independently of the control of the army, which certainly muttered about SS excesses but in reality could do precious little about them.

In all, some eighteen thousand from the Leibstandarte, Verfuegungstruppe and Totenkopf units took part in the campaign. Their fighting potential, given the comparatively easy odds, could not be judged fairly. Indeed, many members of what was to become the Waffen-SS had not realised that they were going to war at all, believing they were involved in just another of the SS officer-training schools' endless manoeuvres.

Largely with Wehrmacht support, the young volunteer SS groups had fought with a fanatical fury every bit as great as that of the Poles. With the fluency of intensive training, the majority of the SS moved steadily forward in section and platoon formations, sweeping the Poles from their positions.

Armoured cars sporting the SS runes and the Death's Head symbol so beloved of Theodor Eicke had stormed through the fighting at Danzig, but Totenkopf had another infinitely less glorious role. It was to act, in essence, as a murder band.

In the wake of the German armoured columns knifing into Poland came the lorries and motor cycles of the Einsatzgruppen, the 'action groups' of the security police and SD. These were under the control of SD chief Reinhard Heydrich who, with characteristic cynicism, immediately embarked on what he called a campaign of 'little terror'. It was a description which had a certain awful truth about it. For the activities of the Einsatzgruppen between September and November 1939 were mild compared with what was to come.

One particular Einsatzgruppe was to gain the devoted attention of Theodor Eicke.

A high-level meeting of 'Chefs der Sicherheitspolizei und des SD' was held on 12 September concerning the deployment of SS units in Poland. Here orders were given for units to be organised into five separate Einsatzgruppen to operate in conjunction with Eicke's manpower. SD-Einsatzgruppe 2, operating behind the German Eighth Army, was placed directly under the command of Eicke.

The Totenkopf Regiment Brandenburg, which moved into Poland on 13 September, was to make a particularly gruesome name for itself.

Originally formed in April 1935 as SS-Wachtruppe Brandenburg, it had been put to work as a guard unit for the concentration camp at Sachsenhausen. It achieved regiment status the following year and by the spring of 1939 could boast four battalions.

Standartenfuehrer Paul Nostitz had been one of Eicke's earliest protégés and was eager to build on the goodwill of his chief. There were plenty of opportunities.

With patent pride, Nostitz was soon submitting a report outlining with clinical exactitude how his Totenkopf men had conducted a campaign of house searches, securing villages from 'insurgents', and had arrested and shot large numbers of 'suspicious elements, plunderers, insurgents, Jews and Poles'.

There were sections of the Wehrmacht which attempted vainly to isolate the duties of Brandenburg to routine security assignments, in particular combing the forest which lay to the south of the city of Wloclawek. However, the SS considered the city itself offered a far more fruitful field of activity — tormenting the local citizenry, above all the Jews.

To make sure that his trusted subordinate did not rest on his laurels after that, SS-Gruppenfuehrer Gunther Pancke was despatched by Eicke to Nostitz's headquarters with further instructions. These were to send battalions of SS-Brandenburg to Bydgoszcz and conduct an 'intelligentsia action' there.

It was a strange phrase to describe a blueprint for murder, but that is precisely what it amounted to.

Within two days, eight hundred Polish civilians were hunted down, arrested and shot. Nostitz did not attend the 'intelligentsia action' in person. He was too busy mopping up his other adventure in Wloclawek.

Synagogues were set on fire; prominent Jewish citizens were arrested and tortured into confessing that they had personally started the blazes. Nostitz thus had a good excuse for fining his prisoners for starting the fires and a further two hundred thousand zlotys was levied against them for breaking the rule which forbade use by Jews of the pavements.

General Alfred Boehm-Tettelbach of the German Eighth Army was so disgusted with SS excesses that he submitted an indignant report to Eighth Army Commander Generaloberst Johannes Blaskowitz, who in turn protested to Generaloberst Walther von Brauchitsch, the German Army Commander-in-Chief.

The report was ignored. Boehm-Tettelbach had to contain his anger, scarcely helped by a remark made in his presence by the unrepentant Gruppenfuehrer Pancke: 'Totenkopf does not obey army orders. It has special tasks to perform that lie outside the competence of the army.' If news of the protests reached Eicke, it is doubtful that he did anything about them.

Some important fresh news from Himmler made far more agreeable listening.

The Reichsfuehrer-SS, the fervent admirer of the Jesuit Loyola ('My Ignatius', Hitler had fondly dubbed his devoted 'Heini') had created in his SS an organisation which, like the order of Jesuits, was a complete law unto itself, answerable only to its 'Pope', in this case the Fuehrer. Himmler, of course, had gone further than creating merely a cadre which would do Hitler's will. Romanticism of a twisted sort inhabited the sparse frame of the Reichsfuehrer. Himmler had read deeply the ancient legends of Teutonic knights wielding holy wars against the sub-human Slavs. He went even further. Was he not, he convinced himself, the actual reincarnation of the Saxon duke called Henry the Fowler, who became Heinrich I, founder of the German state?

In pursuit of this extraordinary conceit, he founded the 'new Teutonic' castle of Wewelsburg in the forests near Paderborn, an ancient town in Westphalia with historic associations going back to Charlemagne. Here at the cost of some eleven million marks was built a monastic-like establishment where privileged members of the SS met for a ritual of spiritual exercises. The design and association of the rooms were supposed to conjure up the spirit of Germany's greatness; each was named after a historic figure such as Frederick the Great. Needless to say, Himmler's own room was called Heinrich I.

Hitler, when told of these activities and Himmler's insistence on SS 'spiritual exercises', is reported to have burst into contemptuous laughter at what he regarded as 'arrant nonsense'. Indeed, if Himmler had stuck to his researches into the origins of Germany and the efficacy of garden herbs, he might have been less dangerous. But Himmler was seized with another obsession — his ruthless, driving ambition that bode ill for anyone who got in the way.

And, following the military success of the German campaign in Poland, Himmler was very ambitious for his

SS indeed.

He was fortunate, during the first week of October 1939, to find the Fuehrer highly sympathetic to his suggestion that new SS field divisions should be created for the forthcoming campaign in the west.

Such acquiescence on the part of the Fuehrer could by no means be taken for granted. Hitler reasoned that an armed SS was all very well, but it essentially had a policing role and it was desirable that it should return to this function once the brief war in the west was over and won. Besides, it was necessary to tread carefully. The deeply conservative army had no love for any groups of Nazis anxious to play at soldiers; the very suggestion of an expansion of SS activities was regarded with a shudder.

Hitler confessed to Himmler: 'I don't want to upset the generals by raising up the spectre of a party army.'

Himmler possessed the sort of serpentine ingenuity to supply an answer. In his capacity of Reichsfuehrer and Chief of the German Police, he transferred sufficient men from the SS-Totenkopf regiments, with their concentration camp guard duties, and the German police to form two new divisions. These men were then replaced by a new intake of volunteers not subject to military conscription. Himmler was thus able to enlarge Hitler's Praetorian guard, the Leibstandarte-SS Adolf Hitler, into a reinforced motorised infantry regiment and form the three pre-war Totenkopf regiments into yet another division. This was at first called the SS-Verfuegungs Division and later Das Reich.

Such methods of cunning and stealth in expanding the Waffen-SS (its future title) scarcely concerned Theodor Eicke. The fact remained that, no matter how it was constituted, he had been placed by Himmler to assume command of the brand-new Totenkopf Division.

As for Poland, one by one the centres of resistance crumbled. The three original Death's Head regiments which had gone to Poland were pulled out to be replaced by new Totenkopf people, many from the 12th SS-Totenkopf Regiment. They were enthusiastic recruits to terror, moving into Poznan province hot on the heels of the departing SS-Brandenburg.

But now Poland was shrugged aside impatiently as past history, a mere brief interlude in the far more serious business of preparing for war in the west.

As for Theodor Eicke, he had more immediate problems. Where, for example, was he to train his new division consisting of 6,500 members of the Totenkopfverbaende, some Verfuegungstruppe members and a few Allgemeine-SS?

The obvious answer was Dachau. The unfortunate inmates, who were under the illusion that they would be released to make way for the new division, speedily had their hopes dashed. Prisoners were transferred to camps at Flossenburg and Mauthausen.

Not even Himmler's guile in juggling with personnel and statistics could overcome the obvious distaste of the army for the new division.

Himmler was not above rubbing in his triumph with a certain grim satisfaction. Whereas members of the Totenkopf Division who had served in the pre-war Totenkopf regiments were allowed to retain their old insignia — Death's Head on the right and badges of rank on the left collar patch, together with regimental cuff-band — newly recruited personnel were issued with *army* uniforms. The field-blouse had collar patches with the Death's Head on both sides.

A small patina of military respectability for his Death's Head units was greatly valued by Eicke, who resented widely expressed opinions that his men were essentially nothing but a bunch of concentration camp sadists, and killers and looters of defenceless civilians. The fact remained, though, that however much Eicke may have craved a more respectable image, his methods of forging his new division into a weapon of war remained every bit as unsubtle as might be expected from this essentially crude one-time police nark.

The commander of the SS-Totenkopf Division knew little or nothing about tactics or strategy or the history of warfare. It all seemed childishly simple to him. War simply meant concentrating as many troops as possible on the objective. Each man was given a weapon; it was his duty to hurl himself at the enemy until there was total annihilation of himself or his objective, or both.

Sufficient of a realist to know his own limitations, Eicke did not hesitate to delegate. His choice of 'shadow' fell on SS-Standartenfuehrer Cassius Freiherr von Montigny.

Anyone seeking a model for the classic Prussian militarist, arrogant, humourless and totally without pity, could scarcely have made a better choice than this icy aristocrat who had served in the U-boat arm of the Imperial Navy in World War I.

It was easy to see what had attracted Eicke to the Freiherr. The latter had been steeped in political intrigue since 1918. He had served in the right-wing, pre-Nazi movement of the Freikorps, switched rapidly to the police and then found his niche in Hitler's Wehrmacht.

Montigny soon was shooting off a strongly phrased letter to Himmler in which he accused army leaders of being anti-Nazi, torpid and bureaucratic. When it is remembered that the army loathed and detested Himmler's very name, it has to be granted that Montigny was a master opportunist.

Himmler read: 'What the officer corps needs is a thoroughly politicised cadre of new men to infuse the army with the proper National Socialist spirit.'

It was indeed the sort of language that Himmler liked to hear. He scribbled some complimentary remarks on the memo and forwarded it to Hitler.

Reaction was not long in coming. On 1 April 1938, at the request of Heinrich Himmler, Montigny joined the SS with the rank of Obersturmbannfuehrer and was assigned to the SS-Junkerschule at Bad Tolz as instructor in military tactics. Just over a year later he found himself working as operations officer for Theodor Eicke.

Meanwhile, there were other pressing problems facing the new division. It was all very well for Himmler to be nagging away at the Fuehrer, insisting that the new SS divisions should be out there in the front of the first attack waves of the western front. What would be the good of that without a decent supply of weapons?

Himmler had issued orders that the Totenkopf regiments should be equipped in the same way as the regular infantry regiments. It was very easy for the Reichsfuehrer to make his airy pronouncements; getting the material was something else entirely.

A grumbling Oberfuehrer Heinrich Gaertner, Chief of the SS-Procurement Office, who had the job of getting the necessary equipment, told Himmler that a request to OKH (Oberkommando des Heeres, the Army High Command) 'under the authority of the Decree of the Fuehrer and Reich Chancellor of 18 May 1939' for eighty-four light pieces and 126 anti-tank guns for the Totenkopf regiments 'had not been answered'. SS field formations were drastically short of artillery, particularly guns of large calibre.

Gaertner put to Himmler that the SS should bypass the Wehrmacht and secure for itself the plentiful stock at the Skoda works in occupied Czechoslovakia. But the Wehrmacht was not going to be caught by that one; it had already taken the equipment 'under its own protection' and had no intention of surrendering it.

Eicke boiled at what he regarded as particularly childish domestic squabbling. To him, there appeared no problem. The only way to get weapons was plainly to hijack them. In a single operation, he mustered a team to swoop down on the motor pool of the concentration camp inspectorate at Oranienburg. The haul was modest but acceptable — twenty-two Opel-Blitz trucks and nineteen motor cycles were seized.

It was all done under the polite term 'requisitioning'; the truth was that Eicke became an expert at begging, borrowing and, if necessary, filching the supplies he needed.

Endlessly throughout the days and nights, convoys belonging to the new division shuttled in and out of Dachau. They penetrated into every corner of the Reich, seizing whatever items were needed.

Complaints about Eicke's high-handed methods were inevitable. Oberfuehrer Richard Gluecks, now the Head of Concentration Camp Inspectorate, rebelled when

Eicke in late December despatched a convoy of thirty drivers to Oranienburg to seize any additional trucks and vehicles not urgently needed for the inspectorate. Such high-handed behaviour, he stormed, was not to be tolerated.

Himmler, for all his ruthlessness, had a horror of rows among his executives. He readily agreed to censure Eicke for the sake of smooth relations. The commander of the Totenkopf division, he declared in a letter, was to be forbidden any more vehicles from the motor pools of the SS. He would just have to make do with existing supplies until the army was prepared to release more vehicles to the Waffen-SS.

Insensitive though he was, Eicke smarted under the indignity of his position. Here he was, as commander of a division, having to adopt ludicrously underhand methods to secure the supplies he desperately needed. True, he was flooded with armoured cars, motor-cycle side-cars, Czech-made trucks and a clutch of field howitzers, but of more essential ironmongery such as 150 mm artillery pieces, let alone the medium half-tracks to transport them, there was no sign. It was necessary to motorise three infantry regiments and the reconnaissance battalion.

There appeared to be virtually no prospect of getting essential armaments.

However, in one sense fortune smiled on Theodor Eicke. The end of 1939 gave him the valuable breathing-space he so badly needed. There was a deceptive calm. On 12 December, the Fuehrer had issued a top secret directive which postponed the attack in the west. It was stipulated that a fresh decision would be made immediately after Christmas; now the earliest possible date for 'A' Day was 1 January 1940. Then on 27 December came yet another postponement 'by at least a fortnight'. On 13 January there was yet a further delay, due to 'the meteorological situation'.

It was frustrating for those Germans spoiling for a fight, no doubt, but for the under-equipped, under-trained Totenkopf Division it was a blessing.

The internal affairs of Totenkopf were far from well. Discipline within the division was nothing less than appalling. Certainly there was on hand a lot of belligerent talent capable of getting drunk in the Munich bars and generally making a nuisance of itself, but Eicke could scarcely muster troops capable of taking to the battlefield. Furthermore, he realised that, however unpalatable it might be, he had to produce manpower which would be subservient to Wehrmacht discipline.

For the most part he had on his hands a bunch of thugs, and he had only a matter of months, possibly weeks, to lick them into shape; members of the Ordnungspolizei and the Allgemeine-SS were of a different calibre from those who had served in SS-Oberbayern, SS-Brandenburg and SS-Thuringen.

One of the troubles was peculiar to troops the world over and not just to the SS. The barracks were near Munich, where the temptations of bars and brothels proved overwhelming. Cases of syphilis were something Totenkopf officers preferred not to be faced with on the eve of war.

On 13 November, Eicke acted. Violations of the criminal code would be dealt with by a species of internal discipline that was nothing less than Draconian. Courts martial, instituted solely by the SS, would deal with all offenders against discipline and Eicke himself would be the sole arbiter of sentences.

He had acted just in time. On the night of 20-21 November, men of the Totenkopf Division distinguished themselves in one scandalous act of misconduct that could have caused Eicke his job or worse.

It was the 14th Company of 2nd Infantry Regiment of the division which let its commander down. Six enlisted men in a stolen Opel-Blitz truck paid several visits to bars in Munich. The outcome was inevitable. The truck, making for home, weaved out of the city and smashed head-on with a streetcar. Damage to both vehicles was serious. Not that the offending Totenkopf men were worried or, indeed, were aware of what had happened. The police, surrounded by an inquisitive crowd, found the men totally comatose in the back of the stolen vehicle.

With a mixture of cajolery and threats, Eicke managed to avoid any publicity. Once that was achieved, he turned the full force of his rage on the offenders. They lost rank and were expelled from the SS. For Eicke it was not enough. He despatched them to Buchenwald.

This was tricky territory; Eicke had no power to throw into concentration camps those who had offended against the military code. But the commander of Totenkopf was determined to give his own interpretation of the law. The sentence against the malcontents went either unnoticed or unchallenged.

Eicke grew in confidence — other troublemakers who dared to disobey him also went the same way.

Punishments such as these were accompanied by maximum humiliation. Offenders from Totenkopf were paraded in convict garb. The incarceration period was indefinite, but even when he came out of jail a disgraced Totenkopf man soon found that his troubles were far from over. To be expelled from the SS meant virtual ostracism from the German community. Such a pariah would only have the most menial of jobs open to him.

Aside from discipline, the nagging problem of equipping the new SS-Totenkopf Division persisted.

Himmler soon discovered that it was not merely a question of issuing instructions to the armaments factories. There was the entire army establishment with which to contend; predictably, it had no love whatsoever for Totenkopf with division status or not.

The Reichsfuehrer made fresh approaches to Armaments Minister Fritz Todt. Immediately the army smelt a rat.

To the fury of the owlish Himmler, who nursed an almost pathological sense of inferiority, military chiefs ignored him altogether and protested volubly to Hitler. The protest was not simply because of detestation of the SS; the Wehrmacht, it again argued, had extreme difficulty in securing enough supplies for itself.

Why, fumed Eicke, should Totenkopf be treated in this scurvy fashion? It was common knowledge that the

Verfuegungs Division was equipped and motorised with the best of German weapons, and the Leibstandarte was if anything over-supplied. Although Eicke was anxious to live down the early days of the Totenkopfverbaende, arguing that his new division was of totally different calibre, the association with concentration camps remained obstinately in the minds of the Wehrmacht officer corps. Eicke and his band were regarded as beyond the pale.

The only way in which the Wehrmacht was prepared to unbend was to throw Eicke a few Czech weapons to keep him quiet. The army, as it turned out, was in for a surprise.

On 2 April 1940, just over a month before the assault on the west, Totenkopf received a visit from Generaloberst Maximilian von Weichs of the Second Army, to which Totenkopf Division had been assigned.

In preliminary talks with Weichs and his staff, Eicke had to swallow his pride and listen to patronising remarks about 'this outfit that has been organised and equipped like a Czech division'. It was plain to Eicke that the snobs in the Wehrmacht knew nothing of how he had secured the ironmongery he needed. Well, they were about to find out.

The inspection left Weichs astonished. Here beyond dispute was a modern, motorised infantry division. Furthermore, this was a time when only seven of the German Army's 139 infantry divisions were motorised. Eicke was also able to add the information that a heavy-artillery section was also being organised.

Weichs was jerked out of his contemptuous lassitude as he paraded past the ranks of SS who were to go into battle with the Death's Head insignia on the right collar patches of their uniforms. His inspection of the troops left him noticeably impressed. He finished his visit in a frame of mind somewhat different from when he arrived.

Others were not so sure. Generaloberst Franz Halder, Chief of the German Army General Staff, commented that the Totenkopf Division presented 'a nice appearance' but was not really to be trusted with front-line duty.

Theodor Eicke was no doubt all very well in his way, but he was after all only a 'police general'.

Humiliation could surely go no further. In fact it could and it did. The disposition of the SS divisions assembled for the invasion of France really rubbed Eicke's nose in it. The Leibstandarte and Der Fuehrer regiment were to be poised on the Dutch border to link up with troops assigned to snatch key fortifications, while the remainder of SS-Verfuegungs Division remained alongside 9th Panzer Division. Totenkopf was to be kept in reserve on the Rhine.

The SS Division Polizei fared even worse. It was on static duty to Army Group C under General Wilhelm von Leeb. Indeed, it was to spend most of the campaign glaring balefully at the Maginot Line.

Totally against his nature, Eicke had to compose his soul in patience. The astonishing speed and success of Hitler's 1940 advance in the west was to ensure the delay would be brief.

5

The massive throaty roar of heavy German bombers, orchestrated by the high-pitched screech of German Stukas, shattered the calm of the May dawn.

Soon a great Anglo-French army was hurtling northwest from the Franco-Belgian border to man the main Belgian defence line along the Dyle and Meuse rivers east of Brussels. The success and speed of the German advance, entailing the despatch of panzers through the hilly, wooded country of the Ardennes, stunned the Allies.

The assault on the west had been envisaged by Hitler and the German High Command on a scale hitherto unknown in the history of warfare. Here were the finest armoured motorised divisions in the world; ninety-three divisions arrayed in three army groups stretching the entire length of Germany's Rhine boundary from Holland to Switzerland.

Seldom could a would-be conqueror have faced so complacent an enemy. After all, was there not the impenetrable Maginot Line? German tanks? Certainly these were known to be formidable, but, after all, the Allies could more or less match the Germans as they did in the number of divisions — 136 Germans against 135 French and British (only nine divisions).

But the Allies did not have General Erich von Manstein, chief of staff of General Gerd von Rundstedt's Army Group A on the western front. Manstein, with whom the Totenkopf was to become much involved during the war with Russia, was a beaky-nosed, icy-eyed disciplinarian; the army was quite literally the dominating passion of his life.

It was Manstein who proposed that the tanks should be launched through the Ardennes with a massive armoured force, which would then cross the Meuse north of Sedan, breaking out into the open country for a helter-skelter dash to the channel ports. Manstein further proposed that a feint by the right wing of the German forces would bring the British and French armies speeding to Belgium. Then by cracking through the French at Sedan and heading west along the Somme's north bank for the Channel, the Germans would entrap the major Anglo-French forces along with the Belgian Army.

Manstein had sold the idea to Hitler and done it so skilfully that the Fuehrer ended by believing that he had proposed it in the first place.

Above all, it was going to work.

And what of the role of the Totenkopf Division? At the time of the invasion Theodor Eicke reckoned himself to be the most hard-done-by fighting soldier in the entire Reich. What was it Halder had sneeringly called him? 'A police general'. The insult had smarted and plainly it had been the army's intention that it should. For on 10 May, the date of the invasion of western Europe, Theodor Eicke had been firmly put in his place.

On the previous evening, Second Army had signalled him to have the Totenkopf Division on full alert by dawn the following morning. Movement, he was further told, would be at short notice. That sounded like business. Eicke was even more delighted when he received instructions to despatch a truck column to Kassel to pick up sixty tons of field rations which the division would need. Enough for a ten-day march were issued. Commanders received their orders to be at the ready within twelve hours.

Eicke waited for the summons that must surely come. It did not. Or, rather, such orders that were issued merely told him to be prepared for march instructions from the relevant army group. March instructions! Already, Eicke reflected bitterly, the invasion had begun. The SS was represented by SS-Leibstandarte and SS-Verfuegungs Division. His Totenkopf was no less combat-ready than the other two. Halder had continued sarcastic and distrustful. Clearly, the impressionable Weichs had counted for nothing. The hours spent in begging, borrowing, filching and stockpiling guns, ammunition, vehicles and other materials had been nothing less than a waste of time.

Eicke saw his treatment as a calculated insult by the snobs in the army. To judge by later experiences, when the Wehrmacht would attempt to slap him down time and again, he was probably right.

Months of scheming and chicanery had enabled the division to be built up to its present strength. And for what? All the Totenkopf could do was listen to the almost monotonous catalogue of German triumphs.

But as it turned out, bitterness could not be nursed for very long. Success in war, as in everything else, carried its penalties. The advance of 7th Panzer Division under General Rommel, for example, had been at terrific speed. But, while it kept going, it urgently needed the services of infantry to clear points of resistance and occupy ground.

By the late afternoon of 12 May, Guderian's tank

columns were in possession of Sedan and the north bank of the Meuse; the progress of Rundstedt's advance forced the army to make the first change in the status of the Totenkopf Division.

Orders came to move westward forthwith to a new reserve staging-area on the frontier of Belgium. By 8 p.m., Totenkopf Division was on the move, driving through the night in twenty-mile-long columns, passing through Cologne in the early-morning darkness.

Then had come four days of further frustration; four days before final marching-orders were forthcoming. Eicke passed the time in characteristic style: the men of Totenkopf were made to exercise and drill. There were ideological harangues on National Socialism. There were compulsory baths and hair-cuts.

By the night of 14 May, the spearheads of Army Group A were preparing to break out of the Meuse bridgeheads; Eicke was alerted to stand by. Sedan and Dinant were soon far behind. Hitler's armoured divisions fanned out and careered triumphantly towards the Channel ports.

Eicke's instructions were to move west along the southern tip of Holland and through Belgium, to link up with the 15th Panzer Corps of General Hermann Hoth. He was moving with breakneck speed; in went Totenkopf Division to add much-needed muscle.

The march through Holland and Belgium involved no fighting as the British and French had been pushed back. But there were other problems. The swift progress of the armies led to a number of traffic snarl-ups. Eicke was no respecter of the Wehrmacht, certainly not of its rankers. Countless times, he leapt from his command car to bluster and threaten passage for his own men. Desperately tired and footsore troops replied to the SS upstart with interest. The delay seemed eternal; indeed it was not until the early evening of 19 May that the truck columns of Totenkopf Division were able to roll foward again.

Orders for the first combat assignment were of a kind which time and again were to characterise the role of Totenkopf Division in this war. Eicke's men were pressed into service as Hitler's 'fire brigade', racing to pull other units out of the fire.

Seventh Panzer needed help — and fast. Rommel's crack division had been halted between Le Cateau and Cambrai. The French were pinning it down in a savage counter-attack.

For the task, Eicke peeled off Totenkopf Division's 1st Infantry Regiment, together with anti-tank, engineer and artillery companies. They were pressed into attack across the Sambre River towards both Le Cateau and Cambrai.

Small villages were defended by French Moroccan troops. With such opponents there could be no question of taking prisoners. They were hauled from the houses and slaughtered in their hundreds after vicious hand-to-hand fighting.

Next there came a concentrated series of tank attacks, but by mid-morning on 20 May, Eicke had cleared the enemy from east and north of Cambrai. Advance could be resumed by 15th Panzer Corps.

Allied divisions were later trapped between Rundstedt's Army Group A and Generaloberst Fedor von Boch's Group B. Eicke's orders now were to mass in force, cross the Scarpe River and advance due north to the highway running west out of Arras.

Eicke may well have reflected grimly that he need scarcely have worried about inaction. The British had concentrated two battalions of the Royal Tank Regiment and an infantry brigade of the Expeditionary Force. Soon after 2 p.m., leading British tanks hurled themselves at the flank of Rommel's infantry and armoured regiments and proceeded to batter them mercilessly.

Tanks, armoured cars and infantry made up the confusing battle, which was as deadly as anything Totenkopf Division had yet encountered. In dismay, Eicke saw his shells bouncing harmlessly off the tanks. His gun-crews were blasted to pieces by the thirty-ton British Matildas. Men died horribly as they fell screaming under the treads. But many of the anti-tank gunners held on, hurling themselves at the British, singly or in pairs, with hand grenades. It was a futile gesture, calculated only to send the casualty figures mounting.

In the manner of Rommel, the British attack were led from an open car by Major-General Giffard Le Quesne Martel, who had been one of the greatest advocates of tank development in the inter-war years.

Two mobile columns struck southwards around the west of Arras. Both consisted of a tank battalion and an infantry battalion of the Durhams. Shorn of all air cover, their objective was to arrow at speed for the river Cojeul. The right-hand column had suddenly come to grips at Duisans with motorised infantry of Rommel's 7th Panzer advancing north-west.

Cursing, Martel realised that there had been a serious fault in Franco-British reconnaissance; an eventuality of this kind should have been anticipated. Duisans was plainly not going to be saved without a fight. Its eventual clearing was not without cost to the British; companies of infantry and some anti-tank guns had to be left behind to hold the place.

This sort of sacrifice could ill be afforded by the British, but worse lay in store for the columns pressing onto the Douellens-Arras road. Heavy machine-guns and mortar fire cascaded onto Martel's forces. The Luftwaffe streaked gleefully into the act with a twenty-minute assault.

The next objective was Wailly, where tanks hit SS-Totenkopf Division. The conflict was brief and bloody. The British got the worst of it, and fell back ignominiously.

Luck was to desert the British with a vengeance that day, but the next disaster was not inflicted by the SS formations. A detachment of French tanks opened fire on British anti-tank guns, mistaking them for Germans. Before the error was discovered there was furious fire in which one British tank was knocked out, several men killed and more than one French tank hit.

The confusing battle of tanks, armoured cars and infantry that followed was to prove a sobering experience indeed for Totenkopf Division. The engagement ended abruptly with the scream of Stukas; the remaining British tanks were beaten off. The cost to the Germans was considerable: thirty-nine dead, sixty-six wounded and two missing.

Although the uncomfortable truth tended to become blurred later, Eicke's role in this particular engagement was not covered with glory. Some of the units had panicked in the early stages. In the supply columns, men had been seen to abandon their vehicles and flee in the path of an approaching group of British tanks.

Unfortunately, the rot spread to Rommel's men. The general described how in Wailly he found 'chaos and confusion among our troops in the village and they were jamming up the roads and yards with their vehicles, instead of going into action with every available weapon to fight off the oncoming enemy. We tried to create order.'

A chronic attack of rattled nerves was suffered by the Germans after the unexpectedly vicious attack delivered at Arras. Totenkopf Division henceforth was regarded with caution and in some cases open hostility.

Just how hostile, Eicke was destined to find out when the next 'fire brigade' role presented itself — transfer to General Erich Hoepner's 16th Panzer Corps which also accommodated the SS-Verfuegungs Division and 3rd and 4th Panzer.

Orders to Eicke were blunt. Personal ruthlessness where his men's lives were concerned was to be held in check; he was carefully to reconnoitre a designated area. And do nothing else. There were to be no heroics, no grand slam. The commander of Totenkopf Division toed the line.

Hoepner then proceeded to his next objective. A full-scale attack across the line of the La Bassee Canal was planned. Its object was to prevent the retreating British from digging in on what was a natural defence line. Eicke's role was spelled out with a complete absence of ambiguity: advance on the town of Béthune and probe the waterway for a likely crossing-point. At no time was he actually ordered to make the crossing, but that was a mere detail he forthwith decided to ignore.

Numbers of battalion strength were ordered across; the elementary precaution of reconnoitring the opposite bank

59

was totally dispensed with. The men of Totenkopf then proceeded to go hunting for trouble.

They found it quickly enough. The British were dug strongly into the town and started firing forthwith on the interlopers. The SS scuttled back across the canal. Eicke pressed on with his main preoccupation, which was moving artillery and anti-tank batteries into position along the canal. Engineers were brought up to prepare bridges for a large-scale crossing.

British resistance continued to be fierce and any ideas of getting his men across were patently futile. So Eicke had to fall back on his original instructions: find a weak point where crossings might be possible. In flagrant disobedience of Hoepner's instructions he had achieved nothing beyond copious blood-letting.

Hoepner had made his feelings felt. The inevitable reprimand left Eicke completely unmoved. What really smarted was that his men had been forced into the indignity of withdrawing to defensive positions.

As if to rub salt in the wound, the British kept up fierce artillery and mortar fire for the next two days, while the SS could do nothing but sit and take it all.

The moment came when Eicke could no longer bear the strain on men and materials. But there was the need to proceed tactfully with Hoepner. Cautiously, a few selected SS men were sent to look over the British positions on the opposite bank, putting as many mortar batteries as possible out of action.

Obersturmfuehrer Harrer's combat group made the journey across the water safely enough. The danger came as they were making their way along a road on the other side, when they spotted the motor-cyclist. He was a British courier, and once the SS had seen him he had no chance. Almost as a reflex action, the Mauser was raised and its bullet caught the rider in the right shoulder. The men of Totenkopf hauled the badly injured man out of his ditch and began their interrogation. It was a fruitless exercise because the prisoner refused to say anything even when Harrer addressed him in halting English.

Harrer shrugged impatiently as if to indicate that the whole business was taking far too long. He aimed his weapon at the head of the wounded man and pulled the trigger at point-blank range. Then his Totenkopf comrades threw the body and the motor cycle into a drainage ditch and carried on with their interrupted march.

The British remained glued to the canal line; there could be no scruples now about the use of the rest of the Totenkopf. It would have to cross the canal and get in the thick of the fighting with everybody else.

Standartenfuehrer Friedmann Goetze, helped by Eicke's heavy artillery to soften up the British positions, crossed with his Totenkopf regiment to secure a bridgehead. On the left, Standartenfuehrer Heinz Bertling began his move across under the cloak of darkness and ran straight into heavy opposition.

All at once nothing seemed so important as the pre-dawn completion of those pontoon bridges. Shortly after daybreak on 27 May, Eicke received additional orders from Hoepner. There was to be an attack in force across the canal line. Béthune was to be seized, along with the villages of Estaires and Neuve Chapelle. But Hoepner had miscalculated; nobody had grasped the extent of the fire-power of the British. It raged and stormed in one of the most bitter engagements in the entire battle of France.

Somehow — nobody quite knew how — Eicke's men on 27 May managed to swarm across the canal on the skilfully constructed pontoon bridges, while a vicious artillery assault was unleashed on the seemingly tireless British.

Hold Béthune! That was the message for the 1st Battalion of the Royal Scots Regiment, the 2nd Battalion of the Royal Norfolk, the 1st Battalion of the 8th Lancashire Fusiliers. There was a bid to follow the orders with grim exactitude; it was interpreted by the British as meaning not just the obvious defensive positions, but every brick of every building.

Not an inch was uncontested in street, alley, darkened building, shack or barn. Ammunition ran out. It mattered not a jot; Eicke's enemies fought on with knives, bayonets, entrenching shovels.

The onslaught began to tell. By noon it was clear that Heinz Bertling's situation was nothing less than desperate. Like so many demented lemmings, his infantrymen, only lightly armed, had hurled themselves at heavily camouflaged machine-gun nests. They paid the price for their commander's impetuosity and inexperience. The British gleefully pressed their advantage. They began breaking up Bertling's regiment into separate, isolated pockets. Soon all was chaos and radio contact with a fuming Eicke hopelessly lost.

Orders were issued, countermanded, reissued. Dazed staff commanders wandered around like chickens without heads.

The next disaster was so devastating and so unexpected that it left Eicke emotionally pole-axed along with the rest of his senior staff.

That brilliant dour aristocrat, SS-Standartenfuehrer Cassius Freiherr von Montigny, who had been one of Eicke's most valued associates and in France was the commander's operations officer, suddenly keeled over and collapsed. This was not from an enemy bullet but a haemorrhaging stomach ulcer. The only course was to evacuate him quickly to a rear-dressing station and from there back to Germany. At a stroke, SS-Totenkopf Division had lost its best military mind and not through the fortunes of war, either.

Eicke had no time to reflect on the irony before misfortune bludgeoned him again. A British sniper got Standartenfuehrer Goetze into his sights outside the village of Le Paradis. Another senior officer had been snatched from the scene.

A curtain of silence now fell around Goetze's battalion, which had been on a mercy mission on behalf of the luckless Bertling. It took hours to re-establish radio contact and resume the attack.

Morale in the division plummeted. There was also a cold furious anger against the British. The pride of the arrogant black knights had been dented, the stuffing knocked out of them.

Fury when it finally exploded centred on the village of Le Paradis, about one mile west of the fortified defensive line.

A battalion of the 2nd Royal Norfolks was hanging on tenaciously throughout the day, beleaguered in a group of farm buildings near the pretty hamlet. This battalion, together with the Royal Scots, held the villages of Riez du Vinage, Le Cornet Malo and Le Paradis, where battalion headquarters was situated.

The 2nd Infantry Regiment of Totenkopf concentrated all its energies on Le Cornet Malo; its reward was nothing short of a bloodbath. According to one German account, 4 officers and 150 men were killed and 18 officers and 480 men wounded. This was the first taste of battle for 2nd Infantry Regiment; its men were enraged at its losses and even more incensed at the impossibly slow advance.

Emil Stuerzbecher, Adjutant of 1st Battalion, witnessed resistance at Le Cornet Malo being gradually worn down. But what was the extent of the British strength still holding the villages? Stuerzbecher sought what information he could from ammunition-carriers, returning wounded and assorted other stragglers.

Somebody shouted: 'There are wounded British lying at that burning fire over there.'

Stuerzbecher, together with the assistant medical officer, was soon looking at a group of around twenty-five lying and sitting British wounded. Orders were hastily given for the men to be removed from the burning building.

Then all at once Stuerzbecher was stiffening to attention at a brisk command from his superior officer, Hauptsturmfuehrer Fritz Knoechlein, who snapped: 'These prisoners are nothing to do with you. They belong to me.'

Stuerzbecher later commented disgustedly: 'The man was storming and raving like a lunatic. He obviously wanted to add the prisoners to his list of captured, for his own credit.'

Obersturmfuehrer Max Schneider, a mortar-layer, knew

63

that there was a lot more to it than that. At noon, he had witnessed the complete encirclement of the area around Le Paradis. Heavy mortars pounded the remaining positions.

But it was neither the fighting nor the devastation which had rooted Schneider's attention. When his unit moved towards the village he saw a group of British troops. They had been disarmed and lined up in marching order on the road, escorted by SS riflemen. Among the knot of officers was Fritz Knoechlein.

An officer gave the order for the heavy-mortar section to cease firing. The prisoners were ordered to move through a gateway into a meadow. It seemed to be a welcome diversion for the mortar-crew, who sat down thankfully to rest. Besides, there was nothing for them to do now.

Theodor Emke, section commander in charge of a machine-gun platoon of No. 4 Company, moved with his men along rue de Paradis, crossing an open field and reaching the meadow. Then from Untersturmfuehrer Petrie, who was Emke's superior, came the abrupt order: 'Halt!'

Emke thought: 'The fellow seems rattled. What's wrong?'

His expression must have conveyed as much, because here was Petrie snapping: 'I'm taking command of the section. Hurry up. Get the guns in position.'

The machine-gun team opened fire; defenceless troops were mown down. There were moments of individual horror in the mass slaughter; one man pointing to his chest, desperately begging for the *coup de grâce*.

There was not much time to take in those heaps of shattered bodies or to listen to the screams of the dying. Emke was conscious that Petrie was at his elbow, ordering him to take back command of the section. It resumed its progress; the last thing Emke heard was shots that came either from pistols or rifles.

Fritz Knoechlein, on the other hand, was in no hurry to move on. He gave himself a full hour to determine that the British prisoners were dead. But then he was a thorough man; thorough, above all, in the enthusiasm with which he had embraced the SS. It had probably been inevitable, in an ambitious youngster trapped in a series of dead-end jobs during the dreary years of the Weimar Republic preceding Hitler. By the outbreak of war, the former errand-boy, insurance agent and clerk had become a company commander in Dachau. Then providentially had come the formation of Totenkopf Division.

Theodor Eicke could scarcely have had a more industrious disciple — a man who after the shooting at Le Paradis had ordered a squad of his men to fix their bayonets. Then they had set to among the bodies, stabbing and shooting in the head anyone who might have survived.

It had been a highly successful day's work for Knoechlein, the product of Dachau who loved killing so much. He ordered his company to quit the spot and push on to Estaires and Merville, where the British had dug a new defence line.

6

When it came to waging war conventionally on the battlefield, Generaloberst Erich Hoepner of 16th Panzer Corps yielded to no one in ruthlessness as a tank commander. But he was no callous killer; his contempt for the SS crystallised into naked hatred over the likes of Eicke and his Totenkopf Division.

From the start, Hoepner was cynical about the ability of Totenkopf to behave efficiently in action. An order had been transmitted to Eicke that his armoured formations along La Bassee Canal should be halted so that they could rest and refit. This also helped to ensure that lives were not wasted needlessly.

Eicke's reaction had been one of cold fury. He stormed

at Hoepner: 'What do losses matter? One must hold one's position and not retreat in the face of the enemy.'

Hoepner had stared at him coldly, only trusting himself to comment: 'That is a butcher's attitude.'

Few other exchanges between SS and Wehrmacht pinpointed their differing philosophies quite so neatly.

News of the Le Paradis atrocity was soon spreading throughout 16th Panzer Corps and neighbouring divisions. Varying accounts reached Hoepner, who promptly issued an order; all officers and men were warned that killing prisoners either as reprisal or punishment would be considered murder by a court martial. In the meantime, he intended to launch an exhaustive enquiry as to just what had happened at Le Paradis.

Sifting rumour from fact hindered any investigation. But there was one man capable of throwing useful light on what had happened. Gunter d'Alquen, a Third Reich journalist who had been the first editor of the Nazi newspaper *Das Schwarze Korps* and who in March 1940 had formed a War Correspondents' Company, visited Divisional Headquarters on the day following the massacre.

He learnt from a medical officer of heavy fighting by the Totenkopf Division and of even heavier casualties.

A divisional officer, assigned to take him round, let drop the news that the British soldiers had been mown down at the side of a road.

Startled, d'Alquen queried: 'Why?'

The officer told him: 'It seems these soldiers had displayed a white flag with a swastika painted on it and had fired on our men after agreeing to surrender.'

The journalist and his driver eventually found their way to the crude little farmhouse where the men of the Royal Norfolks had held out for as long as possible and from which, dog-tired and unshaven, they had stumbled out to surrender.

D'Alquen noticed the bodies of some fifty soldiers, apparently slaughtered where they stood. The corpses were promptly photographed as a record for the Totenkopf Division.

The evidence of witnesses and others who had seen

either the shootings or at least some of the bodies was forwarded by Hoepner to Sixth Army Headquarters and headed *Subject - Shooting of English Prisoners by SS-T-Div*.

After the discovery of bodies by d'Alquen and the divisional officer on the day following the massacre, the Totenkopf Division was ordered to put in a report. This was a masterpiece of evasion, couched in terms which plainly suggested that the army should get on with the war and leave the SS alone.

The Wehrmacht retaliated with a demand for a fuller report. This and all the subsequent questions were greeted with further evasions or ignored altogether. Highest levels within Totenkopf were obviously playing for time. The reason was clear; early in June Totenkopf quitted the corps command.

But German military archives contained devastating testimonies which were to surface in 1948 at the trial of Fritz Knoechlein. Along with the documents, there confronting him were Albert Pooley and William O'Callaghan, both privates in the Royal Norfolks who had miraculously survived the massacre and made good their escape.

A report from Corps Headquarters referred to 'prisoners who had been shot, by way of summary execution in the head; which shots must have been fired at very close range. In some cases the whole skull was smashed, a type of wound which can have been inflicted by blows from rifle butts or similar weapons . . . I ordered my driver to count the corpses. He recorded eighty-nine.'

Doctor Major Haddenhorst, in a document headed *Report regarding the Shooting of English soldiers by SS Inf*, stated:

'The bulk of the corpses lying together in heaps immediately gave the impression of a mass shooting. Upon examination of the individual wounds it was ascertained that they were mostly head wounds caused by rifle ammunition resulting in the blowing off of the cranium and exudation of the brains. Some of the shots were from behind. Many of the dead showed several wounds and some of them also had wounds in the back. A few corpses had pistol-shot wounds from close range, which is taken as meaning they were given the *coup de grâce*.

'In a stable attached to the house there were fourteen wounded. They were attended by an M.O. and later removed; when questioned he said they had been wounded at another spot and carried into the house by German soldiers.'

Faced with these details and the pointed questions which Totenkopf refused to answer, the army demanded a court martial for Fritz Knoechlein. Eicke lost no time in running to Himmler, who promptly decreed that what had happened at Le Paradis was henceforth to be designated 'a state secret'.

After the war, when the intelligence services in London came to investigate the case of the Le Paradis massacre and start the hunt for Knoechlein, they came up against one phrase with monotonous regularity: *'Es war eine geheime Reichsache.'* ('It was a state secret.')

Knoechlein did eventually stand in the dock of a Hamburg military court to claim that the British had sported an enemy flag and, furthermore, had been using 'dum-dum' bullets — ammunition with flattened, filed, blunted or otherwise distorted points to cause excessive injury. Unproven claims did not save Knoechlein from the gallows.

But in 1940, his career was only just getting into its stride. By 1944, he would be commanding a regiment of volunteer SS in Norway as an SS-Obersturmbannfuehrer, a holder of the Knight's Cross.

Generaloberst Hoepner was obliged to contain his indignation at SS excesses; it was necessary to get on with fighting the war. And there was plenty of work for the men of the detested Totenkopf Division.

From a position along the Lys Canal, Eicke received his orders. The attack on Estaires was to be launched early on the morning of 28 May and a bridgehead secured across the canal. Sixteenth Army Corps was intent on forming a new canal-defence line. Enemy resistance would receive a gigantic clout; German forces would arrow to the north-east, and further withdrawal of Allied forces would be impossible.

As the centre division of Hoepner's corps, Totenkopf would lead the attack and, so Eicke confidently asserted, grab all the glory.

But it was not to be. The arrogant, supremely self-confident products of the barrack square with their fresh faces and immaculate uniforms had been taught that they were the members of an élite and therefore invincible. But the men of Totenkopf Division were worn down with fatigue from the previous day's fighting. British artillery counter-attacks in and around Estaires were so violent that Eicke's tired forces were all too soon on the defence.

Throughout the day, vehicles were set ablaze while the casualties spiralled. It would not have been so high a cost if there had been some tangible advantage. But by darkness the Totenkopf Division could chalk up an advance of precisely half a mile.

Hoepner's fury knew no bounds. He had always known that the SS were animals. But they were shown to be incompetent as well.

Over the telephone, Eicke received the full brunt of his superior's fury. Hoepner snapped: 'You will resume the attack at dawn tomorrow morning. Shift your position over to the west and see you don't fail me again.'

Estaires was on Totenkopf Division's right as lead units of engineers, riflemen and anti-tank gunners swarmed across the canal. With mounting excitement, Eicke saw that the British were drawing back.

General Hermann Hoth, Hoepner's superior as Panzer Group Commander, gave the Totenkopf no rest. It was made to snap relentlessly at the heels of the retreating British at Bailleul, north-west of Armentières and east of St Omer. At that point, Hoth directed, they would halt and await the units on their flanks.

On sped the advance, but it soon became obvious that there were limits to British withdrawal. At first grey light came the deadly stream of artillery-fire from positions north of Estaires and Bailleul. Eicke had the ignominious experience of having to scuttle for cover with his staff. The British, as soon as they could, made good their escape.

The main trouble was the sheer power of British artillery-fire. Eicke pleaded for the Luftwaffe to bomb the menace so that the Totenkopf advance could proceed.

But there were destined to be more frustrations; the source of it had nothing to do with either Hoepner or Eicke.

There was no shortage of fierce inter-service rivalry within the German High Command. The bombastic Hermann Goering, head of the Luftwaffe, proclaimed: 'The British are trapped in the Dunkirk pocket. Don't waste your valuable Panzer formations. My aircraft will finish them off.'

On the whole, the Wehrmacht had enjoyed a surprisingly smooth passage through France; the air arm had grabbed precious little kudos. Now was the time, Goering reasoned, to redress the balance.

Hitler allowed himself to be persuaded. Goering saw the destruction of the British as a simple mopping-up operation that the army should leave alone. As for the Panzers, it would be enough for them to stand by at a safe distance to keep the British Army hemmed in.

The order to halt was withdrawn after forty-eight hours. But it was by then too late. The British evacuation plans were under way; the panzers found themselves faced by three British divisions separated by heavy artillery.

Goering's meddling was cursed roundly by the Luftwaffe. And with reason. It had proved disastrous. Bad weather had frequently grounded the aircraft which failed to fly by night when the evacuation was continued. And there had been the added factor of the Royal Air Force. It was the Messerschmitt against the Hurricane. The British fighters were disputably outnumbered, but their performance turned out to be better.

The boats of the British made it home, even though 243

of them were destroyed over ten terrible days.

Eicke of course remained at this time ignorant of what appeared at first to be an incomprehensible order to stand down. All he knew was that the Toptenkopf Division was to be detached from 16th Panzer Corps and assigned to the area around Boulogne.

Eicke spat his disgust in the presence of other SS officers: 'They're talking about coastal defence duties. It's nothing but a rest-cure.'

Eicke was diplomatic enough, though, to keep his protests within bounds. For he had been summoned to a conference in Bailleul attended by no less than Reichsfuehrer Himmler, who had stepped from his *Sonderzug* to inspect the Totenkopf formations.

It was not a pleasant experience; even someone as monumentally insensitive as Eicke smarted for days under Himmler's withering strictures.

The matter of the Le Paradis massacre had been — Himmler had chosen the word carefully — 'unfortunate'. As a result of it, the Waffen-SS was detested in military circles. There had also been the matter of the appallingly high rate of casualties, due largely to Eicke's impetuosity and sledgehammer tactics.

Himmler, ever the efficient bureaucrat, produced his figures. Between 19 and 29 May, for example, the division had suffered 1,140 casualties. That was bad enough, but the loss of around three hundred officers was almost more serious. From where were the replacements to come? The army had not exactly fallen over itself to oblige.

In the end, Eicke had to put up with three hundred half-trained cadets from the SS-Junkerschule at Bad Tolz.

And he had not just been wasteful with manpower. The loss and damage to equipment was colossal; forty-six trucks, a score of anti-tank guns and motor cycles, together with assorted armoured cars, mortars, heavy machine-guns and rifles was serious. But the real point was that the degree of damage to material was so great that, by the time the division reached Boulogne, mechanics were obliged to work non-stop for a week to make

Eicke's formations mobile again.

But Eicke was soon recovering his old bounce. Lack of material, after all, was a problem he had faced before. It had been solved by the simple process of requisition. Such measures would plainly be necessary again.

French transports, of course, were a handy source, but there were not enough of them. Bypassing Himmler, Eicke managed to lay his hands on no less than thirty-six trucks from his units still based in Poland. By the time that the Reichsfuehrer discovered what had happened, it was too late.

The episode put Eicke in a far better mood. Here was a victory of sorts. He had scored in another matter, too. News of the Le Paradis massacre had made the army noticeably reluctant to distribute any medals to the division, at least before any enquiry. Eicke complained bitterly to Himmler. Eventually the Wehrmacht gave in; the required consignment of medals reached the Totenkopf Division.

Eicke derived the most satisfaction from his own Iron Cross, First Class, for his role in commanding the Totenkopf Division in northern France.

Generaloberst Erich Hoepner made the presentation; it must have gone against the grain.

Eicke, in the mind of Heinrich Himmler, had disgraced the name of an élite. The Reichsfuehrer, who had been chief of his beloved SS for over a decade, took this as virtually a personal insult. Calculatingly, he set out to teach Eicke a further lesson.

Always suspicious of anyone who might even remotely prove a threat to his immense power, Himmler had in May made an attempt to clip Eicke's wings by creating the post of 'Inspector of Replacement Units of the SS-Totenkopf Division'. The job had gone to SS-Brigadefuehrer Kurt Knoblauch, a trusted subordinate who could be depended upon to do as he was told — a quality emphatically not possessed by Theodor Eicke.

The post had the effect of separating the replacement units of the Totenkopf Division from the reserve Death's Head formations. The reserves therefore became Knoblauch's province — which, of course, in practice meant Himmler's.

Now Himmler dropped a fresh bombshell. He declared: 'It is my belief that the Totenkopf Division is in need of an operations officer. I shall find you one.'

On 1 June 1940, Kurt Knoblauch presented himself for duty. Eicke greeted him in precisely the same way as he dealt with all opposition: he ignored it. When it became necessary to speak to the detested encumbrance, Eicke treated him as an office-boy barely worthy of notice.

His correspondence with Himmler had always, right from the early days in Dachau, been frank. Now he deluged the Reichsfuehrer with a catalogue of grumbles about his new operations officer.

Himmler let Eicke sweat out his punishment until December when, mercifully, Kurt Knoblauch was moved on. It is hardly likely that he was any less delighted than the commander of the SS-Totenkopf Division himself.

Nevertheless, the knowledge of Himmler's displeasure did have a sobering effect. It was pointless to argue that the atrocities at Le Paradis were the work of men of a mere company and that the division as a whole had no responsibility for such excesses. Every Totenkopf man was now tarred with the same brush, and Eicke's reputation for brutality back in his concentration camp days scarcely helped.

When the division moved to Boulogne for a period of coastal duty, Eicke warned his men to behave impeccably towards the French, since 'we find ourselves under sharp criticism wherever we go'.

Le Paradis had demonstrated tragically that, whatever may have been the attitude of Totenkopf towards the subjugated French, they had no scruples in persecuting the British.

Rifleman Adrian Vincent of the King's Royal Rifle Corps was taken prisoner by Eicke's men in the Calais area. He recounted:

'They were swaggering, arrogant and flamboyant,

73

and personified to the life Hitler's new race of *Herrenvolk*. Nearly all of them carried rubber truncheons, which they used on the slightest pretext. If a man wandered slightly out of the column, or stumbled, or was not moving fast enough, one of the Panzer troopers would be on him, around the head with a fine disregard for his skull . . .

'Those in the rear of the column — my usual place — were particularly unfortunate. With fewer men to hide among, one was more vulnerable there. Consequently, whenever the guards in the rear started on us, we would indirectly set the whole column into a panic. With someone laying into you with all his might, the only thing to do was to try to push through the others in front of you. As soon as we tried to go forward, those in front would also begin to run rather than be caught up in the trouble behind them. This running spread through the whole column, until in the end we were all stumbling along the road as fast as our legs could carry us. By that time other guards had joined in the sport, and were also joyfully helping us along with their truncheons.'

Inevitably, the long hours on the road induced boredom — relieved, in the case of the Totenkopf, by brutality. There was mild fun to be gained from the machine-gun placed on the truck at the front and rear of the column. Fore-and-aft fire for defenceless prisoners might scarcely have seemed necessary, but it did provide the front gunner with his own specialised brand of amusement.

This was to let fly over the prisoners' heads at the slightest whim. A dive to the ground was the cue for the rear truck to accelerate; the prisoners had to spring to their feet to get out of the way. The resulting chaos, fear and inevitable injury helped the SS to pass the time agreeably.

Eicke's men forced prisoners such as Adrian Vincent to walk twenty or thirty miles a day — invariably on an issue of scraggy German rye bread, green with mould.

The lightning thrust through France to the Channel

ports, a triumphant ride on the high tide of conquest, was something to look back on with a terrible yearning once 1940 had gone. Those were the days when Eicke's men were out there in front, harrying the sadly depleted French armies south of the Marne. The division, now serving as a spearhead of 14th Motorised Corps, fanned out in two battle columns to advance on Orléans. Here progress was unchecked, memories of past humiliation forgotten. So sparse was the opposition that it was not even thought necessary to encode messages.

Eicke crossed the Seine at Nogent, falling in echelon to the rear of 9th Panzer Division. The next assignment was to seal off a possible French escape route in Alsace by striking for Dijon and Lyons.

Progress was not always unimpeded. Inevitably, the roads were jammed with the sad flotsam and jetsam of war — French troops wandering around in a daze, wrecked and burnt-out vehicles, and pitiable groups of refugees in eternal fear of strafing.

But these were mere irritations; German successes were becoming monotonous. It was not long before the division was spoiling for a fight once again.

French troops had long departed from the village of L'Arbresle near Dijon, but they had not left it undefended. Prepared to fulfil their role as rearguards with a blend of savagery worthy of the Totenkopf itself were Moroccan troops who delighted in skewering their enemy with foot-long, razor-sharp knives in hand-to-hand fighting.

Such temerity threw Eicke into a blind rage, particularly as it was the work of racial inferiors. There could be no question of non-white troops being taken prisoner. It was a fight to the death with these black soldiers in French uniforms. Those who were ill-advised enough to surrender were shot where they stood.

In a similar action involving negroes, the Totenkopf report declared with sinister brevity that the day's fighting had yielded 'twenty-five French prisoners and forty-four dead negroes'.

*

75

It was not just that the French were defeated in battle. The whole country suffered the death of pride.

On 5 June, the morning after the fall of Dunkirk, the Germans launched their massive assault on the Somme. They attacked in overwhelming strength all along the four-hundred-mile front which stretched across France from Abbeville to the Upper Rhine. Against the enemy, the Germans flung 143 divisions, including ten armoured. The resistance they encountered was puny to the point of embarrassment — only sixty-three divisions and most of those second-rate.

Defeatism, as strong as a physical presence, stalked the ranks of the French High Command. The short and dapper Commander-in-Chief, General Maxime Weygand, once so supremely confident, bewailed: 'I am helpless. I cannot intervene for I have no reserves . . . *C'est la dislocation.*' And with the news of the fall of Paris, the writer André Maurois recalled: 'At that moment, I knew everything was over. France deprived of Paris, would become a body without a head. The war had been lost.'

And the Totenkopf Division? On 22 June, it learnt that the French were capable of at least one last kick at the SS. A reconnaissance battalion romping with arrogant abandon towards Villefranche ran head on into an ambush. The French machine-gun nests kept up their defiant barrage; Totenkopf casualties were numerous. But it was the very last engagement for Eicke's men in the triumphant battle of France.

From then on there was the routine of rounding up large groups of French soldiers, who were soon filing into captivity. Later, a total of 6,088 prisoners was claimed to have been taken between 17 and 19 June. War material was to be had in abundance; notably 23,000 litres of petrol. Casualties at this time of the war were puny and Eicke, whose position and reputation as a fighting man remained decidedly shaky, must have been grateful for it.

Events for France moved fast and with a tragic inevitability. The new French government of Marshal Pétain began armistice negotiations. Eicke received instructions to follow the 14th Motorised Corps to the area south of

Bordeaux; his men would be positioned in a strip of territory between the Atlantic coast and that part of France which was to remain unoccupied by the Germans. Responsibility for security at this point was to be shared jointly with the SS-Verfuegungs Division.

The war in France for the Death's Head legions was over. The army might not like it, but had to admit that the professionalism and ruthlessness of the SS fighters were qualities with which it was necessary to reckon. Here was now a combat-hardened, supremely self-confident formation that remained utterly indifferent to the extent of the sacrifices it was called upon to make. And these had been very heavy indeed. In seven days of heavy fighting, the division had suffered 1,152 casualties. Eicke might shrug them off as unimportant since victory had been achieved, but even he could not deny the arithmetic. More than ten per cent of the effective combat strength of SS-Totenkopf Division had been wiped out.

And already Adolf Hitler was thinking about turning east.

7

That summer of 1940 was to be a brief period of euphoria for the men of Totenkopf Division lounging in the pavement cafés in Bordeaux and shedding the tiredness, grime and fear of battle in the beguiling blue waters of the Bay of Biscay.

To wallow in such luxuries, however, was far from being to the taste of Theodor Eicke. True, he was due some leave, but before that he had to attend the magnificent victory parade to be staged in arrogant triumph in Berlin. Adolf Hitler, who had brought Europe to her knees at the relatively cheap military cost of forty thousand German lives, wanted to gloat.

And the Fuehrer wanted Eicke there. The personal invitation was accompanied by a private plane, not just for the commander of the Totenkopf Division but, in a shrewd piece of morale-building, also for an SS-Ober-schutze, picked at random.

The official party newspaper, *Voelkischer Beobachter*, for 19 July 1940, was at its most florid in reporting the parade:

'The capital of the Reich honoured its returning sons in a manner that befitted the occasion. The impression gained was certainly one the soldiers would have wished for. They showed the laughing faces of joy and pleasure — undeniable joy of the hour which showed the Fatherland spiritually and physically intact. . .The entire square and two gates of the Brandenburger Tor were decorated with swastika banners, the flag of the Reich and the movement. Pine garlands decorated with gold, beautiful eagles provided the decorations. But the real decorations of the event were the glowing eyes of the men and women, the boys and the girls of Berlin. Their joy and excitement were reflected in their songs. . .

'One of the most beautiful sights was the marching youth of Berlin, hundreds if not thousands of their children marched past the stand on the Pariserplatz, down Unter den Linden, the white and black uniforms of the young girls and the brown of the Hitler Youth. Today, the youth did not show excessive discipline and controls on the square were not very strict. Over and over again, boys and girls burst through the cordons throwing flowers and bouquets and flags to the men.'

The vehicles of the parading Wehrmacht were decorated profusely with summer flowers. Soon after six, when Berlin Gauleiter and Reich Minister Dr Joseph Goebbels and Commander of the Reserve Army General Friedrich Fromm had taken their seats, there came the first strain of marching songs, reaching the square through the Brandenburg Tor. Then could be seen the gleaming sea of swastika flags at the head of the procession.

The style of Goebbels' speech matched the general euphoria. He began: 'As Gauleiter of Berlin, I bid you welcome on the soil of your Fatherland. The capital of the Reich has put on a festive garment to welcome you. Hundreds and thousands of the population have come out to watch your marchpast, to receive you with enthusiasm . . .You shall enter the capital of the Reich through an avenue flocked by the people. For you it should be your proudest hour, for your relations the happiest of their lives. We know and we feel it in our hearts how ecstatic your joy must be. You have deserved this day of honour.'

For hour after hour, the various motorised divisions passed the reviewing stand and the suitably subservient reporter for the *Voelkischer Beobachter* enthused:

> 'Even the ordinary onlooker realises what an enormous force the Wehrmacht is. . .How right the Gauleiter was when he praised and described the shining equipment that the National Socialist soldier had at his disposal. This equipment guaranteed the Fatherland, this equipment assisted the army. That is why today we have "avenues of victory" in Berlin.'

It was highly impressive showmanship, first-class material for the front page of the *Voelkischer Beobachter* but it was, after all, the house journal of the Nazi party. Far more impressive and useful was the speech Hitler made on 19 July to the Reichstag in which it was made clear that the German people meant business by waging war.

The Fuehrer thundered: 'Thanks to their National Socialist training, the people of Germany did not enter this war in a spirit of superficial and blatant patriotism, but with the fanatical grimness of a nation aware of the fate that awaits it should it be defeated. The efforts of our enemies to shatter this unity by means of propaganda, were as stupid as they were futile. Ten months of war have only served to strengthen our fanaticism. It is a great misfortune that world opinion is not formed by men who see things as they are, but only by men who see them as they wish to see them.'

Of even more satisfaction to the servants of Himmler's SS was Hitler's praise of the German forces involved in the war. For the first time he stated that within the framework of these armies, fought the valiant divisions and regiments of the Waffen-SS.

The point was underlined even further: 'As a result of this war, the German Armoured Corps has inscribed for itself a place in the history of the world; the men of the Waffen-SS have a share in this honour.' He even praised the 'reserve formations of the SS' without which 'the battle at the front could never have taken place'.

Praise was heaped particularly on the organising ability of 'Party Comrade Himmler', an exclusive tribute the significance of which could not have been lost on Theodor Eicke.

Despite the invitation from Hitler and the lavish praise, Eicke was well aware that all was far from being satisfactory within the SS-Totenkopf Division. The army sniped and sneered with redoubled enthusiasm. A healthy portion of its hatred was reserved for Eicke himself, the chubby Alsatian bully who, ever since he had been put in charge of an SS division, had exercised power and influence way beyond his rank and abilities.

Eicke returned the detestation with interest. To Himmler he stormed: 'It's high time that our men were released from the grip of a malicious jealous gang.'

The Reichsfuehrer-SS had no love for Eicke. He feared him as a rival but at the same time had need of him. For one thing, Eicke had access to vast stockpiles of weapons, vehicles and supplies. These were hidden away until Eicke needed them; he made it very clear just what would happen to any camp commander who could not come up instantly with the regular material.

Himmler, who seemingly wielded absolute power but whose opposition to personal bullying extended little beyond blinking from behind prissy spectacles, was hardly proof against Eicke's arrogance. The Alsatian regarded SS manpower as his own particular fiefdom.

Men serving in the Totenkopf concentration camp units were simply syphoned off into the division without so much as a single-sentence memo being sent to the Reichs-fuehrer-SS.

Himmler was too scared to tackle Eicke direct. Characteristically, he went behind his back and began to insinuate his poison among the Alsatian's many enemies.

Chief among these was the pompous forty-five-year-old Swabian Gottlob Berger, whom senior SS-officers, in an apposite pun on his first name, contemptuously dubbed 'Praise God'.

A saw-mill owner's son who had been severely wounded in World War I as a second lieutenant commanding a battle group, 'The Duke of Swabia' (another nickname bestowed by the SS with anything but affection) had been one of the earliest recruits to National Socialism and the SA. Opportunistic, shrewd and ruthless, he was regarded with a mixture of fear and loathing by his colleagues.

They had good reason. For Gottlob Berger had scant interest in anything that did not advance Gottlob Berger. He had once given SA headquarters the written assurance that 'I shall always regard the SA as Number One and shall never be on the side of those who wish to destroy the SA.' It was a declaration that could have meant death at the hands of Sepp Dietrich's firing-squads at the time of the Roehm purge. Berger was clever enough to disown his allegiance rapidly. He lost no time in joining the SS. The man was a survivor; more important, he now enjoyed the complete confidence of Himmler as the chief recruiting officer of the SS.

One of his greatest enemies was Theodor Eicke.

Berger saw his main task as building up the SS divisions to battle-strength for the forthcoming campaign in the east. But from where was the manpower to come?

The Wehrmacht continued to block every attempt to swell the ranks of the Waffen-SS. As Berger saw it, the only solution was to intensify recruitment outside the Reich. In a top-secret memorandum, entitled *Population Movement*, Berger wrote to Himmler on 7 August 1940:

'No objections against a further expansion of the Waffen-SS can be raised by the other armed service if we succeed in recruiting part of the German population not at the disposal of the Wehrmacht. In this I see a task yet to be accomplished by the Reichsfuehrer-SS.'

He went on to ask Himmler 'for an authorisation to organise a recruitment office for foreign countries'.

Permission was granted. But it was by no means to prove as easy as that. Vocal in his objections was Theodor Eicke.

The head of the Totenkopf Division refused to believe that the recruitment of foreign troops was merely a device to build up the Waffen-SS. No, here was a conspiracy by Berger and Himmler to obstruct the growth of Totenkopf and adulterate it with foreign rubbish. He hit back. He opened the first round by flatly refusing to accept many of the SS replacements which were sent him during the summer of 1940. The man who had been instrumental in murdering Roehm and torturing concentration camp inmates was soon telling Berlin: 'Most of the young men you are sending me are criminals and obvious racial inferiors incapable of discipline and unworthy of the SS uniform.'

He went even further in challenging Himmler. His next move was to instruct Standartenfuehrer Dr Wilhelm Fuhrlander, the racial expert of SS-Totenkopf Division, to conduct examinations of all incoming recruits and reject those who would damage the racial susceptibilities of the division. Individual unit commanders were also told to screen all arriving replacements and send back to their respective reserve units anyone with a criminal record.

It was insubordination of the most blatant kind. Anyone who dared to challenge Eicke face-to-face received a volley of abuse and threats. Even Himmler was told to mind his own business; characteristically, the Reichsfuehrer-SS lacked the courage to settle the whole affair by dismissing Eicke. Himmler preferred other means.

Eicke's immediate superior as chief of the SS-Fueh-

82

rungshauptamt (SSHA) — the Operations Office, which Himmler had created to co-ordinate the military activities of the SS — was Brigadefuehrer Hans Juttner. He was given the task of assembling as much damning evidence as he could on the record of the Totenkopf Division's commander.

It was not a particularly hard task. The division, after all, had been guilty of the first major war crime in the west with the murder of British troops at Le Paradis.

Eicke had been known to obtain secretly additional weapons for his division from the Dachau and Oranienburg concentration camps; he had made unauthorised purchases of trucks in unoccupied France because the Wehrmacht had declined to motorise his division.

But, worst of all, Eicke had been known to demand a declaration from certain of his men that they would never utter complaints about conditions within the SS-Totenkopf Division.

Eicke was conscious of the intrigue swirling around him. He stormed: 'Ever since I left Germany certain circles have been doing their best to undermine the Reichsfuehrer's confidence in me which I have enjoyed for years.'

It was no use; Juttner had already taken things too far. Under his orders, SS legal officers interrogated those who had carried out Eicke's missions to seize unauthorised weapons; consequently, vehicles which had been hijacked were seized and taken away from the division. Furthermore, Juttner stated that if there was any more of such insubordination those responsible would be hauled before specially convened courts.

Even Eicke's methods of command were questioned by the legal beavers of the SS-Fuehrungshauptamt. To Juttner, Eicke indicated 'expert pen-pushers on your staff and silly gossip by their spiteful friends. . .

'When enquiries are made regarding conditions in an SS operational division which has left twenty-three officers and 370 NCOs and men dead on the battlefield, and when the purpose of the enquiry is simply to obtain incriminating evidence against decent SS officers and men, this is pure Marxism and the result is to undermine confidence.'

There were occasions when Eicke seemed to be quite deliberately building up the case against himself by issuing stupid orders that served only to make himself resented within the SS-Totenkopf Division. Even regimental commanders had been punished for trivial offences; the names of senior officers who contracted venereal disease were being announced in public. This last measure, which came to be know as 'gonorrhoea orders', provoked not only indignation throughout the SS, but ridicule. This was far worse, since it served to undermine Eicke's authority.

Still Himmler could not bring himself to act. He fell back on bluster and wrote:

'Dear Eicke, when I read something like this, I doubt your reason. There are moments when I question your capacity to command a division.'

The remedy was in Himmler's hands, but he lacked the courage to dismiss his protégé despite the evidence which Juttner had assembled. And Eicke? He swallowed the reproof and hung on to his job.

But moves were afoot within the Waffen-SS which even Eicke could do nothing about. For above Himmler and Juttner and Berger their squatted the malign presence of the Supreme Commander himself. The querulous caco-phony of gossip and backbiting was being drowned by something far more drastic — the chatter of teleprinters as the Fuehrer's headquarters spewed out new orders.

Adolf Hitler had decided to attack the Soviet Union.

On 22 April 1941, Himmler, riding roughshod over every sensibility, named the units of Totenkopf as an integral part of the Waffen-SS. Up to now, the Reichsfuehrer had been prepared to accept the decision of OKW (Army High Command) that the Waffen-SS was to be made up solely of the fighting formations, their replacement units, the Totenkopf regiments and the three cadet schools at

Brunswick, Bad Tolz and Klagenfurt.

All this was in the past. Himmler as Reichsfuehrer-SS was approaching a position of absolute power. Was he not now in control of four divisions and on the eve of the greatest National Socialist adventure of all, the invasion of the dark Slavs of the Soviet Union?

The Waffen-SS must be expanded. A directive declared that from henceforth 179 units and agencies were to be within the embrace of the armed Schutzstaffel. These would include the concentration camps, their administrative staff and the Totenkopf guard units. In other words, he had gained complete control of those organisations formed in 1939 when Eicke's Totenkopf-verbaende (a term eventually abolished) were relieved from concentration camp duty.

Camp guards now came within the control of the Waffen-SS. At one stroke, Eicke had been relieved of his own 'private army'; some 6,500 'good thugs' who could have been kept in reserve for special duties had now been snatched from the former paymaster and *arriviste*. Himmler's revenge was complete.

There was nothing to do but pocket his pride and get on with the job in hand. And that, in all conscience, was formidable enough.

The Totenkopf Division had its fair share of problems; speed and mobility cried out for drastic improvement. Material left much to be desired; there were far too many cumbersome vehicles in the motorised infantry regiments. As for the men themselves, their arms were too light; it was highly unlikely that a major campaign could be fought with what was available.

To secure the vehicles was the big headache. Matters had not been helped by an embarrassing episode on 4 October when Eicke's chief 'requisition officer', SS-Sturmbannfuehrer Weinhoebel, was caught red-handed at Dachau with a convoy of supplies which he had been intent on smuggling to the Totenkopf Division. Weinhoebel cheerfully admitted to acting on Eicke's direct orders and was arrested. The whole thing had proved decidedly uncomfortable; the most awkward aspect of the affair was that it made the procurement of further vehicles from the Wehrmacht out of the question.

But ever resourceful, Eicke turned to the vehicle parks, which were crammed with captured French army trucks and armoured cars. The haul was eminently satisfactory. By the spring of 1941 he had all that he wanted. Admittedly, his columns would look a little peculiar with Peugeot, Renault and Citroen cars and trucks, to say nothing of a handful of American-made Dodge, Ford or Studebaker trucks, but that scarcely mattered.

The question of how manpower could be armed more effectively was largely a matter of reorganisation. The motorised infantry regiments were given added punch by their conversion into aggressive Kampfgruppen or battle groups, organised around an infantry regiment and strengthened with motorised light and heavy artillery and anti-tank batteries.

Eicke realised that the time was approaching when there would be no further need for subterfuge. There would be no more commando swoops on army property. The Reichsfuehrer-SS was kept informed of all developments.

It was a wise move. Soon Eicke had his chief eating out of his hand — to such an extent that by April 1941 Himmler had authorised the formation of a full-sized flak battalion for the Totenkopf Division.

There was yet another triumph to come. In the final weeks before the invasion of Russia, Himmler's new-found generosity extended to giving the division twelve 150 mm heavy-artillery pieces. Eicke immediately assembled a separate heavy battalion of the artillery regiment. There then sprang into existence a fully motorised reserve battalion drawing on available men and equipment.

Of equal importance was the forging of strong links with the Wehrmacht that, despite its previous opposition, had now been forced to fall in line with Himmler's directives. The Reichsfuehrer-SS had the full backing of Hitler, who realised that the imminent invasion of the Soviet Union would suck vast manpower from all available sources; rivalry between SS and Wehrmacht was the sort of irrelevance that now, in the realities of total war, belonged to the past.

Eicke for perhaps the first time in his stormy career was getting allies and disciples. Few were more dedicated than Max Simon, the future Obergruppenfuehrer whom the Russians after the war were to accuse of being responsible for the extermination of twenty thousand citizens of Kharkov. Simon was given a key training job — planning a series of exercises to reduce sharply the time needed for a motorised infantry regiment to be deployed into battle formation from marching columns.

Another of Eicke's stars was former construction engineer Hans Lammerding, a colourless individual but a serviceable administrator who was to go on to command the Das Reich Division at the age of thirty-nine. He had served his apprenticeship on the staff of Eicke's concentration camp inspectorate. It was a measure of how times had changed that such an individual could now be accepted as the Totenkopf representative at the weekly staff conferences by Rudolf Schmidt, Chief of Staff of 39th Army Corps.

While other adherents of the Waffen-SS went on to make names for themselves in the campaigns of Yugoslavia and Greece, Eicke took his men on simulated battles in the forests, small villages and rivers of Germany. Predictably, the exercises were no rest-cure and, since Theodor Eicke was in charge, there were inevitable fatalities.

But a few months before, Himmler would have protested at such a profligacy of lives. But now everyone was thinking in terms of a military machine — a vast ideologically fuelled juggernaut which, it was firmly believed, would in a short, brutal campaign devastate the Bolshevik bacillus.

Of course, Eicke's men had been stuffed with Himmler's racial doctrines, which held that Marxism was Jew-dominated and that the Bolsheviks were somehow in league with Freemasons, gypsies and liberalism. If the ranks of Totenkopf swallowed all this impetus of hate, that alone did not account for the spirit almost of exaltation which swept through their numbers at the prospect of their coming adventure.

There was something else, a sense of new purpose, which had turned an ancient fossilised social order on its head. These new soldiers were not required to address their superiors with the prefix of 'Herr'. Officers ate with their men and used the same sort of barrack oaths.

In the old days, half of the traditional Wehrmacht officers sprang from professional military families, but the SS men had often left school at fourteen and had come from the humble farming families of the north. No longer would the stiff-necked Wehrmacht refer to them contemptuously as 'asphalt soldiers'.

They were new men, marching proudly in their field grey towards a new dawn.

8

The men of the Totenkopf Division knew that the pleasant period of mild fraternisation with the cowed French could not last forever. Nevertheless, the abrupt order from 'Papa' Eicke that all contact with the people of Bordeaux was to cease forthwith came as something of a shock.

What did it mean? Eicke gave a small hint when he added: 'Anyone who even mentions that the division could be on the move will be shot as a traitor.'

On the move? Where to? At around the time Eicke's men were pondering their fresh order, in Berlin Nazi Foreign Minister Joachim von Ribbentrop was locked in secret conference at the former residence of the Reich President in Wilhelmstrasse.

On the table lay the intelligence all had suspected for months and many secretly dreaded. The Wehrmacht was intending to move against Soviet Russia.

Yet less than two years before Ribbentrop had said:

'This treaty with Stalin will keep our rear covered. It will ensure us against a war on two fronts which brought disaster to Germany last time.'

Now Ribbentrop surveyed the faces of the anxious ambassadors, envoys and ministerial officials. Plainly, he had to come up with some justification.

'Gentlemen, I can tell you that the Fuehrer has information of a build-up of forces by Stalin so that he can strike at us at a favourable moment.

'The Fuehrer has proved that he is always right. Furthermore, he is confident that he can bring the Soviet Union to its knees in eight weeks.

'As for our rear, that will be safe enough without Stalin's goodwill.'

The goodwill of Stalin was a commodity that Adolf Hitler had long been quite prepared to do without. At a conference given in his Bavarian home, the Berghof, the Fuehrer had told his audience:

'There is no time to lose. War must come in my lifetime . . .We will crush the Soviet Union.'

But eight weeks! Nobody dared ask what would happen if it took longer. The die was cast. And a large number of the troops who would have to implement Hitler's astonishing about-face were sweating out their last few hours of early summer in hectic exercises around Bordeaux.

Then at 1 a.m. on 23 May 1941, it came. Here was a coded, top-secret telegram from Seventh Army HQ. Eicke was to be prepared to move by rail no later than 3 June.

Secrecy was paramount. The following week an advance party of officers and NCOs were smuggled secretly out of France to prepare new quarters for the division.

Then came the movement of Totenkopf manpower. This was done, naturally enough, under the cloak of darkness, with units being sealed into the cars for the long trip through France to Germany.

Members of the resistance and alert civilians were suspicious that something was in the wind; after all, all stations on the route had suddenly been declared off-limits. To the families of the SS men, their husbands and sons no longer existed. No letters or communications of any kind were allowed. Not the slightest hint could be given that SS-Totenkopf Division was on the move.

In cramped, airless, dust-coated wagons they travelled a distance of over one thousand miles, rumbling across the Reich to divisional headquarters at Marienwerder, a muggy forest set deep in the most inhospitable regions of East Prussia.

For four days and nights they had been cooped up like cattle, yet even on arrival there was no respite. They piled out of the wagons and began a long weary march to their new location to face an unknown enemy fuelled by an ideological fanaticism that equalled and frequently surpassed their own.

Every Totenkopf man stumbling that summer towards Marienwerder to fulfil his individual destiny with Unternehmen Barbarossa (Operation Barbarossa) could recite Theodor Eicke's oft-repeated litany of hatred. The enemy was a Jewish-Bolshevik subhuman, intent on annihilating the Reich unless he was prevented. Such prevention was to be achieved without mercy or pity; commissars were to be slaughtered along with prisoners.

Eicke confided to his more intimate cronies that the trouble with the new SS intake, as favoured by Himmler and Berger, was that it lacked the necessary ideological training. You did not make a good Totenkopf man by hustling him into uniform, giving him some basic training, and pushing him into the front line, where he probably would not last long. What was necessary was political education; that alone would inspire the fanatical determination necessary to slaughter Bolsheviks.

It was certainly true that ideology and sheer brute physical strength were useful weapons for waging war, but those in command needed something else in equal measure. And that was an appropriate sense of timing.

Hitler had originally envisaged invasion for the middle of May — directly after the normal end of the muddy season. But then had come the April diversion in the Balkans which had involved the formations of Das Reich and Leibstandarte.

This campaign, which many believed fatally delayed the invasion of the Soviet Union, had been necessary to bail out Italy, Germany's ally. The previous October, Benito Mussolini, who was rapidly becoming Hitler's most embarrassing liability, had launched an attack on Greece. The Duce received a bloody nose; Italian forces were forced back into Albania. Hitler had to go to the rescue of his Axis partner.

In the way of wars, one disaster proved merely a prelude to another. Diplomatic pressure had been brought to bear on Yugoslavia; on 25 March, Paul, the country's Prince Regent, agreed to co-operate with Germany. He never got the chance. The following night, he was ousted by a coup, the seventeen-year-old King Peter was rushed into power, and Yugoslavia promptly renounced the agreement. Such impertinence had to be dealt with speedily.

The resulting victories were gratifying, certainly. But they fatally held up plans for the invasion of Russia. Four weeks of good weather had been thrown away.

One man who was decidedly not inactive during this time was the ever-industrious Himmler, obsessed with extending his already formidable power-base. After all, there was Hermann Goering, whose Luftwaffe was still boosting his power and prestige. Even Joseph Goebbels was finding a satisfactory wartime role for his propaganda ministry.

Himmler felt vaguely dissatisfied. There was the Gestapo, certainly. There were the concentration camps, the cloak-and-dagger activities of his entire security apparatus. But these were secret affairs; in no way could they gain public prestige for the SS or, more to the point, for Heinrich Himmler.

The Reichsfuehrer-SS began redoubling his efforts to

enlarge the Waffen-SS, to seek ways of increasing its role in the looming eastern campaign.

But how? Himmler cast covetous eyes at the Totenkopf regiments, as distinct from Eicke's division, which was a field formation in the Waffen-SS. These regiments consisted largely of youths below conscription age and of older SS reservists called up as 'police reinforcements'. Technically they were part of the Waffen-SS but they did not come under military control. As a sort of semi-military political police, they were extremely useful when it came to keeping order in German-occupied Europe. With a strength of forty thousand, they were Himmler's own and he guarded them fanatically, equipping them like regular army infantry regiments with the field-grey uniform and the Death's Head on the collar tab which took the place of the usual SS runes.

The time had come to give them more important work to do.

Their previous security functions could be handled perfectly well by members of the Ordnungpolizei; they could now become proper soldiers. Himmler, though, was determined that a healthy section of them would remain under his personal control. Like a wilful small boy who had no intention of sharing his toy-box with anyone, Himmler hugged five Totenkopf regiments to himself. These even had their own private training-ground in Poland. Thousands of Poles were ejected from an area near Debica; into the territory marched Himmler's pets, equipped with a full complement of infantry weapons. They were fully motorised and were eventually redesignated SS infantry regiments and organised into combat brigades.

The myopic Reichsfuehrer-SS, who in World War I had not risen above officer cadet and whose poor physique was a martyr to disabling stomach cramps, managed eventually to gain control of a 'private army' — a virtual Waffen-SS within the Waffen-SS — comprising five infantry and two cavalry regiments. Only the demands of the battlefront and the heavy drain on manpower put paid finally to Himmler's grotesque ego trip.

Not that recruitment was unimportant before the start of Barbarossa. The battle of France had seen to that. Between 12 and 18 June, more that nine hundred SS recruits poured in from Nuremburg, Dresden, Breslau, Prague and Brno. They were destined to swell the infantry regiments and the reconnaissance and engineer battalions.

The German offensive front for the invasion of Russia was divided into three sectors — North, Centre, South.

All along that frighteningly long frontier of 930 miles, from the Baltic to the Black Sea, three million troops were to lie waiting.

The Totenkopf Division was attached to Army Group North under the aristocratic and austere Feldmarschall Wilhelm Ritter von Leeb, a veteran of the old Prussian General Staff whom Hitler had heartily distrusted. And with reason. Leeb had taken part in crushing the Fuehrer's famous Munich Putsch of 1923 as commander of the Bavarian Artillery. Early in 1938, he had been retired but Hitler had called him back.

Leeb's task was to advance with two armies and one Panzer group from East Prussia across the Memel. The overall task of Army Group North was the annihilation of the Soviet forces in the capture of Leningrad.

The armoured spearhead of Leeb's forces was Panzer Group Four, under the command of Eicke's old adversary, Hoepner.

Eicke's orders to move the division into the assembly area of the group came on 19 June. They were accompanied by tight security measures from the Army High Command (OKH). Eicke complied by keeping his columns of vehicles concealed under camouflage netting in the wooded areas near Kreuzingen on the frontier between East Prussia and Soviet-occupied Lithuania.

The day before, Fuehrer Headquarters had issued *Directive No. 21 Case Barbarossa*, whose preamble read:

'The German Wehrmacht must be prepared, even before conclusion of the war against Britain, *to overthrow Soviet Russia by a rapid campaign. . .*'

A rapid campaign? Well, why not? The recipe, after all, had been a triumph in the west. To the complete surprise of the French, Hitler had broken rapidly through the terrain of the Ardennes, which the enemy had fondly supposed to be impregnable. The much vaunted Maginot Line had been pierced with breathtaking ease and the campaign had seemed to end almost before it began.

The same sort of plan was to be applied to the Soviet Union. All available forces would attack in an unexpected area. The enemy front would be ripped apart. Vital centres of the Russian defence — Moscow, Leningrad and Rostov — would be seized. German forces would sweep on in high triumph on a line from Astrakhan to Archangel. The possibilities of failure would not exist.

Shortly before 3 a.m. on 22 June, Hitler's proclamation to his forces was read aloud to the men of Totenkopf by their unit commanders.

'Soldiers of the Eastern Front!. . .Weighed down for many months by grave anxieties, compelled to keep silent, I can at last speak openly to you, my soldiers. . . About 160 Russian divisions are lined up along our frontier. For weeks, this frontier has been violated continually — not only the frontier of Germany but also that in the far north and in Rumania.'

Hitler went on to describe Russian patrols which had penetrated into the territory of the Reich and had been driven back after prolonged exchange of fire. The proclamation concluded:

'At this moment, soldiers of the Eastern Front, a build-up is in progress which has no equal in world history, either in extent or in number. Allied with Finnish divisions, our comrades are standing side by side with the victor of Narvik on the Arctic Sea in the north. . .

'You are standing on the Eastern Front. In Rumania, on the banks of the Prut, on the Danube, down to the shores of the Black Sea, German and Rumanian troops

94

are standing side by side. . .If this greatest front in world history is now going into action, then it does so not only in order to create the necessary conditions for the final conclusion of this great war, or to protect the countries threatened at this moment, but in order to save the whole of European civilisation and culture.

'German soldiers! You are about to join battle, a hard and crucial battle. The destiny of Europe, the future of the German Reich, the existence of our nation, now lie in your hands alone. May the Almighty help us all in this struggle.'

It may seem strangely old-fashioned, this purple rhetoric from the Supreme Commander of the German forces who, in the twentieth century, addressed his troops like some warlord out of the middle ages. But it is also worth recalling remarks made about the same time by the Soviet Marshal Nikolai I. Krylov. He proclaimed: 'The Russian loves a fight and scorns death.' He gave the order: 'If you are wounded, pretend to be dead; wait until the Germans come up; then select one of them and kill him! Kill him with gun, bayonet or knife. Tear his throat with your teeth. Do not die without leaving behind you a German corpse.'

The easy victories in the soft west had, understandably, led the Germans to suppose that they had the sole monopoly of brutalism. They were soon to learn otherwise.

The last hours before the assault ticked away; the men of Totenkopf behaved much like any soldiers on the eve of battle. They played cards, smoked, wrote letters. Some were able to come to terms with the tightening of the stomach muscles, to take advantage of the shroud of the night. They slept.

It is unlikely that Theodor Eicke was among them. His officers had noticed a change in the brutal one-time supremo of the concentration camps who had expressed contempt for what he saw as the fustian traditions of the Wehrmacht. Now he kept to his office desk, poring for hours over maps from which vast sections had been snipped for study.

Theodor Eicke was belatedly playing war games.

The statistics were certainly impressive. On 21 June 1941, the German forces in the east were poised for the attack with seven armies, four Panzer groups and three air fleets. That meant 3,000,000 men, 600,000 vehicles, 750,000 horses, 3,580 armoured fighting vehicles, 7,184 guns, and 1,830 aircraft.

Just what those figures meant in human terms was demonstrated between 3 a.m. and 3.30 a.m. on 22 June when a three-mile strip of territory stretching the length of eastern Europe from the Baltic Sea to the Carpathians erupted in a torrent of fire and flying steel. In went the German aircraft, artillery and armour, blasting into the Soviet frontier.

Six thousand gun flashes had lit the eastern dawn. The bewildered Russians were overwhelmed in a tumult of fire and destruction. There was ample evidence that the assault had caught the enemy totally by surprise. Again and again the Germans intercepted the same message: *'We are being fired on, what shall we do?'* The head-quarters of Stavka (the High Command) could give no satisfactory reply. General Gunther Blumentritt, Chief of Staff of the Fourth Army, picked up the retort: *'You must be insane? And why is your signal not in code?'*

On the evening of the invasion at German HQ at Lotzen in East Prussia, General Franz Halder, Hitler's Chief of Staff, wrote in his diary:

'The enemy has been taken unawares by our attack. His forces were not tactically in position for defence. In the frontier zone his troops were widely dispersed and his frontier defence was weak overall.

'Because of our tactical surprise, enemy resistance on the frontier has been weak and disorganised. We have been able to seize bridges over the border rivers, and slightly further on, to overwhelm any positions fortified by deep earthenworks.'

In Moscow, blissful ignorance reigned. In his biography

of Stalin, Emmanuel d'Astier de la Vigerie, a French general turned historian, wrote:

'At dawn on June 22 1941, on the day before the anniversary of Napoleon's crossing of the Nieman, 120 divisions speed towards Kiev, Leningrad, and Moscow, where the theatre is performing *A Midsummer Night's Dream*.

'Stalin, living in a dream world of hope, has spurned warnings and refused advice. During the first hours of the attack he issued orders that German firing is not to be answered. He would like to think he is faced by nothing more than a provocative act from a few ill-disciplined German units.

'On June 21, a German Communist worker deserted and revealed the date and time of the attack. Stalin is told but refuses to believe the evidence. Fifteen years later, Nikita Kruschev recounts the episode; and another historian adds that Stalin ordered Korpik, the deserting worker, who could only in his view be an agént provocateur, to be shot.'

The Russian official history of World War II, *The Great Patriotic War*, tried to explain away Stalin's refusal to believe or prepare for a German invasion:

'One of the reasons for the error made in the appreciation of the situation is that J.V. Stalin, who alone decided the most important political and military questions, was of the opinion that Germany would not break the Non Aggression Pact in the near future.

'Therefore he considered all the reports of German troop movements were intended to force the Soviet Union into counter-measures.'

Even when Winston Churchill, who had at his disposal decodes by British Intelligence of German signals sent via Enigma machines, forwarded Stalin a warning the Soviet leader chose to ignore it. He feared that Churchill had concocted elaborate forgeries in a bid to create a split between Berlin and Moscow and to divert the weight of German arms from Great Britain to the Soviet Union. There was plenty to corroborate the British warning, including information received from Stalin's own sources. It made no difference. He preferred to sit tight.

And now the war had come to Russia.

There were accounts of bewildered Russian frontier guards, jerked into consciousness by the squeal and clatter of tank tracks. They wandered half-dressed through the reek and were promptly shot. The Wehrmacht recorded that it encountered undermined and incomplete fortifications that the Russians held on to grimly until they too were cut down.

Eicke found himself at first in the position of a man who enters a room, sees two acquaintances but is unsure which of them to approach first.

Hoepner's Panzer Group Four was made up of the mass of the armoured and motorised units in Army Group North. On the left, was the Panzer formed by General Max Reinhardt's 41st Panzer Corps. The right wing of Hoepner's armoured fork consisted of the 56th Panzer Corps led by General Erich von Manstein. As for SS-Totenkopf Division and the 269th Infantry Division, they were to be held in reserve for Hoepner. The idea was to commit them either to Reinhardt or Manstein, according to need.

Eicke fretted, waiting his moment. At first, the presence of Totenkopf scarcely seemed necessary. The two Panzer Corps of Erich Hoepner hurled themselves at the Soviet frontier positions and annihilated such resistance as there was on the border. A wide gap was torn between the right wing of the Russian Third Army and the edge of the Battle Military District area. Through the gap that had been wrenched open poured the full strength of Panzer Group Four.

It spelled death to three Russian infantry divisions. Five more were licking their not inconsiderable wounds. General Dmitry Pavlov, a renowned Soviet tank expert, had lost half his strength in a matter of hours and was later shot on the orders of Stalin for the lapse. German bombers next swept down on the Russians's 14th Mechanised Corps and effectively removed it from the scene. Ahead lay the Dvina River, one of the most formidable natural obstacles on the road to Leningrad.

Eicke heard of the triumphs with mixed feelings. He had a suspicion that it was going to be France all over again, with seemingly eternal waiting in the wings. The stark truth was that, with the campaign a mere eighteen hours old, the armour of General Manstein and the motorised infantry had punched a miraculous fifty-three miles into Soviet territory and had reached the Dvinsk highway at Wilkomierz, 105 miles from the East Prussia border. The city of Dvinsk was reached in a day; after that there was nothing to stop Manstein reaching the Dvina.

In the town itself came stiff Soviet resistance. Fighting lasted throughout the day. At the end of it, the Russians were edging back. Anxious that the Germans should gain the very minimum from their advantage, the Soviet troops put a torch to the town. On 27 June, the 3rd Motorised Infantry Division succeeded in making a surprise crossing of the river, north-west of Dvinsk. The first stage of the German plan on this front was over.

Even years after the event, when he came to write his memoirs, Manstein could not conceal his triumph. He recorded:

'Before the offensive started I had been asked how long we thought we should take to reach Dvinsk, assuming that it was possible to do so. My answer had been that if it could not be done inside four days, we could hardly count on capturing the crossings intact. And now, exactly four days and five hours after H-Hour, we had actually completed, as the crow flies, a non-stop dash through two hundred miles of enemy territory.'

In fact, it was a lightly opposed Blitzkrieg advance, helped by the fact that the Russians had been incompetent when it came to placing explosives effectively on the road and rail bridges across the river.

Manstein's satisfaction though was tempered by the realism of the professional soldier. The Wehrmacht's boldest and most calculating strategist had no patience with ideology, with Hitler's dreams of flattening the Soviet Union out of existence. There must be a short sharp campaign; allow things to drag on in the seemingly limitless reaches of this vast country and ultimately Germany would lose.

Speedy advance was all very well, but it had its drawbacks. The lightning progress of 56th Panzer Corps meant that the rest of Panzer Group Four and the slower infantry divisions of Sixteenth Army were soon being left far to the rear. This entailed a frustrating halt on the Dvina while the rest caught up. Manstein's rapid dash was Totenkopf's gain. Totenkopf and 269th Infantry Division were committed to action.

They were badly needed.

Manstein had reached Wilkomierz shortly before dusk on 24 June. At that time, Eicke received his orders. These were to move Totenkopf Division east before midnight, then to proceed fast to plug the gap that was lengthening between Manstein's right flank and the wing of Busch's Sixteenth Army.

The task? Eicke was told that the initial combat assignments would involve mopping up isolated groups of enemy stragglers and repairing damaged roads. All the time, the division would be moving forward to cover the resumption of Manstein's advance. It was essentially a mopping-up operation: ruthless extermination of surviving remnants of the Red Army which had been smashed on the very first day of Barbarossa. That assignment concluded effectively, orders came for the move on Wilkomierz.

It was tame stuff, though. Eicke had seen a more effective role for his Totenkopf Division than simply that of a dustpan sweeping up behind the main advance. Fortunately, fresh orders came. Totenkopf was to proceed to Deguciai and across the Dvina at Dvinsk on 29 June.

That, as it turned out, was no easy task. With good

reason, the Russians had become seriously worried. It looked to headquarters as if the entire north-western front was in danger of collapse.

Frantically, the luckless Pavlov began shifting divisions out of the Soviet Tenth Army areas northwards to stiffen the shaky Third Army. Meanwhile, Eicke led Totenkopf Division east through central Lithuania — and cannon-aded sharply into the stiffest resistance it had yet encountered in any theatre. At one point, the reconnais-sance battalion was forced to halt in the face of a suc-cession of Russian armoured counter-attacks.

The tanks rolled over the German columns again and again. What struck the awed men of Totenkopf Division was not so much that the Russians were unswayed by enormous losses, but that they did not appear to notice them. The wave of assaults went on. But the time came when the Russians had had enough and they melted into the forest. Eicke's battalions were miraculously without casualties, but they had met a foe whose fanaticism and fighting prowess uncomfortably matched their own.

What sort of men were these who were prepared to fight themselves into the ground rather than to recognise the invincible might of the élite SS? The Germans reacted to this new sort of enemy with a mixture of anger and amazement. Far more to the point, the men of Totenkopf Division began to experience an emotion which was entirely new to them.

It was fear. But fear of what?

Fear of strange Mongolian types with brutal, close-cropped heads and deep-set expressionless eyes. Fear of an enemy that itself seemed to know no fear.

Instances of the battlefield implacability of the Soviets were legendary. There was the story of the Soviet tank at the citadel of Brest Litovsk which, it was comfortably assumed, had been put out of action the previous week.

Incredulous observers inside German Divisional Head-quarters suddenly saw a turret head begin to swing, a gun aligned directly at them. When the tank was disabled once and for all, the bodies of three of the crew were found to be in an advanced state of decomposition. The fourth man, appallingly wounded, without food or water or medical attention, had held onto life within the foetid cocoon for over a week.

While an Allied prisoner of war, Obergruppenfuehrer Max Simon produced a paper on *Soviet Russian Infantry and Armoured Forces* in which he discussed the Russian infantry soldier; many of whom took the men of Totenkopf by surprise:

'. . .the officers. . .exercise firm authority over their regiments and are able to create from the mass under them a manoeuvrable body, the individual members of which will hug the terrain when working their way forward, will quickly dig in and as quickly push forward again or allow themselves to be slaughtered if so ordered. The native frugality of the Russian and Asiatic not only favours the restriction of the supply train of combat troops to the minimum, but also makes it possible to exploit the strength of the individual in a measure which seems impossible to the European. The insensitivity of the men to weather conditions, their craftiness and closeness to nature, likewise facilitate training and increases the value of the infantry.

'The simple needs of the Communist soldier are also reflected in his equipment. A lightweight suit in summer, a padded jacket and trousers in winter. . . sturdy leather waterproof boots for the summer and simple winter boots which are made of felt. . .Cooking utensils, a wooden spoon and shaving equipment are all that is taken along besides weapons and ammunition.

'The advantages and disadvantages inherent in the national characteristics peculiar to the peoples of the Soviet Union naturally set their imprint on the tactics employed. On the one hand will be found a clever use of terrain. . .ruthlessness and mercilessness towards friend and foe. On the other hand will be found a rigid insistence on carrying out plans. . .'

The Russian infantryman, he went on, always defended himself to the last gasp and even crews in burning tanks kept up their fire for as long as they had breath. Wounded men reached for their weapons at the very moment of regaining consciousness.

When it came to defence the Red Army infantrymen were equally remarkable:

'They blended into the terrain and they could dig in themselves in an amazingly short time. Their defensive positions were simple and effective.

'Trenches were discarded to a very great extent and instead deep narrow holes were dug which held two or three riflemen. Machine guns were skilfully sited so that dead angles were avoided and snipers, of whom there were often as many as forty or fifty to each company, were given the best positions.

'Trench mortars were available in all calibres and flame throwers, often fitted with remote control, were used in conjunction with mortars so that the attacking troops ran into a sea of flames. Well-concealed tanks stood by to take part in counter attacks or were dug in at intervals. This was defence in depth protected by wire entanglements and numerous minefields, and was a defensive system applied to all kinds of terrain.'

The extent of Russian guile and ingenuity was something else the SS legions had failed to appreciate. They were to be given plenty of opportunities to learn.

'Russian battlefield discipline was most impressive. German patrols were allowed to penetrate Soviet lines and even to withdraw without having seen anything. Spotter aircraft usually saw nothing of the enemy who made no movement in their well camouflaged positions.

'Experienced German officers driving through a seemingly deserted village would swear that there were neither troops nor inhabitants in the place but other troops following up would find themselves faced with a fortified position, defended by an infantry regiment, reinforced by all arms. The positions had been so well camouflaged and the Soviet soldiers had remained so still that the officers as they drove through had noticed nothing.'

Faced with so formidable a foe, it became obvious that new heart had speedily to be put into the men of Totenkopf.

Max Simon proclaimed in an order: 'These Russians are bandits, whipped into fanatical frenzy by the Bolshevik commissars and fanatical Red Army officers. They must be slaughtered ruthlessly.' There could be no question of prisoners, of abiding by the accepted rules of old-fashioned warfare.

In justice, it has to be recorded that the Russians suffered from no such scruples, either. In a report forwarded by Eicke to 56th Panzer Corps on 6 July, Max Simon recorded that a group of two hundred Russian soldiers had approached Totenkopf units with their hands raised.

The Germans accepted this as a mark of surrender, particularly as the Russians dropped to the ground. Then, a mere twenty yards from the SS positions, the Russians opened fire.

The Totenkopf men showed no quarter after that. They fired volley after volley into the Russian columns, killing even those who implored to be allowed to surrender.

There was undoubtedly satisfaction to be gained from the mopping up of 'Soviet bandits'. But Eicke saw his men these days as far more than punishment battalions. He itched for further orders from Hoepner. They were not slow in coming.

9

Glittering prizes beckoned for Hoepner on the northern front. Greatest of all, of course, was the city of Leningrad. To the senior personnel of OKW, hunched over the situation maps and cocooned from the grimy realities of battle, the Commander of Panzer Group Four must seemingly have had an easy task.

But the objective of striking hard at the cradle of Bolshevism was only part of it. He had at the same time to protect not only his own right wing, but that of the entire Army Group of von Leeb. Progress was hindered by a whole series of encirclement battles, not the least of which were the unrelenting attacks on the bridgeheads over the Dvina.

Clearly, there was work for Eicke. Totenkopf was assigned forthwith to Manstein's 56th Panzer Corps and ordered to send a single infantry battalion and the tank-destroyer battalion forward to Dvinsk. The object was to help secure the flank of 3rd Motorised Division, taking horrific punishment from the fierce Russian counter-attacks.

Hoepner declared: 'The advance of 56th Panzer Corps must be held up no longer.'

It was all very well. The Russians were proving as ruthless in the air as on land. The Red Air Force flew in squadron after squadron. In they came at tree-top level, to be picked off by the Germans.

For three days, Totenkopf Division slogged forward amid stiffening resistance and mounting air attacks. Eventually, the division reached Dvinsk; before dark on 30 June Eicke's men were rushing across the Dvina.

There was general relief. Things on the northern wing

seemed to be running broadly on the lines laid down by Hitler's original directive.

So far, punishment of the Russians had been nothing less that appalling. Leningrad's fate seemed obvious. Seriously alarmed, general headquarters, the Stavka, had been compelled to constitute the Leningrad theatre virtually as a separate command. Totenkopf Division just kept going, its orders to knife ahead through the towns of Dagda, Kraslau and Skorlopova to Rosenov and Opochka and the Lovat river.

The Panzer Army had resumed its march on 2 July, and now the axis of the two corps was separated. Reinhardt was directed on Ostrov and Manstein was flung into the yawning void on the right flank, buttressed by Totenkopf Division.

A fresh ebullience swept through Eicke's ranks. In schoolboy high spirits, Max Simon dashed off a highly colourful report of his seizure of Kraslau. Especially proud of himself was Matthias Kleinheisterkamp, a pet of Himmler, who had seized an agreeable quantity of petrol, guns and abandoned ammunition.

The SS may well have been pleased about the achievement at Kraslau. The Wehrmacht's emotions were decidedly different. Generalmajor Lancelle, no lover of the Waffen-SS and a man who lost no opportunity to make his contempt of the black legions clear, read through Simon's report of Kraslau with mounting anger.

Simon had been full of self-congratulation. The truth, however, was that Lancelle had to break off the task of command to untangle a vast traffic jam of SS vehicles. The men were so ill-disciplined and ill-led that the entire advance had been put in jeopardy. 'I literally had to prod them forward,' Lancelle grumbled.

He did more than grumble. In went a blistering report in which he revealed that in Kraslau itself he had come across a group of SS men in the main street engaged in nothing more warlike than tinkering with an ancient Russian gramophone. Elsewhere, those implacable fighters of Theodor Eicke were amusing themselves in an orgy of looting and window-breaking. Lancelle declared:

'Virtually every training rule was violated. The men exposed themselves to needless dangers and the losses were consequently heavy.'

The casualty figures were to spell out a frightening message for the Waffen-SS. Between 22 June and 19 November 1941, the five divisions of Himmler's paladins, which had gone into the battle of Russia 100,000 strong, were to lose 1,238 officers and 35,377 men, of whom 13,037 were killed in action.

In a report to corps headquarters, Eicke wrote:

'The losses suffered so far in battle have deprived this formation [Totenkopf] of nearly 60 per cent of the vital officer and NCO cadre. Losses in NCOs are catastrophic. . .a company which has lost its old experienced NCOs and section commanders cannot attack. It is unreliable in defence because its backbone is not there. There are already companies in this division incapable of reconnoitring in front of their sectors.'

It was all the army's fault, of course. Men like Lancelle had to be put in their place. It was a measure of the mutual hatred between Wehrmacht and SS that, at the height of the German Army's fight in Soviet Russia, the private war between Himmler's men and the military establishment should break out with renewed fury.

If Lancelle could sling mud, so could Eicke. The Totenkopf commander got Oberfuehrer Simon to provide positive proof that OKH had deliberately not passed on an order from the Fuehrer's headquarters to relieve a select group of Danish SS volunteers from the line. The outcome had been the slaughter of the Danes with the army sitting back on the sidelines and not committing its own men.

Manstein, however, had no patience with what he plainly regarded as the dangerously childish squabbles and jealousies which broke out periodically between the Wehrmacht and the Totenkopf Division. Ever a pragmatist, his main concern was the calibre of Eicke's men as fighters.

In his memoirs his praise for them was couched in the dry, unemotional terms of an official report. He wrote:

'As far as its discipline and soldierly bearing went, the division in question undoubtedly made a good impression. I had even had reason to praise its extremely good marching discipline — an important requirement for the efficient movement of motorised formations. The division always showed great dash in the assault and was steadfast in defence. I had it under my command on frequent occasions later on and think it was probably the best Waffen-SS division I ever came across.'

Nevertheless, his bouquets were by no means unstinting. He also declared:

'Yet bravely as the Waffen SS divisions always fought, and fine though their achievements may have been, there is not the least doubt that it was an inexcusable mistake to set them up as a separate organisation. Hand picked replacements who could have filled the posts of NCOs in the army were expended on a quite inordinate scale in the Waffen SS, which in general paid a toll of blood incommensurate with its actual gains.'

And now that toll of blood was being extracted mercilessly as the division closed with its adversaries at the village of Dagda. The 21st Armoured Group of General D.D. Lelyushenko was in danger of disintegration. The need for a counter-attack was desperate. First to experience the full brunt of a spirited new offensive was Max Simon's lead battalion; Totenkopf lost ten men and nearly one hundred of the SS were wounded.

Tanks and artillery hastened to buttress the Soviets. It was a novel experience for Eicke to yield ground, but he had no choice. The result was to postpone the proposed advance until 3 July. By then, he hoped, the Luftwaffe would have dealt with the Russian artillery.

But the Stukas were of limited help. The going was still undeniably slow; Dagda was not retaken until after 10 p.m. on that same evening. The Russians then withdrew to regroup along the so-called Stalin Line, which stretched in its entirety from the Gulf of Finland in the north to Kiev in the south.

Even in withdrawal the Russians kicked back viciously with an artillery barrage harassing Totenkopf until daylight. The SS forces, perhaps for the first time, knew the real meaning of tiredness, the sort of total fatigue which was almost a physical pain made exquisitely worse by the realisation that sleep, even for the second or third night, was out of the question. And this was only the beginning.

Manstein's mission was to launch a direct offensive on the heavy fortifications which dotted the Stalin Line. The role assigned to Eicke was eventually to swing north behind the town of Opochka so as to cut off the Russian retreat, which would be hastened by the attentions of the Germans' 3rd Motorised and 8th Panzer Divisions. The outcome was to demonstrate both the strength and weaknesses of Totenkopf as an effective fighting force.

In common with most of the Germans hurled into Hitler's adventure, they knew nothing of this extraordinary land of unbearably hot summers and abnormally cold winters.

And there were the Russian troops. The calibre of these fighters, as Max Simon was to describe it, was utterly beyond the understanding of the German soldier. Time and again the men of the Totenkopf Division were deceived by columns of abandoned trucks, supply wagons and the general litter of war. This, the SS men believed, was proof of a demoralised defeated foe. An ecstatic Eicke declared: 'Enemy resistance is on the verge of collapsing altogether.'

It was nothing of the sort. The events of 6 July 1941 were to ram the lesson home as nothing else could.

At dawn on that day, Totenkopf Division delivered its first great hammer blow on the Stalin Line and came up against a network of defences, the strength of which had not even been imagined.

A Wehrmacht Intelligence report, made after the line had been run over, described it as:

'A dangerous combination of concrete field works and natural obstacles, tank traps, mines, marshy belts around forts, artificial lakes enclosing defiles, corn-fields cut according to the trajectory of machine-gun fire. Its whole extent right up to the position of the defenders was camouflaged with a consummate art. . . Along a front of 120 kilometres, no less than a dozen barriers, carefully camouflaged and proofed against light bombs and shells of 75 and 100 mm, had been constructed and sited in skilfully chosen fire positions.

'Thousands of pine trunks masked ditches which the attacker could not discover until it was too late. About three kilometres behind, over stretches of ten or twelve kilometres, three ranges of pines had been driven more than a metre into the ground. Within this obstacle stretched out abatis ramparts made of trees sawn to within a metre of the ground, and whose tops, turned towards the enemy, had been entangled with barbed wire. Concrete pyramids strengthened this barricade.'

The Russians had begun constructing this leviathan of defence as early as 1936; German Intelligence was woefully ignorant of its extent.

Totenkopf knifed into its centre; all at once, progress was halted. Now movement was to be measured in yards. Each bunker had to be prised apart, the defenders rooted out. Even then advance was feeble as the division was peppered with relentless artillery fire. Reliance on assault groups was heavy; in went infantry and engineers with their flame-throwers, high explosives and hand-grenades. As the precious hours ticked away, the path ahead was blown open.

Throughout the entire day, the attack ground forward. It was only at nightfall that there was any sense of real achievement, with the engineers slinging the first bridges across the Velikaya river. Now there seemed no reason why the advance around Opochka should not go ahead.

Again, the men of Totenkopf were allowed no rest as the Russian hammering continued. It was a death-watch beetle chipping away at the division's morale.

Totenkopf had learnt to accommodate high casualties; then came another blow. While returning to the front from his HQ at around midnight, a mine erupted beneath Eicke's car. Seriously wounded, he was rushed to a rear island hospital, but not before he had appointed Matthias Kleinheisterkamp as interim commander.

There was no time to fuss over 'Papa' Eicke; the battle for Opochka wore on until it seemed impossible that there could be any more villages to raze or vehicles to destroy. Each side had five days of it. On 11 July, Totenkopf seized the town, sharing the glory with 13th Infantry Division.

Tanks of 21st Army Corps had withdrawn into the swamp forests lying to the east of Opochka. There was some small consolation for their exhausted crews; they were joined by fresh Soviet divisions.

The reward of Opochka for Totenkopf went beyond mere capture; for an exquisite few hours there could be sleep. But there was no rest for Kleinheisterkamp. His job was to send Himmler the casualty figures; predictably, they made grim reading. In sixteen days of fighting, the division had lost eighty-two officers and 1,626 NCOs and men. That meant a casualty rate of around ten per cent of the combat strength.

The reaction of Manstein was blunt: elementary precepts of practical warfare had simply not been learnt. In *Lost Victories*, he wrote in schoolmasterly vein:

'The division suffered excessive losses because its troops did not learn until they got into action what armoured units had mastered long ago. Their losses and lack of experience led them in turn to miss favourable opportunities, and this again caused unnecessary actions to be fought. I doubt if there is anything harder to learn than gauging the moment when a slackening of the enemy's resistance offers the attacker his decisive chance.'

Soon Manstein was facing his own problems, one of which, ironically, put him badly in need of the SS division that he regarded with a mixture of admiration and disapproval.

At military headquarters, the success of the breach of the Stalin Line was studied. Plainly, the last great obstacle before Leningrad had been removed. Then came the order: Hoepner's Panzer Corps was to strike north between lakes Peipus and Ilmen, then close in on Leningrad. Manstein was to make north-east to Novgorod on Ilmen's north shore, where he would be expected to sever the main Leningrad-Moscow highway.

Fifty-sixth Panzer Corps moved into action on 12 July, but for Totenkopf Division there was a surprise. Hoepner detached the SS men and sent them north to Porkhov as part of Panzer Group reserve.

Whatever his reservations about the SS, Manstein deplored the move and said so.

As events turned out, he was not to suffer the deprivation for very long.

Klimenti E. Voroshilov, appointed to represent the Soviet High Command at the Leningrad front, was prepared to hurl all available forces against this dangerous German armoured spearhead aimed at Novgorod. Manstein's Corps, consisting of 8th Panzer Division and 3rd Motorised Infantry Division, suddenly came under attack by numerous divisions of Soviet Eleventh Army. A wedge was driven between the two German divisions; their supply route was severed. Manstein retaliated by withdrawing 8th Panzer Division and preparing for all-round defence.

Three critical days followed. Voroshilov was desperate for victory, and to annihilate the surrounding German divisions. The crucial area was a forest clearing, two miles behind the foremost infantry line at Gorodische. Here impassable swamps lay to the right and left of the road. Mortar shells put paid to the machine-guns in the German battery. For nearly two hours the fighting continued. Nearly all the ammunition was spent. Most officers and NCOs had been despatched. The Germans had resisted with spades, pistols and bayonets. Now they roped in for combat duty tractor-drivers and other general-service personnel. A mere 120 men were fighting an entire battalion.

Communications within Manstein's Corps had been disrupted. Previously, Totenkopf Division, in its period of withdrawal, had enjoyed a brief span of relative quiet. Engineer battalions went to work repairing damaged roads and bridges. The reconnaissance battalion and infantry regiments picked up stragglers and partisans; it seemed as if Totenkopf would revert to its old habits of venting spite on the civilian population.

But there was to be no such luxury. Totenkopf was stuck firmly with a role as a full fighting force. Earlier, Manstein had grumbled: 'I often had to break off to get the Waffen-SS out of trouble.'

Soon he would complain no longer.

10

The news when it came was so incredible that for a time Manstein had stood paralysed, the telephone in his hand. What was it Hoepner had actually said?

'The attack on Leningrad is off.'

He had then outlined the crisis which had suddenly developed for Sixteenth Army on Lake Ilmen, south of Novrogod in the Staraya Russa area.

The Soviet Thirty-fourth Army had, on 14th August, arrowed out from Novgorod around the eastern edge of the lake and slammed straight into the flank of General-oberst Busch. It was necessary for Manstein's 3rd Motorised Infantry Division to turn round, dart south-east and link up with Totenkopf Division, which had instructions to await his arrival. It was a fire brigade role all over again.

Manstein bitterly recalled von Leeb's optimism a few days before. At Hoepner's headquarters he had crowed: 'Leningrad can't escape us now.'

Well, it was no good remembering *that*.

For Totenkopf, fighting around Lake Ilmen had already proved a particular species of hell. Under Brigadefuehrer George Keppler, appointed the division's commander until Eicke's return from hospital, the SS had found itself in terrain beyond its remotest experience.

Small wonder that the land here had scarcely been mapped. The Germans could well be forgiven for thinking they had blundered into some nightmare of the Middle Ages — a phantasmagoria of seemingly limitless forests, vast lakes and dense thickets, fractured by a riot of rivers and streams.

When it came to combat, the Red Army outsmarted the Germans every time. Here the Russians were at home and the men of Totenkopf in the kingdom of the blind. Here was an enemy who was an expert in camouflage, ambush and — particularly galling for Totenkopf — specialised close fighting.

But with the situation now facing Manstein, there was a chance for Totenkopf to get some of its pride back.

The full clout of 3rd Motorised Infantry Division and Totenkopf struck at the Russians on 19 August. The army's flank was rolled up; its rearward communications shattered. Totenkopf's reconnaissance battalion had raced ahead of the division, nosing in on the most critical sector and hurling everything it had at the Soviet spearheads, which were shoved in ignominy across the Lovat.

In the annals of Totenkopf bravery the name of the commander of the reconnaissance battalion, SS-Sturmbannfuehrer Walter Bestmann, was to be singled out for special honour. He was the first in the division to be garlanded with the Knight's Cross.

The Soviet command was paralysed by shock and surprise. General Hansem with his 10th Corps, previously held down in heavy fighting, broke loose and was thrown at Voroshilov's Third Army. The disaster for the Soviets appeared total.

Sixteenth Army had achieved a fantastic success. Of that there could be no doubt. But just precisely where did this put Manstein? Certainly, the threat to the right wing of Army Group North had been averted for a while. But there was no question of Manstein returning to the push on Leningrad by rejoining the offensive forces of Hoepner. Voroshilov was obviously going for a fresh scrap — and with interest.

Now was revealed one of the most striking characteristics of the Russian fighter. He could suffer the most appalling casualties, his loss in material could prove catastrophic, his retreats seemingly the ultimate in shame.

But where he scored was in sheer numbers. This made the men of Totenkopf dumfounded. The bulk of one army had seemingly been destroyed, yet here were the units of three more. And they were at full strength for Voroshilov's task of blocking off the neck of land between lakes Peipus and Ilmen.

Nevertheless, the pressure had to be maintained; Totenkopf and 3rd Motorised Division charged to meet this new threat.

The entire 21 August turned out to be truly appalling for the Russians. They faced unrefined slaughter from Totenkopf Division.

The SS fanned out and advanced; the ground was raked with machine-gun fire. In desperation, the Russians struggled to escape encirclement around the Polist river, just south of Lake Ilmen.

The orders given to Keppler had been specific: the push on the Polist was to take precedence; once there he was to seize as many bridges as possible to stop the Soviet escape east. Every building, bunker and suspected enemy position was destroyed with grenades and high explosives.

By the end of the day, the division had captured more men and materials than at any time since the battle of France. More than one thousand prisoners had been taken. Into the hands of the Germans there fell a healthy quantity of heavy-artillery pieces, trench mortars and ammunition trailers. There could be no doubt of Manstein's unstinted admiration for the Totenkopf Division now.

But what had really been achieved? There was a victory, certainly; Voroshilov's plan had been to outflank the army group and take Hoepner in the rear. That particular scheme had been set at naught, but Manstein's forces and those of Totenkopf Division had been tied down in this particular exercise for five days. The Soviets elsewhere had not been cowed; indeed, they had been free to get on with the task of deploying additional reserves in infantry, armour and artillery in the outskirts of Leningrad.

And no amount of victories, however triumphant, could alter the fact that the Germans were hopelessly outnumbered. Russia could produce limitless reserves; how much blood was let in the process of killing the fascist enemy was a matter of indifference to Stalin.

To replace his shattered forces along the Kholm-Ilmen front opposite the Germans' Sixteenth Army, the Soviet leader rushed in three new armies - the Twenty-seventh, Thirty-fourth and Eleventh. There would have to be another attack but now Manstein was faced with additional aggravation. It was the end of August and the first rains of that summer were setting in. The rain turned every road into a quagmire so that the motorised divisions were stuck like flies in a gluepot.

To make matters worse, enemy resistance was stiffening. On the Lovat river, the Russians dug in and Manstein's divisions were harried by the Red Air Force, which strafed the area between the Lovat and Pola rivers.

In vain, a fuming Keppler begged for Luftwaffe retaliation. His job had been to throw the Russians back across the Pola, and now all he could do was to stand and watch his vehicle columns being shattered. Eventually, the Soviet air attacks ceased, but the Germans could claim no credit for this. Gathering thunderclouds forced the Soviet aircraft out of the sky.

Keppler had other worries. Himmler might consider the Totenkopf Division to be made up of ideological automatons, but the cruel reality of war was that these men had become almost totally exhausted. Their lack of physical resistance inevitably led to a sharp rise in disease. More than four thousand men had laid down their lives, and there was every prospect that casualty figures would go still higher. Defensive armament was woefully deficient; vehicles and equipment were shattered and worn out.

Keppler was not in the least intimidated by Manstein. The two met at the SS commander's headquarters during the afternoon of 29 August. Keppler lost no time in getting to the point.

He said bluntly: 'The division is being bled to death. The condition of my men is so debilitated that any further advance by them is out of the question. Army Group North must withdraw the division for a rest.'

Manstein shrugged: 'Well, the weather should soon help you. I'll postpone any further advance until it clears. Your men can sit and rest on their positions on the river.'

It was not good enough, as Manstein well knew. It was vital that Totenkopf Division and 3rd Motorised Division should be detached and rested from Sixteenth Army altogether.

He stated as much in a pleading letter to Generaloberst Busch. The reply was swift and abrupt:

'Totenkopf Division is no more tired than any other formation on the eastern front. Fifty-sixth Panzer Corps will proceed forthwith to the Demyansk area.'

The riposte provided a nice welcome for Theodor Eicke when he returned to duty on 21 September.

At a series of briefings, Eicke listened grimly to reports of stiffening Russian resistance along the Demyansk-Staraya Russa highway in the area south-east of Lake Ilmen. There had been some spectacular mopping-up assignments by Totenkopf, certainly. But offensive operations — the essential move forward — had been all but abandoned because the Russians had lashed back with such effective viciousness.

An initial inspection of his men appalled Eicke. Here were emaciated wrecks who were expected to fight in rotten, soggy clothing. Furthermore, the number of NCOs who had either been killed or forced to go on leave because of sickness was running so high that the command structure of the division was being undermined.

In his strongest language, Eicke dashed off a series of demands to Himmler's adjutant, Karl Wolff. He stated bluntly: 'You must intercede with the Fuehrer at once so that my men can get some rest.'

Even if Himmler had dared to approach Hitler over such a matter, the whole idea was swiftly rendered academic by the strength of the Soviet offensive.

Eicke was brought sharply back to the realities of the battlefield early on the morning of 22 September.

The urgent message to Totenkopf Division came from 2nd Army Corps: '*Three new Red Army brigades have been identified along the Pola. The Russians are known to be stepping up patrol and reconnaissance.*'

Eicke reflected that a whiff of combat might be just what his men needed, although how skinny scarecrows were expected to fight effectively was something that the army never considered.

Earlier, Manstein, at Sixteenth Army headquarters, had with blunt military coarseness described the immediate prospects as 'shitty'.

Now the top brass of the Wehrmacht was calling on Totenkopf to get it out of the mire again.

Neither Eicke nor his men appreciated that from now on they were to fight two enemies. The first, the Russian, was familiar and getting deadlier all the time. At noon on 24 September, Totenkopf Division received its severest shock since the start of the campaign in the east. Eicke saw his infantry regiments sliced and shattered, engulfed in a human tidal wave of marching formations that catapulted out of a dense forest, swarming across the Pola and falling upon their enemy like crazed wolves.

Gone were the days when all headquarters had to do was listen to a monotonous series of advances. Now the telephones shrilled with calls for ammunition, information and fresh orders.

By mid-afternoon it had become clear that the Russians had made serious inroads into the defences of the division. Individual units and strongpoints had become isolated.

And the other enemy? The first grim hint had been given that the Russian winter was on its way — on 23 September, the ground was covered with thick frost and the temperatures for the first time plummeted to below freezing.

At this stage, if you were fighting, it was possible almost to forget the cold. And there was plenty of fighting. The situation for Totenkopf was at its most critical in the Lushno sector. Here Soviet tanks presented the greatest menace, threatening the very existence of 2nd Battalion of the 3rd Infantry Regiment. The business of the armour was sheer slaughter; twenty or thirty T-34s charging at ranks which were soon torn apart and dissolved into a confused riot.

Eicke's method of retaliation was swift. There sprang into existence specially created 'tank annihilation squads'. Two SS officers and ten more men armed with bags of satchel-charges, mines, grenades and petrol bombs would attack individual tanks on foot.

Inevitably, the legends sprang up. There were tales of brave Totenkopf men obliterating tanks by first shooting at their treads. Then the officer would dash forward, stuffing a live grenade onto the muzzle of the cannon. Or he would place a double satchel-charge on the tank's hull.

Scowling, fanatical SS-Haupsturmfuehrer Max Seela, Company Commander of 3rd Company, SS-Pioneer Battalion, Totenkopf Division, was a young officer determined to set a shining example to his men. At Lushno on 26 September, he personally destroyed the first T-34 by crawling right up to it, placing a double satchel-charge against the turret and detonating the explosives with a grenade.

The remaining six tanks were despatched in the same way. The crews struggled from the turrets of their doomed vehicles; the SS squad mowed them down.

And there was twenty-year-old baby-faced SS-Sturmann Fritz Christen. Every member of his battery was wiped out at Lushno on the morning of 24 September. Only he remained alive, sticking with his gun and firing continuously until six Russian tanks had been knocked out and others driven off.

Three days later, the Russians had retreated. But Fritz Christen was still at his post. Around him lay the corpses and the blasted remains of T-34s. His achievement was straight out of a schoolboy's comic but it happened to be real. He had immobilised thirteen Soviet tanks and killed one hundred Russians.

Eicke personally awarded Christen the Iron Cross, First Class, and recommended him at the same time for the Ritterkreuz (Knight's Cross to the Iron Cross). The young hero was later flown to Hitler's headquarters at Rastenburg in East Prussia to be decorated by his Fuehrer. It was all first-rate recruiting-poster stuff. It encouraged the average German soldier to believe that the Russians were finished. Had he not been assured that it was all a matter of time? By common consent, the Reds had been dealt a decisive blow on the river Pola. But Eicke was already writing to Karl Wolff again, pointing out that, as from 29 September, the Totenkopf Division had suffered 6,610 casualties, a mere third of whom had been replaced. The condition of his men was again giving cause for concern.

And, of course, there was the coming winter.

Hitler was by no means unaware of the need to take Moscow before the onset of winter. Attention switched now to Army Group Centre. Here there seemed much cause for optimism. The fight by the Soviets for the strategically important rail and communications centre at Smolensk — to stem the German sweep into the heart of Russia and to win time to strengthen the Moscow defences — had failed. There was a series of successful pincer movements, all of them designed eventually to converge on Moscow.

In the north it seemed that the Russian retreat into the heavily wooded Valdai Hills near Lake Ilmen was accelerating. Totenkopf, snapping as usual at the heels of the enemy, found that this time it had wandered into territory whose lack of hospitality did not only come from the activities of the Red Army.

For this was partisan country. The bands comprised not just deserting soldiers, but also civilian survivors of SS tyranny in the villages and farms who harried supply columns, field hospitals and the rear areas with total lack of discrimination. It was a new sort of enemy for the cold, dispirited, exhausted Totenkopf Division.

The SS was responsible for disposing of these murder bands, and it enjoyed Wehrmacht blessing.

An OKW order of 16 July 1941 declared:

'. . .The necessary rapid pacification of the country can be attained only if every threat on the part of the hostile civil population is ruthlessly taken care of. All pity and softness are evidence of weakness and constitute a danger. . .'

Although throats of partisans were undoubtedly slit, most of the killing was in the hands of the firing-squads. They had received very precise instructions. They were told to aim at or below the waist, which frequently meant that most of the victims died in agony from stomach wounds.

The partisans had their fair share of success, though, even if it was dearly bought.

It was a thoroughly spent combat unit of Totenkopf which gratefully bedded down in the quiet village of Ilomlya, which nestled below Lake Ilmen. The combing of the adjacent forest in sub-zero temperatures had produced no signs of partisan activities. Nevertheless, the SS men were glad enough to be sharing a billet with a convoy from 30th Infantry Division and two companies of riflemen from the 503rd Infantry Regiment.

Such bedfellows were reassuring, and the senior SS officer present was satisfied that security arrangements were sufficient for a single night.

The Soviet partisans had the knack of being able to melt into invisibility in the woods, emerging equally silently when there was a job to be done. Soon they had reached the German guards. At an agreed signal, the grenades were hurled and the petrol bombs were lobbed at the trucks and supply trailers. The burning vehicles and buildings forced the Germans to evacuate — and as they tumbled onto the streets, the partisan killer groups were ready for them.

In a long memorandum to his superiors at SS-Hauptamt, Eicke lost no time in pointing out that the green reservists with which he was flooded were the most likely to fall victims to partisan guile and the ruthlessness and cunning of the Russians generally. And he took the opportunity to rail against the low standard of ethnic Germans and foreign nationals which Himmler was pressing into the Waffen-SS.

The replacements being sent to him were 'most under-nourished and less suited for physical strain'. Many were not only physically deficient but 'spiritually weak' as well and were 'disobedient and evasive'. They often knew more German than they let on, so that they could avoid unpleasant orders. He sharply reminded Berlin that he commanded an élite division and that he had no use for 'undisciplined and dishonest scoundrels [*Lumpen*] and criminals'.

The need for Totenkopf Division to have a breather before continuing its role as an essential buttress to von Leeb's forces was undeniable. But the blunt truth was that, however much it might dislike Eicke, his troops and their methods, the army needed the men of the Death's Head to fight off the Russians around Lake Ilmen. For Totenkopf Division, there was little prospect of relief.

In the armies before Moscow, officers and troops shivered because they lacked the special winter clothing which would have enabled them to camp and fight on open ground at temperatures which were minus fifty degrees. Such filthy clothes as they possessed were breeding-places for lice that snuggled against the skin. Daily losses due to frost-bitten limbs and intestinal troubles were higher than from enemy action.

Grown men wept with the cold, then had the experience of the ice forming in their eyes. As for equipment, field glasses, trench telescopes and gunsights became useless as their optics faded over.

In the north, it was thirty-four degrees below zero. There was the chill of impending disaster.

11

By early December 1941, the armies of Fedor von Bock, arrowing towards Moscow, lay exhausted under the lash of the first blizzard of the Russian winter.

Onto the vast arena of battle ribboning along a five-hundred-mile front strode the stocky peasant figure of Soviet General Georgi Zhukov. He had secured the laurels of victory two years earlier when Japan had been severely mauled after excursions into Soviet and Mongolian territory.

At a time when the world's attention had been focussed on Hitler's attack on Poland, a little war against the Japanese, involving a mere quarter of a million, had received scant attention in the west. But Japan had taken to heart the lesson that the Germans were soon to learn at a gruesome cost — the danger of underestimating the potential resources of the Soviets.

But, until Zhukov, there was much that the Russians too had not learnt. The war against Hitler was no old-fashioned affair to be fought along the orthodox military principle that what counted was the sheer weight of flesh and metal. The Germans were fighting a technocrat's war with fast-moving, highly trained Panzers.

Zhukov's most effective weapon was manpower, and he lost no time in amassing it. Suddenly, Bock was up against fresh divisions rushed to the battlefront by train from Siberia.

For the first time, something like panic had gripped the German forces. Hitler's orders were explicit: '*The*

German soldier will stand and fight.'

The Fuehrer had assumed the title of Commander-in-Chief. It was no mere ornament. Disobedience or incompetence bought instant dismissal for officers, no matter how senior or how eminent.

Hoepner proved tardy in pulling back the right front of his Panzergruppe. He was publicly cashiered. General Guderian, the architect of German tank warfare, was also dismissed, although he was to stage a comeback later.

Nervous junior officers might have been forgiven for thinking that there had been a putsch in the upper reaches of the army. Thirty-five corps and division commanders were sent back to Germany in ignominy. No one was safe from the Fuehrer's wrath.

Fuel was short and the number of serviceable vehicles limited.

Any retreat would have been woefully slow and the entire German Army annihilated. Hitler kept his nerve while all around him were losing theirs. To his anxious, quaking subordinates at headquarters in Rastenburg, Hitler announced: 'Here we stand and fight it out.'

The Nazi Commander-in-Chief had tenacity and, above all, patience. He had severe need of both. For three months, the Russians kept up their systematic savaging of Army Group Centre. But none of their major encircling moves dislodged the Germans; their territorial gains were limited to a forty-mile belt on the approach to Moscow.

The effects of Zhukov's attentions to Army Group Centre rippled through the north.

Eicke's forward observation post was to discover the first hint of Russian plans for a major offensive in the area of Lake Ilmen. Within twenty-four hours of Zhukov's savage assault on Centre, look-outs had spotted a sharp increase in the movement of the enemy. Eicke decided to probe further. German spotter aircraft were ordered into the air. The reports banished all doubts. Troops and vehicles were moving in vast masses along the former Leningrad-Moscow railway line.

Second Army Corps and Sixteenth Army seemed to get the message. Alert to their warnings, Eicke ordered his men to entrench for strong and continuous Russian attack. Throughout December, the Totenkopf Division remained on full alert; work on the network of bunkers and trenches went on.

Eicke told his immediate staff: 'All this is a sideshow, I'm convinced. There's a much bigger build-up coming from beyond the Valdai Hills.'

Was Eicke being alarmist? There were those in the division who thought so. After all, for the next few weeks the situation was relatively calm. The attentions of small groups of Russian infantry seemed mere pinpricks.

Totenkopf Division was at this time afforded somewhat more than a grudging respect. 'That butcher Eicke' had earned his spurs as a relentless, fearless commander, but that by no means implied that the army could ever regard him or his Death's Head knights as one of themselves.

This was brought home sharply to Eicke when he became embroiled in one of those SS-army squabbles with which he and other Waffen-SS commanders had become woefully familiar.

This time the issue was prisoners. Eicke was determined that most of the construction work on the winter quarters for the Totenkopf Division should be done by Russian captives. It was out of the question for his own severely overstretched contingents to dissipate their energies with such activities.

Luckily, there was no shortage of Russian prisoners. Predictably, those that were available were coveted by 10th Army Corps and others. Eicke employed his familiar tactics. He simply ignored everybody and went ahead appropriating as much forced labour as he wanted.

But by the beginning of January 1942, Sixteenth Army had taken a hand. Eicke was ordered to send a monthly report with information about the condition of prisoners, the number that had been shot escaping or had been turned over to the Einsatzgruppen for 'special handling'. He gritted his teeth and complied, still holding on grimly to the numbers of prisoners he felt necessary to relieve his men.

Serious indeed that January was the situation in the

wooded region between Lake Ilmen, lying to the west, and Lake Seliger to the south-east. Through the centre smashed three Russian armies, the Eleventh, Thirty-fourth and First Shock Army. The aim was to encircle Busch's Sixteenth Army, unhinge the entire right wing of Leeb's army group and prize open what would be a yawning gap between northern and central sectors of the German front.

It soon became apparent that Eicke's reading of the Soviet intentions was only too correct. Totenkopf's front received a bloody nose on 8 January 1942 when the enemy smashed into the 290th and 30th Infantry Divisions on Eicke's left. Twenty-four hours later the situation was even worse. The Russian offensive seemed to be moving like clockwork.

Pressure against Sixteenth Army was relentless. Units of the Totenkopf Division were peeled away and sent to stiffen threatened sectors of the front in the north, west and south. All the signs were that the encirclement of Busch would soon be complete.

Now the writing was on the wall for Leeb but not because of Russian pressure. His request to Hitler was that 2nd and 10th Army Corps should be withdrawn behind the Lovat River to form a new front. Otherwise, Leeb reasoned, they would be annihilated.

Here was heresy of the kind which had already led to widespread dismissals by the Commander-in-Chief. Hitler riposted: 'The request is refused. Sixteenth Army will stand and fight.'

It was too much for Leeb, whose request to be withdrawn from command from Army Group North was granted immediately. General Georg von Kuechler, a traditionalist Junker with forty years' service, took his place.

Immediate effects were not apparent. The situation west of the Valdai Hills grew steadily worse. The powerful Soviet forces, slowly but surely, were squeezing the life out of 2nd and 10th Army Corps.

The site of the constricting pocket was centred around the town of Demyansk. The corps were encircled in an area of 1,200 miles.

By 20 January, all land communications with the rest of Sixteenth Army were cut.

Precisely a month later, Count Walther von Brockdorff-Ahlefeldt, the general commanding 2nd Army Corps, was having the order of the day read to all formations within the pocket:

'Taking advantage of the coldest winter months, the enemy has crossed the ice of Lake Ilmen, the normally marshy delta of the Lovat river, and the shallow valleys of the Pola, Redya, and Polist, as well as numerous lesser watercourses, and placed himself behind 2nd Corps and its rearward communications. These river-valleys form part of an extensive area of swampy lowlands which get flooded and entirely impassable, even on foot, the moment that the ice and snow start to melt. Any enemy transport, especially the bringing of supplies on any scale, will then be entirely impossible.

'Russian supplies during the wet springtime would be possible only along the major hard roads. The inter-section of these roads, however — Kholm, Staraya Russa and Demyansk — are firmly in German hands. Moreover, the Corps with its battle-tried six divisions commands the only real piece of high ground in the area. It is therefore impossible for the Russians with their numerous troops to hold out in the wet lowlands without supplies in spring.

'What matters, therefore, is to hold these road junctions and the high ground around Demyansk until the spring thaw. Sooner or later the Russians will have to give in and abandon that ground, especially as strong German forces will be attacking them from the west.'

It was a novel experience. There had been encircle-ments before, of course, but then it had been the Ger-mans who had been doing the encircling. All that was changed with a vengeance.

The men of the Wehrmacht and Totenkopf did not know it, but military history was being made on this day.

For the first time, an entire corps of six divisions with around one hundred thousand men was to be supplied successfully by air. The first recorded airlift was to get under way, supplying the beleaguered German Army on the Valdai Hills.

The men of 2nd Corps were to be supplied by some five hundred transport aircraft with everything that was needed to fight in this cruel land of blizzards, frosts, fog and winter thunderstorms. Soviet anti-aircraft fire ripped into the transport squadrons, but still the Luftwaffe came — some ten to fifteen of its aircraft every day nosing through a curtain of fire to two makeshift airstrips.

The appalling weather conditions were, predictably, taken by the Russians in their stride. The menace was not just from the conventional fighting man. There was the menace of what Max Simon described as

'. . .the method of infiltration, i.e. the Soviet High Command tries to get troops unnoticed behind the enemy lines, a method which is in line with the general Bolshevik policy, which favours the use of underground channels. . .Once the Russian sector commander has discovered the weak and thinly manned parts of the enemy front, his "infiltration parties", which are led by trained agents, find their way behind that front. No water and no swamp is too deep for these infiltration parties and no forest too dense; for them the word "impossible" is non-existent.

'It is widely known that. . .Soviets in German officer uniforms appeared at the command posts in the East and passed on fictitious orders, thus causing considerable confusion. . .'

The Russians also had a talent verging on the uncanny for being virtually invisible.

Parachutists made brilliant infiltrators. A vast swampy jungle of a forest stretched behind Totenkopf Division's front line. Towards the end of February 1942, Simon's men spotted aircraft giving out flash signals above the forest.

Above: Men of the SS-Totenkopf Division during the French campaign, May 1940.

Below: A wartime example of a Totenkopf collar patch as worn by officers.

Facing page: A Totenkopf unit at the 1936 Nuremberg Rally.

Right: An officer of the Totenkopf Division in action in Russia.

Below: Theodor Eicke visits Hitler's headquarters at Rastenburg. Left to right: Karl Wolf, Eicke, Richard Schulze, Keitel and Julius Schaub, 1942.

Left: SS-Hauptsturmfuehrer
Fritz Knoechlein, May 1940.

Below:
SS-Obergruppenfuehrer
Theodor Eicke and his adjutant
inspect positions in the
Demyansk Pocket, May 1942.

Facing page:
SS-Obergruppenfuehrer
Sepp Dietrich. *(Imperial
War Museum)*

SS-Standartenfuehrer Hellmuth
Becker.

SS-Sturmbannfuehrer Otto Skorzeny.
(Imperial War Museum)

SS-Obergruppenfuehrer Theodor
Eicke. *(Imperial War Museum)*

SS-Gruppenfuehrer Herbert Gille.
(Imperial War Museum)

Right:
SS-Standartenfuehrer
Karl Ulrich at the
Fuehrerhauptquartier
to receive the Knight's
Cross, 1943.

Below: Tank
commander and
grenadiers of the
SS-Totenkopf Division
after the capture of
Kharkov, March 1943.

Above: A copy of a snapshot found on the body of a Nazi soldier showing members of the invading forces during the early days of the attack on the USSR. *(Imperial War Museum)*

Below: An SS NCO on the staff of Belsen concentration camp is searched by a British soldier, May 1945.

Simon related:

'At first, we thought the signals were intended for partisans, although in fact we hadn't encountered any. The next door unit sent out a reconnaissance party and when it failed to return I sent out a stronger force of my own men. This party returned intact, looking puzzled. No one had seen anything beyond some extinguished camp fires. It took some more night patrols before in fact the enemy was spotted and it was possible to draw him from hiding. Then a village was attacked suddenly by lightning forces from the forest and it took three solid days and the use of heavy weapons to drive the Reds back in the woods.

'We took some prisoners and from them we learnt the truth. We discovered that for three weeks Russian parachutists on snowshoes had been infiltrating slowly at various points of the German front and had assembled in the vast forest. Our men had frequently seen snowshoe tracks in the morning, but had paid no attention to them assuming they had been left by our own troops.'

The commander, a parachute specialist and lieutenant-colonel, was in charge of men from Russian I and II Parachute brigade — a strength of five thousand buttressed with hand-arms and machine-guns and mortars.

His assignment was to seize the aerodrome at Demyansk in the heart of the pocket. The parachute forces would then link with other Red Army contingents attacking from outside. The infiltrators had managed to melt undetected into the forest, where they had remained unseen for days, receiving orders, food supplies and additional arms by night from the aircraft seen by Simon and his men.

'The infiltration nearly succeeded. It had not been possible to attack the Russian brigade in the forest itself because we lacked the necessary strength for such an action, but the defence of the vital aerodrome had been well prepared and the Russian attack was repulsed. Later on, the Russians, inside the pocket, supported by forces from the outside, tried to break through towards the south, but we succeeded in annihilating them and capturing their commander.'

There may well have been those who believed that the Fuehrer's steadfast refusal to retreat, his insistence that his forces should stand in perpetual combat, was sheer madness. But that was not for the men of Totenkopf Division to say. They obeyed orders, and Count Walther von Brockdorff-Ahlefeldt had need of them.

Those Totenkopf units under the direct command of Theodor Eicke were separated into two regimental Kampfgruppen. Now it was into a frozen nightmare where the snow was chest-deep and the temperature plunged to thirty degrees below zero.

Within the pocket, the defenders inevitably suffered from the increasingly tight rationing of food. Since supplies were coming in by air, rations for men and horses had to be rigidly controlled.

For the horses, hay or straw was obviously out of the question. The produce of the wretched peasant shacks was no substitute for fodder. Hunger could not be kept at bay indefinitely with tree bark, pine branches and needles, reeds or beans. The animals ate the sand and died of sand colic; they fell victim to mange and founder. Veterinary surgeons could offer nothing beyond the *coup de grâce*, and the horses performed their final service in the field kitchens — with the Russian civilian population jostling for the bones and entrails.

Eicke kept command of the larger of the two mixed SS and army battle groups. It moved into line between surviving units of the 290th Infantry Division at the pocket's westward tip. The essential job was to defend the clutch of villages and connecting roads against Russian attack from the west.

It was at this crucial phase of the Russian war that Eicke's supreme gifts of leadership crystallised and matured. There was still a good deal of the old arrogance, to be sure. But his immediate subordinates noticed a new professional calm, a curbing of the earlier impetuosity that had cost so many needless lives.

There was something else. There was a refusal to allow himself to be above the hardships endured by his men. In the swamps and snows of Demyansk he shared the same meagre rations and donned the same ragged, soggy clothes. He refused any bed but a dug-out.

Above all he spoke the language of the ordinary SS private, with his everlasting oaths from the barrack square.

'Papa' Eicke indeed!

It was the personality of the commander which explained why each Totenkopf soldier was prepared to relinquish his position only in death. If he was beaten back, he merely regrouped. In the burnt-out villages of Tscherentizy, Vasilyevschina and Kobylkina, two companies of the Kampfgruppe held out for more than a month in the chest-high snow and the plunging temperatures.

The frequency and size of the Soviet infantry and armoured assaults increased to a new fury; Eicke discovered that his front was being slashed into a string of small, individual pockets. Once again, the casualty rate was appalling.

Eicke made a direct appeal to Himmler for reinforcements. The Reichsfuehrer was able to oblige, but their arrival inevitably took time. The amount of Luftwaffe traffic available to fly what was needed into the pocket was strictly limited.

But for the Wehrmacht there was another more pressing anxiety — one also shared by the Russians.

Early on 21 March Oberst Ilgen reported to the Fedorovka, Demyansk, headquarters of General Hans Zorn to learn the plans aimed at cracking the Russian ring around the six German divisions in the pocket.

By way of a conversational opening, the Oberst remarked it was the first day of spring. Zorn grunted: 'Some spring! Two feet of snow and fifty degrees below. Frankly, the best thing that could happen to us would be for the frost to hold. Once that thaw comes, we'll get the mud. Not a wheel will be able to turn.'

Both men knew that it was vital for the regiments of General Walter Kurt von Seydlitz-Kurzbach's Corps Group to arrive before that.

At the extreme western end of the pocket Theodor Eicke's men heard the crashes of Soviet artillery. It was 7.30 a.m.

The sound was adrenalin. Here was the real action at last; under way was 'Operation Bridge-building', the German offensive to relieve 2nd Corps in the Demyansk pocket. Seydlitz-Kurzbach was mounting his attack from Staraya Russa with the strength of four divisions. His intention was to blast a corridor right through the pocket, reuniting the cut-off divisions with the main fighting line..

In the pocket's western salient, 'Corps Group Zorn' had been formed. Its task was to launch the breakout attack which had been given the code name 'Fallreep' ('Operation Gangway'). The idea was that the units inside the pocket were to wait until the offensive of General Seydlitz had smashed firmly through the Russian lines and reached the point of Ramushevo on the Lovat. Then the units inside the pocket would attack west with full force.

Spearheads of this operation would be provided by the regiment of Oberst Ilgen, a somewhat patchwork affair woven from various battalions of the surrounded divisions.

At first, there seemed little cause for anxiety. The plan was textbook. There had been the preliminary artillery bombardment and the scream of the Stukas. Progress had been fast and some exultant members of the Wehrmacht were put in mind of the early, heady days of the Blitzkrieg.

It was not long before such optimism was rudely shattered. When the offensive had started there had been no Russian winter but now the temperatures were thirty degrees below, swamps were frozen to stone with the cold. The wintry forest and scrub east of Staraya Russa further impeded progress. Not for the first time the

132

Germans asked themselves: what sort of nightmare was this? What was to be made of a country where, when the thermometer rose to freezing point, it meant a thaw?

By the end of March, the temperature plummeted again, this time to twenty degrees below. By day, there were heavy snowfalls, while at night the swamps and forests were swept by spring gales that instantly froze any living thing lacking shelter. Grown men were grateful to huddle in caves or huts. There were even instances of trees being felled for makeshift refuges.

The great thaw proved no consolation. The snow and ice were a memory, but had left behind water that was knee-deep on the roads. Troops waded waist-high through icy swamps and marshes. Precious time was wasted building rafts from branches of trees and bushes to carry machine-guns which otherwise would have been sucked into the rapacious mud.

The Russians fared little better. Their heavy tanks were unable to impede such German progress as there was. It was not until 12 April that Seydlitz's spearheads caught their first glimpse of the shattered towers of Ramushevo. It became clear that unless this small town which controlled the road and the crossing over the Lovat was held, Fallreep would crumble.

Severe wounds removed Oberst Ilgen from the battle. His replacement, Oberstleutnant von Borries, was firmly in charge at dawn on 14 April. It was six days later that the battalions groped their way at nightfall to the first houses of Ramushevo on the eastern bank of the Lovat. Way out in front was the reinforced SS-Panzerjaeger Battalion of SS-Totenkopf Division under Hauptsturmfuehrer Georg Bochmann.

He and his fellow SS saw a town ablaze with tracer bullets streaking through the night. Over the river drifted the noise of battle, but no one could determine precisely what was happening. The tumult and chaos and smoke and dust all combined with the glare of the fires to kill visibility.

It had taken six days for Eicke's battle group to achieve just this, six days of solid fighting in an advance of little more than a mile a day.

Like a savage dog that clamps onto a human limb and bites still more deeply and viciously with each struggle of its victim, Seydlitz's companies fastened on one particular stretch of the river. Eyewitnesses later stated that they had caught sight of figures on the other side throwing their steel helmets in the air and shouting excitedly: 'They're here! They're here!'

It was 6.30 p.m. on 21 April 1942. Now only the churning waters of the Lovat separated the corridor which would re-establish a continuous front for Army Group North.

The day's work was a triumph.

Hitler did not let the contribution of Totenkopf Division go unrecognised. As well as the Knight's Cross which he had received on 15 January, Eicke was now awarded the additional Oak Leaves, at the same time gaining promotion to SS-Obergruppenfuehrer.

It was all personally gratifying, of course, but for Eicke, who remembered how the Wehrmacht had sneered at his men as a bunch of thugs and had obstructed their endeavours at every turn, there was added satisfaction. The Totenkopf Division was now an outfit which had grown immensely in prestige.

But the decorations, however exalted, had little to do with the real world.

By the end of May, Eicke had submitted a report to Himmler on the division's casualties. During the time of its action on Lake Ilmen, total strength had diminished to 6,700 men. The predicament was not new and neither was the solution propounded by Eicke — either he must receive a replacement of 10,000 men or the unit must be withdrawn for refitting. Furthermore, a decent period must be allowed before the return of the men could even be contemplated. Unless something was done, further resistance against the Russians was out of the question.

Eicke was not the only complainant. On 7 April, a lengthy memorandum had been sent by SS-Hauptsturmfuehrer Dr Eckert, physician of 2nd Battalion of Max

Simon's 1st Infantry Regiment. In late March and early April, stated the doctor, he had carried out extensive physical examinations, which had revealed men in such bad physical shape that he had been reminded of concentration camp inmates.

Eckert's overall conclusion was frightening. It was his belief that at least thirty per cent of the men in the battalion were unfit for any further fighting. As for the other seventy per cent, they were so weak that rest was essential. In short, the entire battalion in its present state was useless.

Eicke might just as well have held his breath. With an ignorance of conditions in Russia which was nothing less than stupefying, the Reichsfuehrer shrugged off the strictures of Eicke, Eckert and others with the fatuous remark that a good nutritional diet of fresh vegetables was what was needed. In any case, Himmler added, the weather would soon be changing and the situation would take care of itself.

What had particularly incensed Himmler was an additional point made by Eckert that the new SS recruits to Russia had been of particularly low racial calibre and lacked ideological enthusiasm.

It was especially painful to Himmler to hear his own racial doctrines preached against him. Furthermore, in his reply the Reichsfuehrer admitted that, under present circumstances, quality within the SS had to be sacrificed to quantity. It was a distressing subject and Himmler, notorious for flinching at unpleasant facts, dismissed the whole matter by simply forbidding any more such reports.

Hitler proved equally inflexible. There was to be no talk whatever of withdrawal; Totenkopf Division's place was on the Russian front and there it would stay.

In one respect, however, the Fuehrer proved more accommodating than Himmler. The need for new formations on the Russian front was clearly genuine. Thus the authorisation for new SS units to be organised in Germany was given, but the biggest disadvantage, of course, was time. By October 1942, the health of the existing formations within the Demyansk pocket was so dire that a virtually new division had to be built.

Meanwhile, Hitler's nightmare was now that the Russians would attempt to cut the Staraya Russa-Demyansk road and try to re-establish their encirclement of the German forces. The job of preventing this was given to Eicke. On paper, it sounded like even further promotion. For he was to be given a corps, no less.

The reality had little prestige about it. On 5 May 1942, Eicke received less than fourteen thousand survivors from the six divisions that had suffered so severely in the Demyansk pocket.

Some corps!

Eicke, looking as bewildered as a child who had been given sweets one minute and a slap the next, had all the confidence knocked out of him. At a hastily convened meeting at his headquarters in the village of Kalitkino with Generaloberst Busch, the new corps commander begged: 'You must either get me replacements or have this lot withdrawn to recuperate and rebuild. You're asking sick and exhausted men to defend a forty-five-mile front. It can't be done.'

Busch possessed decidedly more skill than Eicke as a diplomat. He had been deeply shocked by what he had seen of the condition of the Totenkopf troops, but one had to tread warily with a man like Himmler.

Busch wrote to the Reichsfuehrer in suitable conciliatory tones. Of course, he stressed, the Wehrmacht now realised what a superb fighting-machine the Totenkopf Division was. It was Eicke's energetic leadership which had kept the Demyansk pocket open. But if this magnificent division was to continue its work, at least five thousand replacements were vital.

But Himmler's manpower situation was plainly a good deal more dire than Eicke or Busch had suspected. The Russian campaign was devouring young lives remorselessly. All the Reichsfuehrer could secure was three thousand badly trained reservists from Germany. True, there was a sprinkling of Danish-SS volunteers together with some Volksdeutsche recruits, but most of these were mediocre sweepings from other divisions.

For the men in the Demyansk pocket it amounted to a sentence of death. The Russians had suffered horribly throughout the winter, of course. But they had natural powers of recuperation denied the Germans. The foe now was young, strong, fresh infantry, backed by seemingly endless tank waves and flame-throwers.

Eicke fulminated over the sufferings of his men until early June, when he was presented with what seemed a unique chance to do something directly about the division's plight.

The opportunity was provided, strangely enough, by an order from Hitler via Himmler. Eicke was to hand over command of the division to Max Simon, take a few days off with his family, and then make his way to Rastenburg to receive from his Fuehrer personally the Oak Leaves to his Knight's Cross.

Until the start of Unternehmen Barbarossa, a scheduled passenger aircraft from Moscow to Berlin passed daily over a stretch of territory in East Prussia. It consisted of lakes, swamp area and mixed forests. Despite the attempt at camouflage, pilot and crew were probably not unaware of the extensive building construction apparently going on beneath.

Investigations made by Soviet Intelligence would have revealed the existence of a clutch of buildings intended for the Askania Chemical Works and which, furthermore, held the non-committal code name Installation North.

The Russians would have been tempted to look further. All their enquiries would have led them to a dramatic discovery. Here was a bomb-proof war production plant, no less.

To unearth that discovery would in itself have provided a remarkable intelligence coup. There was, however, one drawback. The intelligence gathered would have been an elaborate Nazi smokescreen.

As early as November 1940, Adolf Hitler had sent out his then Minister of Munitions, Fritz Todt, his staff and a clutch of construction specialists. Their mission had been to pick a suitable site for an HQ from which the war on Russia could be conducted.

Work on the bunkers got under way. A landscape firm from Stuttgart installed artificial trees, camouflage nets and fake 'moss' for the tops of the buildings and above the concrete roads. It was here that Hitler came on 24 June 1941, and here he was to remain, with numerous interruptions, until 20 November 1944.

With a Wagnerian touch of the dramatic, he named the place Wolfsschanze (Wolf's Lair).

A visitor to the place literally entered a minefield. After passing through one checkpoint he would make for an area surrounded by a vast belt of thousands of mines fringing the fenced area of the HQ. Ahead of him lay Sperrkreis I, Sperrkreis II and Sperrkreis III, the restricted zones.

In Sperrkreis I of Wolfsschanze lurked Adolf Hitler, protected by the likely effects of bombing raids by twin reinforced ceilings.

Hitler's interpreter, Paul Schmidt, wrote:

'One recalled the old tales of witches. Not without reason was the HQ known by the code name of Wolfsschanze. The atmosphere of the dark Prussian forest was depressing for people coming up from sunnier parts. The rooms were tiny. You always felt constricted. The humidity which came from masses of concrete, the permanent electric light, the constant hum of the air-conditioning imposed an air of unreality on the atmosphere in which Hitler, growing paler and more flabby every day, received the foreign visitors. The whole place could have been the mystic retreat of some legendary spirit of evil.'

Save to exercise his Alsatian, Hitler seldom moved outside his bunker without a phalanx of SS men — the guards who on Friday, 26 June 1942, escorted Theodor Eicke to be decorated by his Fuehrer with the Oak leaves to his Knight's Cross and have his promotion to Obergruppenfuehrer confirmed.

As Hitler had already pointed out in a telegraph to the commander of the Totenkopf Division, Eicke was the eighty-eighth soldier to receive 'the Oak Leaves of the Knight's Cross of the Iron Cross'.

Predictably, the *Voelkischer Beobachter* made the most of the occasion:

'The life of this man is the life of a political soldier of Adolf Hitler. . .At the decisive moments in battle, the commander was always to be found in the front line. His personal bravery was well known to the whole division. All that was important to him was that an attack would succeed. . .Eicke personally led the breakthrough of the Stalin Line. It took days and weeks of intense fighting against the enemy which outnumbered him and had substantial advantages in weapons. . .

'While returning from a battle, his truck hit a Soviet land mine and the SS-Gruppenfuehrer was badly wounded. He had to give up temporarily commanding the division. After a few weeks he pleaded with the Reichsfuehrer-SS to allow him to return to his troops. His wound had hardly healed — but he was again back with his men!. . .

'The division is proud of its commander. With him they enjoy their glory and high honours. . .'

It was evidently a jovial occasion, and a photograph taken at the Wolfsschanze shows Eicke posing proudly with his decoration, in the benevolent company of Feldmarschall Keitel and other officers.

But it had not all been socialising. There had been the searching interview in the private study alone with Hitler. Eicke patiently submitted to closer questioning on the strength, weaknesses and needs of his unit.

Then, seizing a favourable opening, he had his say. In the bluntest possible language, he outlined the weakened state of the men and the chronic shortage of weapons and vehicles.

Hitler appeared sympathetic, but stressed: 'The first

consideration has to be the situation south of Lake Ilmen. If that remains stable, then the division could be transferred to France in August.'

Eicke also received an assurance that, by the autumn, he would be given fresh and fully equipped units, together with a tank battalion.

As he later wrote to Max Simon, Eicke felt considerable relief. The Fuehrer was plainly a realist, unlike some of the others around him. There could now be no question of the division not being restored to its pre-campaign strength.

Even Himmler was to prove co-operative. Eicke, he declared, badly needed extended leave. The Reichsfuehrer ordered him to stay at home until the Totenkopf Division could be withdrawn from the Soviet Union.

Meanwhile, a stream of orders issued from the Wolfsschanze. Men for the new tank battalion arrived at Buchenwald for a vigorous training programme. The dependable Heinz Lammerding, who had also been sent on leave, was back to lick the new infantry regiments into shape.

Lammerding, in a communication to Max Simon in Russia, was soon asking when the first convoys of the Totenkopf Division could leave the east.

But Simon by now had problems of his own.

12

It was true that a corridor had been re-established in triumph between the main German front of Staraya Russa, which extended south to the small provincial town of Kholm, and the divisions in the area of Demyansk.

But the link was fragile indeed. Second Army Corps held on, barring the Soviets' way across the land bridge between lakes Ilmen and Seliger. Five Soviet armies were tied down; nevertheless, throughout 1942 there was the considerable risk of a build-up of new forces.

All at once, the weather became favourable to the Soviets. Under the convenient cover of unseasonably heavy rain, they began marshalling fresh steel.

Far to the south, the great offensive rolled through the Crimea and towards the Don river and the Caucasus. For the moment, attention shifted away from Demyansk. But not for long. On 2 July, there was a gigantic heave against the salient and the frail supply corridor.

Six days later, the full fury was unleashed against those Totenkopf units remaining.

The month of July was the blackest that Eicke had yet experienced. On the afternoon of 13 July, at a hastily convened conference in Rastenburg, Hitler dropped his bombshell. He blandly announced that it had been necessary to reorganise 10th Army Corps of Generalleutnant Otto von Knobelsdorff so as to widen the supply corridor and straighten out the front of the salient.

The Fuehrer stated: 'There are simply not enough SS replacements. In the circumstances, an attack cannot take place until the end of August. There can, of course, be no question of SS-Totenkopf Division being withdrawn before then.'

Himmler, confronted by the indignant Eicke, attempted to make light of the situation. Obviously, he pointed out, the Fuehrer had to be flexible. The undertaking given to Totenkopf was merely in abeyance, that was all.

The real reason for Hitler's change, though, had little to do with Army Group North. All efforts were being concentrated on the second German offensive, which was to last from June to November 1942. All organised Soviet resistance in the Crimea had ceased. The Germans had taken Rostov and swept into the Caucasus. The main thrust of the German offensive was to be the key industrial city of Stalingrad.

Once Stalingrad had been secured it might make possible a move north to Moscow. German conquest of the Caucasus would deny the Russians a point from which the next stage of the German offensive could be launched the next winter.

Himmler did not spell it out to Eicke so crudely, but the blunt truth was that German forces were so committed in the south that other areas would simply have to wait.

With a mixture of fury and black depression, Eicke wrote to Simon telling him of Hitler's decision.

The Russians meanwhile planned a new move on the severely fractured Demyansk pocket.

It came at 1.30 p.m. on 17 July. The Germans were stunned by the sheer force of the renewed attack. The T-34 tanks were only repelled at enormous cost. Worse, the Russians managed to snatch the vital strongpoint of Vasilyevschina, which lay to the north of the Staraya Russa-Demyansk road.

Two companies of Totenkopf were annihilated. The way was now open to push further south and cut the supply road. Second Army Corps would be trapped again.

Timoshenko's task was to dispose of one hundred thousand Germans commanded by Count Brockdorff. At the disposal of the Soviet marshal were three armies. The Eleventh and Twenty-seventh were to attack the northern front of the northern strip of land from Lake Ilmen. First Striking Army would thrust against the corridor from the south.

Timoshenko had abundant reason to feel confident. His northern group was made up of thirteen rifle divisions, nine rifle brigades, and armoured formations with four hundred tanks.

And the Germans? They could muster three divisions in the north, while in the south they could boast just one.

Count Brockdorff instructed Simon: 'Counter-attack immediately to retake Vasilyevschina. That way we will close the gap on the front.'

Something exploded in Max Simon which made his subsequent action devastating. A few weeks ago — days even — such an act of insubordination born of anger would have been unthinkable.

To Brockdorff he stormed: 'Face facts! The Totenkopf Division has suffered 532 casualties in dead and wounded. It is no longer in shape to attack anything.

'If the army wants Vasilyevschina retaken, then it will have to do the job itself. I utterly decline to obey this order.'

Even while he spoke, Simon's figures were out of date. On a fresh action in the same day yet another SS company was completely destroyed. Totenkopf had now lost thirteen officers and 667 men since the campaign had begun.

Simon reasoned that, if he had ruined his career by his action, he had nothing now to look forward to but the firing-squad. So he might as well make a complete job of it.

The next object of his wrath was no less than the Reichsfuehrer-SS. He informed Himmler by radio of his insubordination, reporting that the army was destroying the Totenkopf Division by deliberately assigning it to the most dangerous work.

Incredibly, Simon's temerity was ignored. Brockdorff assigned the recapture of the town to the 8th Jaeger Division. It made no difference. The Russian infantry there refused to budge — an outcome that gave Simon a moment of malevolent glee, which he speedily transmitted to Eicke.

Elsewhere all was carnage. Timoshenko's attack had begun with a massive artillery bombardment. Then had come carpet bombing; followed by the T-34s, flanked by the rifle battalions.

But still they had failed to dislodge the Totenkopf Division. But at what a cost! Simon had got away with insubordination once; his blood was up and he was in the mood to try again.

This time his appeal was to Feldmarschall Georg von Kuechler, commander of Army Group North. At a conference at Demyansk on 29 July, Simon spelt out the cold statistics — the three battle groups engaged along the corridor's northern side had precisely fifty-one officers and 2,685 men. They were being asked to defend a front twenty-six miles long.

These were men who had already been standing for days in swampy forests. There was no dry clothing, adequate food or proper shelter. Then came the inevitable catalogue of diseases — pneumonia, dysentery, spotted fever and kidney disorders.

By no stretch of the imagination could the tougher training that Eicke had devised prepare his men for anything like this. It was not a question of fighting; here were men who could barely stand.

The Feldmarschall — who had been newly promoted and had just returned from Rastenburg — was in no mood to be sympathetic. He had clearly become infected with the euphoria still felt by his Fuehrer.

What was there to worry about? The front was still holding. Everything would be all right once the supply corridor had been widened, the front stabilised. Then would perhaps be the time to talk about taking Totenkopf Division out of the line.

Theodor Eicke, whose earlier wounds to legs and feet were still painful, now had a new irritant. He read with mounting fury Simon's gloomy account of his fruitless interview with Kuechler.

Few would have thought that relations between Totenkopf Division and the higher reaches of the army could get any worse. But they did, along with the condition of Simon's unfortunate survivors within the pocket.

In the white heat of his fury, Eicke dashed off a letter to SS-Brigadefuehrer Hans Juttner, chief of the SS-Fuehrungshauptamt (SSFHA).

Sarcastically, Eicke proclaimed:

'The army will fight at Demyansk to the last drop of SS blood. I believe it is all part of a determined effort by the army to destroy the Waffen-SS it has always hated. Count Brockdorff's attitude towards Totenkopf Division, his impossible demands and his personal treatment of Simon prove that the army wants to get rid of us.'

It was not just a question of the army's jealousy, he went on. The army was so inept that it wanted to eliminate the remaining witnesses of the winter fighting.

'I beg you to intercede forthwith for the relief of my division. If the SS-Totenkopf Division is not pulled out within three weeks there will be nothing left to build a new division. The SS will emerge from this war as an institution too weak to resume its former tasks and serve the Fuehrer in its intended capacities.'

When news of the letter reached Himmler, the Reichs-fuehrer-SS reacted with something like panic. Internal squabbles of this kind were of no help whatever to the stomach cramps which never ceased to plague him. Eicke was a nuisance who must be kept out of the way, or there would be no telling the results.

The commander of the SS-Totenkopf Division had his convalescence extended indefinitely.

Kuechler had barely departed from Simon's head-quarters before the supply corridor of Demyansk was assaulted from north and south. Once again, the men of the SS-Totenkopf Division took the full brunt.

The Katayusha solid-fuel rocket-mortars arrowed in on the German ranks. This time there was some Luftwaffe support, but it was feeble and was soon driven off.

Simon was forced to round up every even remotely able-bodied man and literally force him into battle at gunpoint.

And then, not for the first time, the ever-capricious Russian weather came as a friend, although appreciation by the men of Totenkopf must have been strictly limited.

Thunder tore the skies apart. The ensuing downpours were sustained and merciless; men shivered and some died. But there was one immense, overwhelming consolation. They could not be called upon to fight; many of them could now rest. The lull in hostilities also meant that fresh supplies of guns and ammunition could get through as valuable replacements. True, it was only a gulp of breath but welcome for all that.

The main problem, however, remained. It was not to do with weapons, but with men. There were not enough of them. And the Russians knew it. This time, they attacked along the south side of the land-neck which led into the salient. Simon was forced to fling in everything he possessed.

Into the hell of battle were pressed mechanics, clerks, field policemen and even medical orderlies. The result was the loss of one thousand lives, but incredibly the line still held. By 4 September the resistance of the summer months was over.

Max Simon had proved himself one of Eicke's most brilliant pupils. When it came to sheer ruthlessness in the closing phases of Totenkopf's involvement in the Demyansk pocket, he had more than proved the equal of his chief.

But of Totenkopf, as at that time constituted, there was almost nothing left. Even Himmler could not deny that. There was reason to believe that by now the Reichsfuehrer was badly frightened. Hitler was not interested in excuses; he would want to know not only why this seemingly impregnable SS division had been shot to pieces but why it also had been necessary to make cannon-fodder of auxiliary staff.

Himmler knew very well that he could not afford to have Simon's head on the chopping-block for such unauthorised behaviour. For perhaps the first time in his life the SS leader went on to the offensive. He joined Eicke in demanding the relief of the pathetic skeletons still stuck in the godforsaken swamps of the Demyansk. The Fuehrer gave in.

The signature was barely dry on Hitler's orders before Himmler and his staff sprang into action.

Provision had been made by Hitler for the reorganisation of Totenkopf as a Panzergrenadier division.

146

The tank battalion at Buchenwald, together with the new units being organised at Sennelager, were to leave forthwith for training in France. With them were to go the new organised reserve, named SS-Standarte Thule. The ingredients of the new SS-Totenkopf Division would include 6,000 men who were on temporary duty in the Reich Labour Service, 15,000 reservists currently based in Warsaw and 500 survivors from SS Regiment No. 9.

Besides building up the manpower of the new divisions, Hitler did not neglect weaponry. His insistence that the Waffen-SS formations should be given the latest and the very best inevitably inflamed the old jealousies between the Wehrmacht and the detested Himmler's 'private army'.

Protests, notably from the military high command, became a flood. There could be no question that absolute priority must be given to the army's Panzer divisions in the Soviet Union and North Africa. The rate of losses in these sectors was appalling; nothing could be spared for outside sources.

At first, the army's strictures were listened to. But the campaign in Russia — that struggle which Hitler had been keen to stress would be over in a matter of weeks — gave no sign of abating. With the Soviets determined to hold on, the fanaticism of the SS would clearly have a fresh role in Russia. Aggression could be channelled into tank warfare.

More specifically, into one tank. This was the much vaunted Tiger, the imposing brand-new behemoth rolling off the production lines.

It was planned that the personnel to fill out the division's new tank regiment were to be co-opted from SS-Nordland, a mountain division hitherto isolated near the Arctic Circle, together with what was available after wholesale plunder of concentration camp guard detachments.

By now, Theodor Eicke had come out of the chill of Himmler's disapproval. The commander's enthusiasm surged. After all, had he not a marvellous division? Provided he got everything that he needed in the way of firepower and vehicles, he would have on his hands one of the most efficient machines for waging war in the entire German Army.

Disillusion was not long in coming. A few hours in Bordeaux were enough to bring Eicke back sharply to the real world.

There was nothing whatever wrong with those who had already served in SS formations; it was simply the old problem of shortage of numbers. But seventy-five per cent of the new strength lacked any form of training, and few looked as if they would benefit from it, either.

What on earth was Himmler playing at? Here was the Reich three years into a world war, nearly two of which had involved a conflict with the Soviet Union. Yet here was a newly reconstituted SS division being sent teenagers who were obviously still wet behind the ears, many of them looking decidedly frightened and wondering where they were.

Nor was that the end of the problems. Hitler had talked airily about supplying limitless Tigers. Barely half of those required by the division were yet in commission. Bureaucratic incompetence and fierce rivalry between the Krupp and Henschel firms were blamed.

General Guderian, the Wehrmacht's outstanding exponent of tank warfare, put the blame fairly and squarely on Hitler's impatience.

In his memoirs, *Panzer Leader*, Guderian wrote:

'In September of 1942, the first Tigers went into action. A lesson learned from the First World War had taught us that it is necessary to be patient about committing new weapons and that they must be held back until they are being produced in such quantities as to allow their employment in mass. . .

'Hitler was well aware of the facts. But he was consumed by his desire to try his new weapon. He therefore ordered that the Tigers be committed in a quite secondary operation, in a limited attack carried out in terrain that was utterly unsuitable; for in the swampy forests near Leningrad heavy tanks could only move in single file along the forest tracks, which, of course, was exactly where the enemy anti-tank guns were posted waiting for them. The results were not only heavy, unnecessary casualties, but also the loss of secrecy and of the element of surprise for future operations. Disappointment was all the greater since the attack was bogged down in the unsuitable terrain.'

Hitler, the supreme commander to whom such domestic difficulties were seemingly beneath his notice, summoned Eicke to the Wolfsschanze on 13 October 1942 to discuss the reorganisation of SS-Totenkopf Division. The Fuehrer declared: 'I expect the division to be ready for smashing the Soviets by no later that 10 January next year.'

It was an impossible order. Even getting the supplies of petrol to carry out the necessary exercises for training his men proved difficult and there was similar obstruction when it came to securing radios, telephones and signals equipment badly needed for the division.

Army obstructionism or general inefficiency? Eicke was inclined to think both.

Precious time, anyway, was being wasted. Just how precious was to be demonstrated on 8 November 1942 with a fresh offensive.

And not inside Soviet Russia.

It was not just on the snowy slopes of the southern Soviet Union that the fates were gathering to undermine the Nazi war-lord.

Reports of Rommel's disaster in North Africa had proved bad enough. In fifteen days of November, the Desert Fox, the darling of the German people and the legend of the Western Desert to whom at one time the badly rattled British had attributed almost superhuman powers, had at last been pushed back. The situation maps spelled out the grim truth: the Afrika Korps had retreated some seven hundred miles beyond Benghazi.

But there had been bad news to rival even this. On 3 November, when the first reports had come in of

Rommel's disaster, the Fuehrer's headquarters received word that an Allied armada had been sighted assembling at Gibraltar.

At first, Hitler failed to grasp the true significance. The Russians, after all, were the main enemy; the obstinate Bolsheviks plainly had no intention of admitting defeat. It took another four days for Hitler to jerk his attention elsewhere and study the afternoon reports flooding into Rastenburg.

All three landings of Operation Torch (the invasion of north-west Africa) had proved successful. Three task forces, one from the United States and two from Great Britain, had landed in the areas of Casablanca, Oran and Algiers. This was French territory, with loyalties divided between General Charles de Gaulle of the Free French and Marshal Henri Philippe Pétain of the collaborationist Vichy regime.

It was obvious to Hitler that the heart of Vichy in France must be immobilised.

Plans were formulated swiftly for an invasion and occupation. The blueprint for 'Directive No 19: Operation Attila' had already been in existence since 1940.

After referring to the need for 'rapid occupation of the still unoccupied territory of continental France' Directive No. 19 went on to state:

'At the same time it will be necessary to lay hands on the French home fleet and on those parts of the French Air Force in home bases, or at least to prevent their going over to the enemy.

'For military as well as political reasons, preparations for this operation will be camouflaged so as to avoid alarming the French.

'. . .The occupation if necessary will be carried out as follows:

(a) Strong motorised forces with adequate air cover will thrust rapidly along the valleys of the Garonne and Rhône to the Mediterranean, will occupy ports as quickly as possible (especially the important Toulon naval base), and so will seal off France from the sea.

(b) Formations stationed on the demarcation line will move forward along the whole front.'

Operation Attila became the new preoccupation of the Totenkopf Division.

Eicke roundly cursed the special instructions which directed him to lead the division across south-west France via Toulouse to the Mediterranean coast. Since his arrival in France, he had conserved scrupulously his meagre supplies of fuel; an unforeseen four days' move across France effectively wiped out the entire stock.

As for the training programme for the new intake, that could only at best be perfunctory. The division's new task was coastal watch duty between Béziers and Montpellier. A decidedly footling role for an SS division garlanded with glory after the hell of Soviet Russia!

It was more than just a matter of an élite being given a job totally unworthy of it. With the training programme abandoned, the division's battle-effectiveness was obviously in jeopardy. For more than a month, Eicke sent a series of pleading requests to Himmler for release from the time-wasting coastal duties.

By mid-December, he was back in Bordeaux. Orders to entrain for Russia came at the New Year.

To hurl the new division back into the eastern front was obviously sheer madness. Not only was it the height of winter, but the division had not even received as much as a whisper of those Tiger tanks which Hitler had promised. Never before had Eicke used such blunt language to the Reichsfuehrer-SS. Unless the orders were countermanded, Totenkopf was doomed; the Soviets would tear it to pieces.

Himmler was equally alarmed. The strength of the SS divisions was something in which he took special pride. It would affect him personally if the most ruthless and effective of them was wiped out.

An immediate trip to Rastenburg was called for. Himmler, who made subordinates quake, normally cut a poor figure before the one man in Germany he recognised as a superior. But now it was a question of sheer survival, his and that of the division. For once in his life, Himmler was blunt and decisive; there could be no question of Totenkopf returning to Russia in under a month.

The reprieve was granted, but Himmler made it clear to Eicke that there could be no extension; the situation on the Soviet front was far too critical.

In fact, it was not until mid-February that the men of the newly hardened Totenkopf Division staggered out of their unheated boxcars into the sub-zero hell of the Ukraine.

Why southern Russia? The short brutal answer was Stalingrad, scene of the most decisive débâcle so far of the entire war.

The morning of 30 January had seen the last phase of the battle with an artillery bombardment from three thousand guns. Then had come the radio message to Hitler: *'Final collapse cannot be delayed more than two hours.'* By 2 February, it was all over. Ninety-one thousand half-starved, frostbitten German soldiers hobbled to imprisonment and almost certain death in the prison cages of Siberia.

The Sixth Army of General Friedrich von Paulus had been encircled. The Soviets had pressed the advantage; slashed open was a huge two-hundred-mile gap between the city of Voronezh and the great bend of the Don river. In a vast, seemingly unstoppable mass, the Russians had poured into the Ukraine.

And now it was the Germans who were fleeing — a retreat from Stalingrad of nearly three thousand miles. The whole area between the Volga and the Donets basin belonged to the Soviets. And they kept on coming.

Compensations there were, even at this time, for the men of Totenkopf Division. Nobody could do anything about the unspeakable Russian climate. But at least some practical measures could be taken to blunt the effects of those appalling winters.

The division was fortunate in enjoying ample and sensible winter clothing — fur-lined parkas, boots and gloves, woollen socks and long underwear.

Predictably, these desperately welcome supplies did not come from the army which had been so niggardly with Eicke over even the smallest items of equipment.

Not for the first time, the division's commander had his own highly ingenious methods for bypassing bureaucracy and securing what he wanted.

On this occasion, he had received more than a little help from a friend. ·

13

While the bitter east winds howled across the treeless Russian steppes and thousands of frozen needles of snow were piercing the faces of his Totenkopf comrades, Homberg-born Obergruppenfuehrer Friedrich Jeckeln fought his war from behind a desk.

Few had sported the Death's Head insignia with greater pride back in those heady, triumphant days when German forces had romped through France. Jeckeln, at forty-five, had only been a battalion commander then but both Eicke and Himmler had taken a fancy to him.

Transfer and promotion had been swift. In the spring of 1941, the Reichsfuehrer-SS had appointed Jeckeln Hoehere SS und Polizei Fuehrer (Higher SS and Police Leader) for the whole of southern Russia.

Such an appointment automatically linked Totenkopf with the SD killer gangs, for Jeckeln now became commander of Einsatzgruppe C, staffed by some of the three thousand individuals with the task of covering the entire rear area of occupied Russia.

The links between Totenkopf and Einsatzgruppen had been forged back at the time of the invasion of Poland in 1939. Then the three Totenkopf regiments, Oberbayern, Brandenburg and Thuringen, had been deployed in upper Silesia as independent SS-Einsatzgruppen under the overall command of Theodor Eicke.

This was far from being an isolated instance. For example, in 1941 Einsatzgruppe A, under the command of SS-Gruppenfuehrer Heinz Jost, had operated in the Baltic states, undertaking an extensive killing programme in the rear of Army Group North. By October of the same year, Totenkopf Division's losses had become so severe and the need for replacements so chronic that a whole company from the battalion serving with Einsatzgruppe A was transferred to the Totenkopf Division. It was rushed into action immediately.

Now the links had to be forged anew. As far as Einsatzgruppe C was concerned, Jeckeln, whose official SS portrait showed a man reminiscent of a benign provincial lawyer, was able to report gruesome success to Himmler — the murder of one hundred thousand people, mostly Jews, in southern Russia during July and August 1942.

His reward was a new post as police supremo of the Baltic states and northern Russia. Here his task was to eliminate the 'Jewish-partisan menace' in the forest region behind Army Group North. In a concerted 'cleansing action' in February 1942, for example, Jeckeln saw to the liquidation of more than ten thousand Jews, partisans and suspected Soviet sympathisers.

Life was undeniably comfortable in the palatial headquarters which Jeckeln had secured in Riga. But it was far from being simply a showplace. Throughout the city were stored valuables snatched as tribute from the conquered — furniture, jewellery, works of art. And — most significant of all to Totenkopf Division — there was clothing.

It was clothes that found their way to Eicke, along with cognac and food parcels. The bulk of these arrived during the traumatic days of the fighting around Lake Ilmen. In that ferocious winter they were especially welcome to Totenkopf Division.

Besides distributing the looted property of Jews, Eicke's ardent disciple found plenty to occupy him in Nazi-occupied Riga.

A sinister threat had hung over the Riga Jews from the German invasion of Latvia in 1941. Aircraft had carpeted the city with leaflets promising large-scale arrests and punishments. Russians or Latvians aiding Jews to evacuate would, promised the Germans, be shot.

Nevertheless, there was a constant stream to the stations, where pitiable groups of Jews crammed themselves into empty freight wagons, or hung about on the platforms waiting desperately for trains to take them to the east. Elsewhere, the sights were only too painfully familiar: knots of cars and bicycles choked the roads.

And out of the clouds came the Luftwaffe, strafing the defenceless columns.

From the very first day of July when the Germans moved in, the occupation of Latvia was not exclusively administered by Nazis. A fair share of 'repatriates' — Latvians allowed home at the price of collaboration — had been returned to Riga. They became useful informers, spies, prison and camp commandants and, in some cases, plain executioners.

A positive orgy of spite was unleashed violently on Jews throughout the summer, but it was an untidy business that Jeckeln later declared he found offensive. It distressed his sense of order that, after the execution of one thousand Jews on 23 July, the anniversary of the original incorporation of Latvia into the Soviet Union, bodies were left to rot in the streets. Special orders had been issued barring the acceptance of Jewish corpses in the morgues.

Jeckeln was soon among those planning in earnest for the complete annihilation of the Jews within a properly organised ghetto. He and his fellow Nazis opted for resettlement of the Jews in the Moscow Vorstadt (suburb) of Riga. A Jewish ghetto had in fact existed there in the Middle Ages, but it was unlikely that Jeckeln was unduly influenced by history. The place was conveniently close to Bickernicki Forest where, incidentally, pro-Tsarist forces had mown down worker revolutionaries as early as 1905.

On 21 October came the order from the Commissar-

General announcing the ghetto's creation, together with a shoal of restrictions. In essence, these meant that Jews were no longer members of accepted society, but mere objects in a racial policy.

The Commissar-General's order stated:

'Jews are forbidden to leave the boundaries of the ghetto. It is forbidden to go out beyond the barbed wire except under armed escort.

'The enterprises at which the ghetto prisoners work are to deliver their workers to the work place and back under guard. The city population is strictly forbidden to talk to the Jews or approach the ghetto fence.'

On the evening of 24 October, the German guards admitted the last Jews through the hastily raised gates. There now followed an uneasy calm. Each morning, the gates of the ghetto were flung open; thousands went to work under escort. The German military units were delighted that so much free labour was available. It became the pride of the Germans administering the Jewish section of the labour exchange that no request for a work party was ever turned down.

A poster hanging on the ghetto gates read: *'Jews given out for a fee. This applies to military units too.'*

At first, conditions — although disagreeable — were at least tolerable. Doctors were allowed to circulate freely within the ghetto, setting up out-patient clinics, shelters for orphans and special restaurant facilities for invalids and the elderly.

Regulations, when they came, were issued so gradually that often their full implications were not realised until it was too late.

On one day it was announced that sewage would no longer be removed from the ghetto. A week later, able-bodied workers were herded into a new 'little ghetto'; at a stroke, nine thousand Jews were cut off from their wives and children.

On 29 November, an emergency meeting of the governing board for the Riga Jewish Community was called. Bluntly, Sturmbannfuehrer Brasch told the community members: 'This ghetto is becoming over-crowded. Therefore some of the Jewish populations must be disposed of. The choice of who is to be selected is up to you.

'I want lists of old men, the sickly, criminals and those whose presence you consider undesirable.'

One of the board's leading members, Dr Rudolf Blumenfeld, stared Brasch out and replied with dignity: 'The council will not give anyone up for execution. I am a doctor and throughout my adult life I have treated the sick — not killed them.

'In any case, our idea of what makes a criminal would not be the same as yours. I suggest you search outside the ghetto.'

In fury, Brasch cut Blumenfeld short and ordered the board to leave.

Desperate attempts were made by the board members to keep Brasch's orders secret. But inevitably rumours began to course through the ghetto.

Then came a terse order from Obergruppenfuehrer Friedrich Jeckeln: 'No Jews will be allowed out of the ghetto for work until a special order is issued.'

The next day, the ghetto gates remained fiirmly shut. Guards who came to escort the prisoners to work were sent away.

What happened next was contained in an official Ger-man report used eventually in evidence by the Allies at a war crimes trial:

'The Higher SS and Police Leader in Riga, SS-Obergruppenfuehrer Jeckeln, has meanwhile em-barked on a shooting action [*Erschiessungsaktion*] on Sunday, 30 November 1941. About 4,000 Jews from the Riga ghetto and an evacuation transport from the Reich were disposed of. This action was originally to have been effected by the forces of the Higher SS and Police Leader alone, but after a few hours the twenty men of the Einsatzkommando 2 who had been attached for security reasons were called in to help.'

The euphemism 'disposed of' concealed an orgy of sheer slaughter by Jeckeln's men. In anticipation of some nameless horror the men of the ghetto tried fruitlessly to conceal their families. There was a rumour of deportation for the men; some of the women attempted to change into male clothing so that they could at least get out of the ghetto.

Then came the order for the men to line up on Riga's Lodzinskaya Street. Eventually, they were led away — some to the 'little ghetto', the rest to the concentration camp at Salaspils.

In the early evening, the women and children were driven from their apartments and tenements in Moscow Vorstadt. Only the old and the sick were left behind. They were shot down where they were found; three hundred in a home for geriatrics were slaughtered. Groups of women and children stood stunned on street corners. Eventually, they too were rounded up and sent to Salaspils, where they were put to work sorting the belongings taken from subsequent transports of Jews, many of whom passed through on the way to death in the forest.

Just what went on there was outlined with considerable pride by Friedrich Jeckeln when he was eventually captured by the Russians. Jeckeln was the inventor of what he termed *Sardinenpackung* (sardine packaging). Graves had been prepared by the inmates in the forest which adjoined the camp. After they had undressed, the victims were either shot immediately at the edge of the graves or else ordered to lie face down between the legs of those already shot and then killed.

Jeckeln later explained: 'It had the merit of saving space.'

Ironically, it was also a method which helped to seal the fate of Eicke's industrious disciple. A few of the more fortunate Jews were able to conceal themselves beneath the bodies of the victims and make their way back to the ghettos after dark. These survivors were to point their fingers of guilt at Friedrich Jeckeln when he came to trial in 1946.

One such fortunate survivor was Frida Frid-Mikhelsen, a seamstress from Riga, who was the only survivor of an *Erschiessungsaktion* in Bickernieki Forest. She wrote:

'. . .I was right next to the pit where the dead were being thrown. I pressed myself to the ground and tried not to move. Half-an-hour later I heard someone shout in German "Put the shoes here!" By this time I had already crawled back a little. Just then, something was being thrown at me. I opened one eye slightly and saw a shoe lying next to my face. I was being covered up with shoes. Probably, my gray cotton smock blended with the colour of the shoes and they didn't notice me. I began to feel a little warmer — there was already a whole mountain of shoes on top of me. Only my right side was completely frozen. The fluffy snow that had fallen in the morning had completely melted underneath me; first it was terribly wet; then the water began to freeze, and I was covered with a crust of ice. I could have put several shoes under me, but I was afraid that the pile would move, and I would be noticed. I lay like that until dark, with ice frozen on my right side. . .

'By evening the shooting had stopped. The Germans left a small guard near the clothing, and they went off to rest. Several Germans stood there, steps from me. They lit up their cigarettes and talked among themselves. I listened to their cheerful, content voices: "We did a great job today." "Yes, it was a busy day." "There are still a lot of them left there. We'll have to work a little more. Well, see you tomorrow." "Pleasant dreams." "Oh, I always have good dreams."

'I decided to crawl out from under the pile of shoes. The first thing to do was get dressed. I crawled over to another pile — it was men's clothing. There was no time to deliberate — I put on someone's pants and jacket and tied a big kerchief around my head. . .

'. . .I had to get as far away as possible from that

awful place while it was still night. But there were guards all around; they could see me in the white snow. Then I remembered. . .soldiers dressed in white uniforms were very well camouflaged in the snow. Not far away I saw a pile of sheets in which some of the mothers had carried their infants. . .

'I came across a blanket cover, wrapped myself in it and began to crawl. . .'

But most were not so lucky. For them, the end came in Bickernieki Forest, where eight enormous pits had previously been dug. As soon as the columns arrived, everyone was ordered to undress; boots were put in one pile, galoshes in another.

Then the SS with the butts of their rifles prodded the naked vitims towards the precipice. The executioner, a Baltic German named Baron Sievers, waited. On hand were two aides to change the cartridge clips on the automatic rifles and take turns in handing them to Sievers. He stood there, spattered with blood, a seemingly tireless killing machine. He was later to boast that on one occasion he had executed personally three thousand Jews.

Friedrich Jeckeln's loyalty to Himmler and Eicke had not extended merely to foraging for the Totenkopf or arranging the setting up of the ghetto and the dispersal of its inhabitants. The collaboration with the Reichsfuehrer-SS, in particular, was closer and more sinister.

Himmler wanted several hundred thousand Jews disposed of, certainly. But there was a limit to how many could be killed on German soil.

An elaborate act of deception was worked out; it was necessary to bring German Jews to Riga under the pretence of resettling them. Smoothly, it was explained that Germany was anxious to colonise the east. A new place of residence would be found; it was suggested that only essential possessions need be taken.

On the body of one of those people slaughtered in the Riga ghetto, the following directive was found:

'Berlin No 4, January 11 1942.

'To Mr Albert Israel Unger and spouse.

'Your departure has been set by order of the authorities for January 19 1942. This order concerns you, your wife, and all the unmarried members of your family who are included in your property declaration.

'At noon on January 17 1942, your premises will be sealed up by an official. You must, therefore, prepare by the designated time your large and hand baggage. You are to hand over the keys to your apartment and rooms to the official. You must go with the official to the police station in the district where your apartment is located, having taken with you both your large as well as your hand baggage. The large baggage you are to surrender at the police station. From there it will be delivered by our baggage compartment by truck to a collection point — Lowetzov Street, 7/8.

'Following the delivery of your large baggage to the police station you are to go with your hand baggage to the assembly point, to the synagogue on Lowetzov Street (the Jagow Street entrance). You may go there by the customary means of transport.

'We will take charge of your belongings at the assembly point and during your train ride. It would be a good idea to take along in your hand baggage some food from your house, especially something for supper.

'Both at the assembly point as well as on the trip, medical and food services will be available.'

The trains which pulled up at the platforms of the Riga station were greeted by Jeckeln's men as well as those of the Allgemeine-SS. The atmosphere was friendly and apologetic.

There had been snags with the arrangements for transport, it was explained. There was a shortage of buses. It was regrettable, but it would be necessary for the men and the healthiest women to walk about five miles to their new homes.

161

All was friendly aboard those buses assigned to carry old people and those with very young children.

As the healthy marched in confident innocence towards the apartments in Moscow Vorstadt so recently vacated by the Latvian Jews the rest were driven to the forest.

From the windows of the buses, the apprehensive passengers spotted the ranks of police. These were unsmiling men. They had received very precise instructions indeed from SS-Obergruppenfuehrer Jeckeln for this latest 'cleansing action'.

Matters were now in the hands of a most efficient deputy, Standartenfuehrer Rudolf Lange, commander of the Latvian police. The Jews were dragged from the buses and rifle-butted; some were shot on the spot.

Then came the order to undress, fold their clothes and walk to the vast pits dug so efficiently in advance.

Friedrich Jeckeln's war ended at Breslau where he was Commanding General and leader of a Kampfgruppe.

Interrogated on 15 December 1945 by a Russian representative of the NKVD — forerunner of the KGB — Jeckeln, who was eventually to be hanged on the site of the former Riga ghetto, confirmed readily enough that he had received his orders to liquidate the ghetto directly from Himmler.

Jeckeln was almost apologetic when asked to be precise about the exact number of Jews who were murdered. He stated that he had taken part personally in three separate mass shootings and had given instructions to senior members of the Gestapo, SD and Schutzpolizei (Security Police). He stated:

'It is difficult to be completely accurate, but I do not think less than 25,000 Jews were liquidated.'

Other Nazis interrogated by the Allies were, for a variety of motives, prepared to condemn Jeckeln. Among these was Rudolf Diels, previously chief of Department 1a of the Prussian State Police, later the Gestapo.

162

Diels, who had also held a civil and military post in Hanover, was questioned at Nuremberg on 4 November 1946. He revealed that, as early as November 1938, Jeckeln had, as a police inspector, been responsible for the burning of a Hanover synagogue:

'On the evening of 9 November, shortly before the pogrom was due, I was informed by the Hanover police that an anti-Jewish demonstration would take place that very night. I contacted Jeckeln who told me that Heydrich had ordered the police not to take any preventative measures against the demonstrators. Burning synagogues was exclusively the job of the SS and I can confirm that this was done by SS personnel.'

Four years later, Jeckeln had passed to higher things. By 1941, he was in the Ukraine, deputy to the notorious Reich Commissioner Erich Koch. Diels revealed during his interrogation:

'In 1941, I had the opportunity to visit the Ukraine and I saw the mass graves of the Jews of Kiev. I learnt from a reliable source that Jeckeln was directly responsible for the murder of the people in these graves.
'Moreover, I had heard that Jeckeln had gone too far in the Ukraine, even in the opinion of Himmler, and that therefore he had been recalled.'

Diels' damning indictment of Friedrich Jeckeln went even further, as the Nuremberg transcript reveals.

'Jeckeln had the reputation of being a cold-blooded but incorruptible murderer. His Chief of Staff, Balke, formerly Chief of Police at Magdeburg, often registered complaints about Jeckeln's terrorist acts. Jeckeln was also involved in anti-Jewish measures in Transylvania and Hungary.'

During the war and long after it, Eicke's men protested that their role in the war — notably on the

Russian front — was as professional soldiers in the manner of their counterparts in the Wehrmacht.

But the Totenkopf also produced men like Friedrich Jeckeln who, seconded from the Death's Head ranks, graduated to specialised tasks within Himmler's Schutz-staffel.

SS-Totenkopf Division could earn the respect and even the praise of men like Manstein and Guderian. But it could never quite lose that stamp of criminality with which it had first been bestowed back in 1940 by Helmut Knoechlein and the massacre of Le Paradis.

14

The sheer weight of the Russian attack after Stalingrad seemed to foretell a whole string of impending disasters. Kharkov — the rail, industrial and communications hub of the eastern Ukraine — was at risk.

Obergruppenfuehrer Paul Hausser with his SS-Panzer groups remembered Stalingrad and the fate of Paulus. It seemed, under this attack, only common sense to pull back. The alternative would be encirclement and an-nihilation.

But Hitler's orders had been both predictable and clear. The Fuehrer had stated: 'Kharkov is to be held at all costs. There will be no withdrawal.'

Hausser sought the permission of his army com-mander, General Lanz, to withdraw. The answer was a blunt and horrified refusal. What sort of treason was this? The Fuehrer had spoken and that was enough.

On 12 February, the Russians were practically breath-ing down Hausser's neck. They were approaching the city from the north-west; the next day the enemy was seen in the suburb of Osnova. Attempts by Leib-standarte division to clear them out proved a failure;

the Tigers were bogged down and unable to move further.

The Russians dug in; further forces entered the city from the north-west and the north-east. History was well on the way to repeating itself.

Yet another appeal to Lanz came to naught. At 12.30 on 15 February, Hausser could hear the rumble of the Russian tanks.

No senior commander of the SS had yet disobeyed an order from his Fuehrer. It was, of course, unthinkable.

Hausser on his own initiative ordered the evacuation of Kharkov.

Manstein, in his memoirs, was to reflect rather ruefully that had this been ordered by the army, Hitler would have undoubtedly screamed for courts martial. But because the action had been carried out by SS-Panzer Corps, nothing of the sort transpired. The unfortunate Lanz, who had weakly opposed Hausser, was eventually to lose his job and be replaced by General Werner Kempf.

The Fuehrer had swallowed his pride. Nevertheless, it was Totenkopf's job to repair the damage and help recapture the lost city.

The division was summoned from France. From Kiev, Eicke was to proceed immediately to Poltava and there link up with the Leibstandarte and Das Reich divisions and make contact with Hausser and 1st Panzer Corps.

The need for Kharkov's recovery was surely obvious. The overall direction, Hitler reasoned, could be carried out under only one man.

Erich von Manstein was a Feldmarschall now. After the advance on Leningrad, he had been promoted to command the Eleventh Army, on the southern wing of the German advance into the Soviet Union. Here there had been fresh glories — the defeat of the Russians in the Crimea and, at the beginning of 1942, the taking of Sevastopol.

The following November, as commander of the newly designated Army Group Don (later Army Group South) Manstein had launched a vain attempt to save Paulus at

Stalingrad, but Manstein had seen to it that the German southern wing had been relieved of much of the brunt of Soviet savagery.

Could Manstein work a miracle and reverse the disasters staring Hitler in the face every time he contemplated his situation maps? The Fuehrer thought so. Manstein was certainly keen enough to retake Kharkov, but he had his own methods.

Hitler was keen to hurl in SS-Panzer Corps straight away. The Feldmarschall, however, favoured something rather more subtle.

Manstein envisaged a vast pincer attack that would converge upon and ultimately destroy the Soviet armies as they reached the Dnieper. It entailed waiting until the Totenkopf Division had joined up with Hausser. Then the SS Corps would serve as the northern prong of the pincer. It would strike south-east from Poltava and slam into the rear of the Soviet Sixth and First Guard Armies.

General Hoth's Fourth Panzer Army would then enter the picture. He and Hausser would link up near Pavlograd, south of Kharkov, and trap the Sixth Army in a mechanised vice from which there would be no escape.

Hitler, however, remained mesmerised by Kharkov itself. The attack, he insisted, should be directed towards the heart of the city. There was the very real danger that the terrible mistakes of Stalingrad would be repeated. Manstein wanted to carry out the defence of Kharkov with fluid, mobile forces. There must not be the risk of being trapped and isolated; the predicament of Paulus!

Hitler could not or would not tear himself away from his old beliefs. The attack, he repeated, should be towards the centre of Kharkov. He continued to mumble the old precepts as if they were some species of religious litany.

'Hold fast, yield not a foot, die where you stand!'

These were the Fuehrer's doctrines, and had they not always been right? But the defeat of Stalingrad had sown the first seeds of doubt in the German people. To Hitler himself it made no difference. *'Hold fast. . .'*

It was not that he refused even to think of Manstein's proposals. On the contrary, he brooded over the Feld-marschall's planned counter-attack. All his instincts rebelled against it. Yet it tormented and nagged him ceaselessly. There could be only one way of resolving the matter; Hitler decided to go and see the situation at the front for himself.

Accompanied by General Alfred Jodl and General-oberst Kurt Zeitzler, Hitler arrived at Zaporozhye, Manstein's headquarters south of the beleaguered Dnie-per, on 17 February.

For two days, both men wrangled. Manstein became convinced that this was one conflict — both for the mind of the Fuehrer and for the defeat of the Russians — that he could not win.

As it turned out, Manstein was wrong. And it was all due to the reappearance of Theodor Eicke.

The commander of the Totenkopf Division arrived back in the Soviet Union after taking full advantage of the month of grace which Himmler had originally granted him.

If the men of Totenkopf Division had previously cursed Eicke's strenuous training programme, they did so with interest now.

From dawn until midnight, the division had submitted to a relentless round of lectures, rifle practice and fire co-ordination drills. But, with the new intake specifically in mind, Eicke had found it necessary to go back to funda-mentals. Exercises had to familiarise unblooded troops with camouflage techniques and the use of varying kinds of light and heavy weapons, to say nothing of basic tac-tical problems, many of them out of the simplest battle manuals.

The securing of an extra month had another big ad-vantage for Eicke: he was able to lay hands on half the allotted Tiger tanks that he had been promised and it was possible to train the crews at least adequately. It was far from being enough, he admitted ruefully, but at least his division had not returned entirely defenceless. The level of combat readiness could fairly be described as effective.

Not for the first time, the weather had its say. The thaw had set in. As it turned out, it was to be nearly disastrous.

At a mid-day conference, on 18 February, Hitler learnt from his intelligence officer, Major Eismann, that Totenkopf, newly designated 3rd SS-Panzer Division Totenkopf of SS-Panzer Corps, had stuck in the mud near Poltava. A warm front had lifted the temperature above freezing. Eicke was soon radioing Hausser that his men were stuck like insects on fly-paper twenty-five miles from the Panzer Corps.

Hitler exploded in impotent fury; plainly, moving on Kharkov was out of the question. The Fuehrer ordered: 'The attack on Kharkov is abandoned. SS-Panzer Corps cannot succeed without 3rd Panzer Division.'

A mere twenty-five miles from the SS formations he so badly needed! It was an additional, highly irritating delay in the essential task of assembling Manstein's armoured trap, but the men of Totenkopf clearly had to be rescued. Hausser's maintenance crews raced to Poltava and joined in the slow, messy task of hauling the division's vehicles out of the grasping, oozing mud.

At last, the forces were assembled; Hausser's armoured and motorised divisions were ready to go.

At a section of the southern front between the Dnieper and the Donets rivers, the divisions, under General Hoth, delivered a gigantic kick to Soviet Sixth and First Guard Armies. With savage glee, the men of Totenkopf, working in tandem with SS-Das Reich Division, swooped upon the Soviet Sixth as if they were working off a personal grudge.

A short time before, a sizeable number of these young men had been tyros in tank warfare. But they had learnt their lessons quickly. The motorised columns drew alongside the retreating Russians, sending unrelenting barrages of fire into the crammed trucks. The lumbering T-34s, out of fuel, stuttered to a halt. The crews received no quarter from the SS, and soon the Russians were quitting their vehicles, attempting to escape on foot they knew not where.

Das Reich and 1st Grenadier Regiment of Totenkopf linked up for the sole purpose of blocking all retreat. Behind them, moving with comparative leisure and with no opposition worthy of the name, were German tanks and infantry. They cut their way through the useless, blackened heaps of abandoned Russian vehicles. Above them streamed the Stukas, flying low and with awesome ease killing hordes of the vulnerable and unprotected Red Army men as they streaked across the steppe.

The scene was set for the most spectacular victory in Totenkopf's history. For the division had a key role in the recapture of Kharkov.

It was vital that, with the destruction of Sixth Army, the Russians should be prevented from flexing any further muscles in front of Kharkov. On the other hand, the Germans had no intention of being sucked into street fighting and running the risk of encirclement.

To the Russians, however, it seemed that both Totenkopf and Das Reich were impatient to get into the city. That was precisely the intention. Earlier, Manstein had commented to Hitler: 'My plan is to allow the Russians to advance until they have well outrun their supply lines. Once they are out of steam, we will slap into them.'

Hausser despatched the Leibstandarte around to the north-west. This division was now in a blocking position *behind* the Soviets. Between 28 February and 3 March, Totenkopf and Das Reich enveloped the Soviet forces. Its armour was slammed back against the Tigers and the assault guns of the Leibstandarte.

The last obstacle between the Germans and Kharkov had gone.

It was indeed an SS victory, but events around the tiny village of Michailovka had already ensured that 'Papa' Eicke was not there to see it.

On the afternoon of 24 February, during the headlong pursuit of Soviet Sixth Army, Eicke became worried by a prolonged loss of radio contact from the division's armoured regiment.

He was not a man who cared for mysteries; the best way of seeing what was going on was from the air.

Pre-reconnaissance before Eicke took off in his Fieseler-Storch aircraft had, to say the least, been perfunctory. The Russians were dug in at a neighbouring village over which the aircraft passed on its way to Michailovka.

A fusillade of small-arms and anti-aircraft fire peppered this tempting target at a mere three hundred feet. In no way could the Storch or its occupants survive; the aircraft was quite literally torn apart.

In vain, SS troops struggled to get near the blazing wreckage, which lay between the two villages. Constantly they were beaten back by the fury of Russian firepower.

The ensuing events were a remarkable tribute to the respect which Eicke, the hardest of men, had evoked in his troops. News spread quickly of his death; the division's Panzer regiment was alerted.

The early morning calm of Artelnoye, the village from which the Russians had fired on Eicke, was shattered by the rumble and snarl of two assault guns, three tanks and a motor-cycle company. These, under SS-Haupsturm-fuehrer Lino Masarie, had been peeled off from the division with instructions to drive the Russians out and recover the bodies. Eventually, Masarie's men carried away the remains of the commander, his adjutant and the pilot.

Of Eicke there was scarcely anything left — merely a fragment of his uniform with the Knight's Cross with Oak Leaves and Swords. To those who had been associated with him and who had sweated and fought on the Russian front, it seemed oddly appropriate.

Announcement of Eicke's death was withheld from the public until 1 March, the day on which he was buried with full military honours in the village of Otdochnina. The Berlin edition of *Voelkischer Beobachter* sketched briefly the highlights of Eicke's career but most of the columns were filled with such laudatory phrases as 'a glowing National Socialist'. He was described as having been 'always a comrade to his men and always an example to them'.

Himmler's hand in the preparation of the obituary could be detected in the frequent use of his word 'hard' when describing the SS and the best of its servants.

Eicke had been 'a great political soldier. He was brave and he was cheerful and he was hard. Such men formed our movement. . .He was hard — iron hard. He once said to his men: "Hardness saves blood. In fact, hardness saves more. It saves bitterness, it saves shame, it saves worry, it saves sorrow."'

Eicke, however, was not destined to rest in peace at Otdochnina. By the following September, the village was overrun by the Russians. To Himmler, the idea that Eicke's remains should be lost to the hated Bolsheviks was unthinkable. He ordered the 'body' to be removed and it was hastily re-interred in the Hegwald cemetery at Zhitomir.

But even the western Ukraine had to be abandoned eventually; Eicke's 'corpse' was left behind to rot in the soil of the state whose system he and his fellow SS had vowed ruthlessly to destroy.

Elsewhere in his obituary, Himmler had endeavoured to strike an optimistic note. Certainly, Eicke's death was a tragedy, but there were other equally ardent members of the Waffen-SS to take his place. The language was flowery: 'The fountain of youth which springs from this movement always sprouts new and capable men.'

The German-language newspaper, *Die Zeitung*, published in London by German exiles, was not so sure. Indeed, it described Eicke's death as the greatest blow to befall the SS since the assassination by pro-Czech forces of Reinhard Heydrich in Prague on 27 May 1942.

This view was echoed unintentionally by a comment from Heydrich's widow who compared Eicke's death with her husband's 'martyrdom' — ironic, since the two men had been sworn enemies and bitter contenders for the job of concentration camp supremo.

Since the war, historians have been less enthusiastic than Himmler over Eicke's military talents. The Reichsfuehrer-SS, referring to Demyansk, stated that Eicke 'with a tiny group of Totenkopf soldiers turned the tide of the battle'.

In his book *Soldiers of Destruction* (Princeton University Press, 1977), Charles W. Sydnor Jnr sums up Eicke as having been, by his last year 'a moderately competent field commander', while Gerald Reitlinger in his classic study, *The SS — Alibi of a Nation* (Heinemann, 1956), concluded that Eicke remained essentially what he had been in his days as a policeman — the equivalent of a detective-sergeant.

Himmler was right in one judgement, however. Eicke had moulded many careers over the years and there was no shortage of talent to succeed him. The job of commander went, initially, to Max Simon.

The time was not for mourning but for assessment. Following the capture of Kharkov, when the casualties were totted up, the cost in blood and bones to SS corps stood at around 11,400 dead, wounded or missing.

After enveloping Kharkov from the north, Totenkopf Division sped south-east to snatch vital bridge crossings over the Donets river at Chuguyev.

Thus Totenkopf had sealed the exits from Kharkov. It had trapped the remainder of the Soviet forces seeking to flee north-east across the Donets from the eager embrace of Hoth's Fourth Panzer Army. Around the area of the Chuguyev crossings, the men of the Death's Head smashed into the bulk of the crack Soviet 23rd Guards Rifle Division, which was slashed to pieces.

There was nothing stopping Hoth now. On 17 March, orders were given for SS-Panzer Corps in its entirety to regroup north of Chuguyev for a new advance. This was to be a gigantic juggernaut offensive against Belgorod, a city striding the Donets thirty miles north-east of Kharkov.

Every moment that the Russians held Belgorod brought Hoth out in a cold sweat. So long as control was maintained, there was nothing to stop the Reds swooping down on Kharkov again.

Hoth had to endure this for somewhat longer; it was

the next day before the entire SS-Panzer Corps —
Totenkopf, Das Reich and Leibstandarte — started the
gigantic rush north. Russian bridgehead positions were
swept aside on the Donets. Belgorod was firmly in
German hands.

To this blessing was added another. At last came the
spring.

One Waffen-SS man wrote of the Russians:

'How pleased we all are with our success. . .We
have thrown them back and Kharkov is German once
again. We have shown the Ivans that we can withstand
their terrible winter. It can hold no fear for us again.'

But there were to be other terrors.

15

A brief, deceptive calm ended the winter campaign on
the Russian front. There came a welcome glow with the
fag-end of that bitter cold which had slashed into men's
skins like a razor. The troops of 3rd SS-Panzer Division
Totenkopf, along with others in the Waffen-SS, basked
for a while in the benignity of their Fuehrer.

Totenkopf was rich in honours — five Knight's
Crosses and higher orders had been bestowed, along
with an honour regarded of particular significance. The
panzer regiment of Totenkopf was renamed 'Theodor
Eicke'.

The triumph of Kharkov, reported Propaganda Minister Joseph Goebbels, had made the Fuehrer 'particularly happy'. But to the mercurial, opportunist war-lord
there could not be tranquillity for long. Hitler had been
more affected by the débâcle of Stalingrad than he cared
to admit. To Manstein, he had made an unqualified

admission of exclusive responsibility for the tragedy of Sixth Army. It continued to gnaw at his sense of pride, at the confidence in his own judgement.

What was needed was another victory.

It would just have to be something on a far larger scale than Kharkov. What was it he himself had said at the time of the initial invasion of the Soviet Union? '*The world will hold its breath.*' It could happen again.

But *where*?

Events on the right flank of Army Group Centre and Army Group South's left wing provided the answer. The groups were threatened by a huge and powerful Russian salient bulging out like a giant hernia around the city of Kursk. It was an area over 400 miles long and 150 miles deep.

Kursk lay between Orel and Kharkov on the north-south line. After Manstein's triumphant victory at Kharkov, Orel was again in German hands. Hitler was desperately worried by what lay between. He planned to sever this bulge, thus straightening the line by trapping hundreds and thousands of the enemy.

The plan was for Manstein to strike north from Kharkov. At the same time, Kluge would be driving southwards from Orel. The aim would be to envelope Kursk.

The shame of Stalingrad would be expunged from the history books; nothing could stop the onward march to total victory after a triumph such as this.

'Kursk,' proclaimed the Fuehrer, 'must be a blazing torch to the world.'

The heroes of the hour in this double envelopment would be Model's Ninth Army (seven infantry, eight Panzer and the Panzer-Grenadier divisions) in Maloar-khangelsk on the northern face. South in the Belgorod area would be Army Detachment Kempf and Hoth's Fourth Panzer Army (seven infantry, eleven Panzer divisions, three assault brigades), together with two air fleets.

It added up to a formidable demonstration of German strength that was to be committed to the greatest tank

battle in history. Here were 2,700 tanks and assault guns
— more than half fielded by Hoth and Kempf in the
south — 1,800 aircraft, two-thirds of the infantry divisions brought up to a strength of 12,500 officers and
men, Panzer divisions with 16,000 men and up to 209
tanks and assault guns in each.

But something was missing. The essential ingredient
was the fire and conviction and ruthlessness of the
supreme commander. But the malign confidence that the
Fuehrer had exhibited so dazzlingly at the start of
Barbarossa was missing now. Stalingrad was burned into
his consciousness.

That was why he confided: 'The very idea of this new
adventure makes my stomach heave.'

Doubtless to convince himself, he began searching for
parallels in his own recent past. In a rambling discourse
with his more intimate cronies, Hitler drew a detailed
comparison with the year 1932, when the Nazi Party,
after victory at the polls, appeared to be going down to
defeat. He proclaimed: 'In 1932, we attained victory
over stubbornness that sometimes looked like madness,
so too shall we achieve it today.'

It was a boast that the men of Totenkopf had been
trained to believe: that the Fuehrer's primary claim to
greatness was an ability to achieve victory against
impossible odds, sometimes almost by will-power alone.

It was only too true that the Nazi war machine had
been mauled and weakened. But there was still plenty to
be optimistic about. The three assault armies were
strong enough, with divisions in excellent shape and well
serviced by the newest tanks.

Armaments Minister Albert Speer had boosted the
Luftwaffe production statistics to an extent which many
faint-hearts had considered impossible. Now there were
about 2,500 first-line combat aircraft on the eastern
front. Certainly, the figures were a few hundred less than
the peak strengths of previous years, but not significantly
so. Half would be committed in direct support of the
tank battle of Kursk.

During the closing weeks of June, long-range bombers

mercilessly pounded the most important Soviet industrial centres within their reach, notably the oil refiner-
ies. At the same time, the railways and airfields around
Kursk shook under the nightly forays of low-level
bombers.

The headquarters of General Konstantin Rokossovsky
was demolished by a single bombload; the general
escaped only because he had decided that the officers'
mess was the best place for his signal group. The Russians were badly rattled. Stalin ordered Soviet fighters to
keep German reconnaissance aircraft away from defences.

The pilot of a captured He-111 informed his in-
terrogators that fresh squadrons were moving up to
Kharkov from the Crimea. All the signs indicated an
attack. The Russians flexed their muscles on the Kursk
bulge.

On the north was Central Front under Rokossovsky,
while in the south Vatutin had charge of Voronezh
Front. Both fronts — the equivalent of army groups —
poured around two-thirds of their artillery and tank
resources into the sectors where it seemed reasonable to
suppose that the Germans would attack.

Hitler had managed to banish his own misgivings.
Others were not so sanguine.

Early on, a new voice had entered the debate on
Kursk.

General Heinz Guderian had been in semi-disgrace;
consigned to the shadows by Adolf Hitler, along with
many of his colleagues in Army Group Centre, after its
defeat before Moscow in 1941.

With mounting frustration, Guderian had watched
German tank production creak and falter. The Russians
were known to be speeding ahead with their T-34s. What
was more, the Russians had learnt a lot from early German successes. New Panthers had failed to materialise.

Hitler became aware of the deficiency. He began to
look around for a saviour; he was prepared to consider
Guderian.

Hitler set out to court him, rather in the manner of a

callous jilt suffering from deep remorse. The Fuehrer was cunning enough to be gradual in his approach. But there were odd straws in the wind and Guderian was able to interpret them.

On 23 January 1943, Hitler addressed an appeal 'to all workers in tank production'. They were urged to intensify their efforts. Hitler made sure that Guderian heard the message. Then he cleverly avoided the subject until 17 February, when Guderian was summoned by telephone to Fuehrer headquarters in Vinnitsa.

It was fourteen months since the two had met. Guderian was struck by the changes in the Fuehrer. This was not the arrogant scourge of the Bolshevik hordes he remembered. True, the gaze was as mesmeric as ever, the charm readily available when its owner chose to use it. But the voice faltered, occasionally the discourse teetered into irrelevance. There was a noticeable trembling of the left hand.

Guderian's books on military theory lay in front of Hitler. The Fuehrer gestured towards them and with a shadow of a smile said: 'Since 1941 our ways have parted. There were numerous misunderstandings then which I regret. I need you.'

If Guderian was touched, he gave no sign. Indeed he made it supremely clear to the supreme war-lord that he would come back on his own conditions. He wanted complete say in the development of new equipment. He wanted control of the armoured units of the Luftwaffe, the Waffen-SS and the tank schools.

On 28 April, Hitler issued what, on paper at least, was a blank cheque:

'The Inspector-General of Armoured Troops Guderian is responsible to me for the future development of armoured troops along lines that will make that arm of the service into a decisive weapon.

'The Inspector-General of Armoured Troops is directly subordinated to myself.'

The last sentence was loaded with dynamite. The

newly appointed inspector of the Panzerwaffe was independent of the authority of the Chief of Staff of OKH. There would of course be some contact over matters of training and organisation within the armoured units, but these were relatively minor topics and did not involve overall command. But such terms of reference carried a touch of superiority which was offensive to General Kurt Zeitzler, the Chief of Staff. If Guderian really thought that he had given himself a free hand in prising these terms of employment from Hitler he was sadly disillusioned.

Understandably enough, the army was resentful. But that was not the main problem facing Guderian. Adolf Hitler would not leave him alone. The supreme commander, the amateur strategist, believed firmly that he knew every bit as much as the professional soldier. It led to inevitable clashes. In the same way that Hitler would seize on a certain person and convince himself that this individual represented salvation, so it was with single weapons.

The weapon of the future, Hitler proclaimed, was the Pzkw VI or, less prosaically, the Tiger. Guderian was repelled by the Tiger's lack of speed at 23.5 m.p.h. and its meagre range of 65 miles, which indicated its limitation at divisional level. Its lack of a forward-firing machine-gun brought condemnation from the tank maestro:

> 'Once they had broken into the enemy's infantry zone they literally had to go quail shooting with cannons. They did not manage to neutralise, let alone destroy, the enemy rifles and machine guns, so that the infantry was unable to follow up behind them. By the time they reached the Russian artillery they were on their own.'

New tank models were on the way, certainly. German tank output rose sharply in the early months of 1943, reaching 621 units in April and 988, including 300 of the new Panthers, in May. But in June and July, production

178

had fallen off to 775 and 811, largely because of production difficulties with the Panthers.

Hitler had a touching faith in the production figures presented to him. But they told only half the story. As was to become apparent, the new models were being rushed to the front before they had been tested thoroughly and without crews who were fully trained.

But it was the Waffen-SS which caused Guderian and others the greatest anxiety. The débâcle of Stalingrad had shaken the Fuehrer's faith in the army. He had come to distrust its leaders and, in any case, he had never felt at ease with them.

Himmler, with his overwhelming desire for seemingly limitless power, had fed these prejudices voraciously. By the end of 1942, there had been eight Waffen-SS divisions. A year later there were seventeen, operational or about to be formed, ten of them Panzer Grenadiers, armoured or motorised. This added up to a strength of about half a million.

But long gone were the days when Totenkopf and Leibstandarte had comprised splendid Aryan volunteers. Conscription was necessary to maintain the figures, and even blatant poaching of army conscripts; Himmler creamed off for himself any young man over five feet nine inches tall.

Himmler was determined that his black legions should have the very best in material and equipment. No one fighting a war could quarrel with that. The trouble was that, under the urgent pressures of manpower, the standard of the training programmes was suffering.

Manstein had declared of the Waffen-SS divisions: 'There is not the least doubt that it was an inexcusable mistake to set up a separate military organisation.' But of course it had long become obvious that it was not military organisations in which Hitler was primarily interested. Spurred by Himmler's terrible ideology, it was his intention to replace the old reactionary army by National Socialist cadres.

If Hitler appealed to ideology, Stalin put the accent on

179

patriotism. The wily Russian leader sensed that this was no time to wax lyrical on the coming paradise of world communism. His propagandists were instructed to dig far deeper back than that. They did Stalin proud; they seized on Dimitri Donskoi, who in the fourteenth century had vanquished the Tartars on the field of Kulikovo.

The Comintern, formed in 1919 to preach world communism, was on the way out; its continued existence was deemed offensive to Roosevelt and Churchill. There were other small gestures. The old battleship *Pariskaya Kommuna* (*Paris Commune*) was for example renamed *Sevastopol*, her original name when launched in June 1911.

The greatest shake-up in 'the Great Patriotic War', though, was in the Soviet Army.

The appalling lethargy and mistakes of two years had to be atoned for. Stalin moved drastically and fast. The Corps of Political Commissars was the first to feel the effects. This organisation, supervising the actions of commanders down to division level and countersigning their orders, ceased to exist. Its often bumbling bureaucrats, whom the army had loathed with industrious contempt, were bundled from office. The more promising of them were selected to become 200 regimental and 600 battalion commanders — enough men to provide officers for upwards of 60 infantry divisions.

But more than that was needed. The splendour and show and dash of the old Tsarist army had been despised by Lenin and his disciples; all officers and men were to be worker-troops.

That was changed too. Back came the insignia of rank and the long Tsarist-style shoulder boards. A veritable shower of decorations was lavished on a variety of magnificent uniforms. No less than six orders were created for the army and the air force, and two for the navy.

On 8 November 1943, the day following the twenty-sixth anniversary of the October Revolution and two days after the liberation of Kiev, the Praesidium of the

Supreme Soviet instituted the Order of Victory. Fashioned of white enamel and encrusted with diamonds, it was given solely to front commanders and those leading front-line units.

But, above all, there was talent in command, formidable brains to replace those which had been bespattered over the walls of execution yards in the Stalinist purge of the 1930s. At the time of Barbarossa, the Soviet Army had only been able to muster three marshals. By the end of the war, Voroshilov, Budenny and Timoshenko had been joined by twenty-seven more.

Nevertheless, among all this enlightenment the baleful shadow of the Communist Party grew no dimmer.

On the contrary, the party had officially-recognised cells in all units and all bodies of troops. Even in the cellars of Stalingrad, political meetings continued, and regimental newspapers with strong propaganda ingredients were printed to recruit new members.

In control — and reinforced by a terror machine that Hitler's Gestapo admired and feared — was one indisputably impregnable individual.

Joseph Stalin was a self-appointed Marshal and Generalissimo of the Soviet Armed Forces. He was also Secretary-General of the Communist Party of the USSR, soon to become undisputed victor of a growing empire.

He faced a dictator easily matching him in cynicism and cruelty. But Adolf Hitler's mental judgement was crumbling along with his physique and his empire was speedily to become a contracting one. The two men's new killing-ground was the Kursk salient.

As we have seen, it did Hitler's digestion no good at all. Guderian was scarcely happier. He wrote:

'. . . the attack was pointless. We had only just completed the reorganisation of our eastern front. If we attacked. . .we were certain to suffer heavy tank casualties which we would not be in a position to replace in 1943; on the contrary, we ought to be devoting our new tank production to the western front so as to have mobile reserves available for use against the

Allied landings which could be expected to take place in 1944.

'Furthermore, I pointed out that the Panthers, on whose performance the Chief of General Staff was relying so heavily, were still suffering from many teething troubles inherent in all new equipment and it seemed unlikely that these could be put right in time for the launching of the attack.'

Hitler did admit that there was some justice in Guderian's view. He was even prepared to listen. In fact, some generals believed that he was taking far too long about it. There was suddenly an alarming indecision as to when to give the nod for the counter-offensive.

One man who could barely conceal his irritation was Manstein. And with good reason. After all, it was *his* Army Group South that was under threat.

He urged Hitler: 'Look at the invasion of North Africa. Sooner or later, the same thing is going to happen on the Continent of Europe. Besides the longer we wait, the more armour the Russians will muster. Their tank production is unquestionably ahead of ours.'

Manstein was keen to go ahead in May. Hitler was obstinate. By waiting until June, he declared, it would be possible to fit out the armoured divisions properly.

In fact, the Fuehrer seized finally on 5 July for the launch of 'Operation Zitadelle' — the battle of Kursk which, it turned out, was to be his last great offensive in the east.

And the location? Kursk lies on a low plateau of Central Russia, situated 330 miles south of Moscow. Although some sort of town is thought to have existed there since the eleventh century, there is not much of interest to detain the tourist speeding to the Black Sea coast from the capital.

Yet, for a few months in the spring and summer of 1943, Kursk could lay claim to being the most important place on earth.

In the middle of a huge salient or arc on the eastern front, it was not ideal tank country; but even so, here the

Germans would assemble 90,000 men, armed with 10,000 cannon and 2,700 tanks and assault guns. The Luftwaffe would weigh in with 2,500 aircraft.

The Soviets could muster 1,337,000 men equipped with 200,000 guns and 3,360 tanks and assault guns. These were to be supported by 2,650 planes.

Furthermore, war was to be waged with a great mass of men and material on a front within about three hundred miles. A stomach-turning prospect, indeed!

It was perhaps understandable that the Fuehrer's preamble to his operations order should have an air of desperate urgency about it:

> 'I am resolved, as soon as the weather allows, to launch Operation "Zitadelle", as the first offensive action of this year. . .Hence the importance of this offensive. It *must* lead to a rapid and decisive success. It *must* give us the initiative for the coming spring and summer. In view of this, preparations must be conducted with the utmost precaution and the utmost energy.
>
> 'At the main points of attack, the finest units, the finest weapons, the finest commanders will be committed, and plentiful supplies of munitions will be ensured.
>
> 'Every commander, every fighting man must be imbued with the capital significance of this offensive. The victory of Kursk must be a beacon to the whole world.'

The trouble was that the prominent position of the huge salient led the Russians to make a number of very intelligent guesses as to where Hitler would strike next. They soon worked out that it was necessary for him to pinch out the salient at the earliest possible date so that his counter-offensive could continue.

It was all very well for the Fuehrer with self-satisfaction to point out the build-up during June of his Tiger, Panther and Ferdinand tanks. At the same time, the Russians were making their own preparations — a corresponding build-up on each side of the salient. They were marshalling forces at Orel to the north and Belgorod to the south.

Around Orel, the Soviets were to face a formidable opponent. A favourite story about the charismatic Generaloberst Walter Model dated back to January of the previous year.

He had appeared then at the severely threatened headquarters of German Ninth Army located at the small Russian town of Sychevka. There was no ceremony about the entry of this small man who yet seemed to personify everyone's idea of the ramrod Junker.

He wore old-fashioned ear muffs and a fur-collared greatcoat that flapped down to his ankles. To complete the picture, he had a monocle.

The staff and officers of the Ninth clicked to attention just in time.

It seemed that they need scarcely have bothered. The little man ignored the courtesy, flinging coat, cap and earflaps on to a chair. Then, as if he had all the time in the world, he polished his monocle vigorously. He turned, and strode towards the vast situation-map with its rash of blue and red pencil marks.

For a while, there was silence. Model looked searchingly at his new command, which had just been slammed by two Soviet armies. A hole nine miles wide had been blasted in the front.

The officers waited. 'Rather a mess', Model commented.

He swept his hand over the Soviet penetrations, stubbing a finger at Sychevka, and proclaimed: 'The first task is to close that gap and turn off the supply tap of those Russian divisions which have broken through. From Sychevka we'll strike at the Russian flank and have them in a stranglehold.'

If Model had been looking for reactions of surprise, he was not disappointed. In fact, the officers gaped at him as if he had arrived from another planet.

One of the first to recover was Oberst Blaurock, who asked: 'What, Herr General, have you brought us for this operation?'

Model stared long and searchingly at the questioner. Then he rapped out the single word: 'Myself.'

A week later, he was as good as his word. The initiative was regained; the two flanks of the front split by the Soviet offensive had been recovered.

And now that same Ninth Army under Model was given the task of demolishing the northern wall of the bulge. At his disposal were three Panzer and two infantry corps — in fact, nineteen first-rate divisions.

However, the southern half of the peninsula dwarfed the resources of Model. Here was the Fourth Panzer Army of General Hermann Hoth with its two Panzer corps (including SS-Panzer Corps) and, on the left flank, 52nd Infantry Corps.

To the south of Belgorod, the wing of the German front, was Army Detachment Lanz with its 3rd Panzer and Eleventh Army Corps. In addition, there were the Panzer divisions, the crack armoured division Grossdeutschland — and the élite of the Waffen-SS.

Only the magnificent and the best represented the black legions: the Leibstandarte, Das Reich and Totenkopf.

How were these forces to be deployed? On 15 April, Hitler put his signature to thirteen copies of Operation Order No. 16. The document, like most of those he produced, was lengthy. The main point read:

'Objective of the offensive: by means of a highly concentrated and savage attack vigorously conducted by two armies, one from the area of Belgorod, the other from south of Orel, to encircle the enemy forces situated in the region of Kursk, and annihilate them by concentric attacks. . .'

Beneath the Fuehrer's confident tone, however, was real anxiety — as Guderian has revealed:

'Model had production information, based largely on air photography, which showed that the Russians were preparing deep and very strong defensive positions in exactly those areas where the attack by the two army groups were to go in.

'The Russians had already withdrawn the mass of their mobile formations from the forward area of the salient; as proposed in this plan of ours, they had strengthened the localities of our possible break-throughs with unusually strong artillery and anti-tank forces. Model drew the correct deduction from this, namely, that the enemy was counting on our launching this attack and that in order to achieve success we must adopt a fresh tactical approach; the alternative was to abandon the whole idea.'

But Hitler would hear of no postponement.

At dawn on 5 July 1943, Operation Zitadelle — the so-called 'Death Ride of Fourth Panzer Army' — was under way.

Within half an hour, the artillery barrage poured on Belgorod, orchestrated by the scream of the Stukas with their blanket of relentless dive-bombing. The leading Tigers poured away into the long, tall grass. There was the nightmare of the mines, but the mine-lifting teams marked their positions by lying down in the gaps be-tween.

Totenkopf had been slotted in on the extreme right flank of Fourth Panzer Army with a brief, not just to screen the flank, but to keep pace with the northerly advance of the SS-Panzer Corps. Opposite the three SS divisions on D-Day were mixed armoured and infantry formations from the Soviet First Tank and Sixty-ninth Armies.

On its progress, the SS came across the most elaborate system of fortifications it had yet encountered; hundreds of Soviet tanks had been dug into the ground in immo-bile pillboxes. With only their turrets visible, they proved extremely tough targets. Prolonged hammering was soon producing a horrific casualty rate.

Yet, despite this vicious resistance, the three SS divisions made smart progress on this first day. Totenkopf penetrated the weaknesses of the Soviet 52nd Guards Division, hugging the groups of Tigers and Panthers.

Indeed, Army Group South overall had a better start than their comrades in the north, thanks largely to impeccable co-ordination between tanks and dive-bombers. In the course of engagements which Manstein described in his memoirs as being extremely tough, Army Detachment Kempf succeeded in smashing through two defence lines. Things looked promising.

But not for long. Soon a solid wall of resistance loomed up. A second defence line held firm. Panzer Grenadier Division Deutschland, which had gone into battle in tight formation, was stopped by fortifications buttressed by anti-tank guns, flame-throwers and T-34s. While Grossdeutschland was stuck fast under the merciless barrage, the pioneers struggled to fix a route through numerous minefields and tracts of marshland. Tanks fell victims to mines and concerted air attack.

On the other hand, nothing, it seemed, could stop Totenkopf. There were times when 3rd Panzer Division appeared to be positively romping towards the high ground. Wrenched from the Russians' 52nd Guards Rifle Division was the village of Yakhontovo, an important forward command post for the Soviet Sixty-ninth Army. Although Leibstandarte and Das Reich had been moving too, their progress was a yard at a time. But the men of Totenkopf lashed out like demons at the Soviet flank defences, hurtling a cool twenty miles to the north.

On the morning of D-Day plus one, the division was across the now severed Belgorod-Oboyan highway. It halted for the night in triumph astride the line of Belgorod-Kursk.

The men of Totenkopf, however, were not too proud to acknowledge that the spectacular tank achievements of the assault had not been theirs alone.

Among the Stuka formations pounding the Soviets on the Belgorod-Oboyan road ahead of the tanks of SS-Panzer Corps was one of the Luftwaffe's most colourful heroes, Hans-Ulrich Rudel.

Swiftly, Rudel took in the Soviet armed might — the dug-in T-34s, the 7.62 cm anti-tank guns on their self-propelled carriages.

On his return, he reported what he had seen with the comment: 'That lot must be got rid of.'

But how? Rudel suddenly remembered earlier adventures in the campaign in the Crimea. There he had experimented with an elderly practice Stuka, below which had been slung an anti-tank cannon. He recalled having a lot of fun with it. Now it occurred to him that the sturdy old warhorse might with advantage be hauled out of retirement.

Here, in the Kursk salient, Rudel's tank-busting wing was born — Stukas with 3.7 mm cannon strapped beneath. Now, armed with this new weapon, entire squadrons of Stukas were able to fly in support of the SS divisions. Onto the Russian columns they dived from behind. The shells ripped into the T-34s, destroying the vital engine-housing.

Ulrich, more than one Totenkopf warrior admitted, was an ally worth having.

But nobody belittled the achievement of Totenkopf at Kursk so far; certainly not Hoth and Manstein when they came to survey the sector situation of SS-Panzer Corps. The twenty-mile advance by the division was impressive; the main road and rail links to the Russian rear had been savaged.

As for the other two SS divisions, they had found the Soviet defences decidedly heavier. But the achievements had been considerable: the sheer weight of Russian carnage was enormous.

Everywhere were wrecked Soviet armour and heavy weapons. There were long dreary queues of bewildered, demoralised Russian prisoners. It did not look as if much could stop 2nd SS-Panzer Corps in its hurtle towards the Kursk salient.

But it was a superficial view — dangerous and misleading and ultimately fatal. The truth was that the SS divisions had raced ahead far too quickly. There was a horrifying gap now on Hausser's left flank; the Leib-

188

standarte had been forced to hold back units with the job of covering the rear of the advance of SS-Panzer Corps. Totenkopf was now also forced to hold back: the right flank of the corps was exposed and threatened.

The advance had been slowed down, but nevertheless it had still proved far too speedy for the Russians. The Germans were getting close to the salient itself. Any further advance would bring the Germans into the rear of the Soviet's First Tank Army across the River Psel.

In a small wood near the village of Gostishchevo, north-east of Belgorod, sixty T-34s and several rifle battalions were assembled. They moved off at noon. The target was the Belgorod-Obayan highway — the supply route of SS-Panzer Corps. But the Luftwaffe had spotted them. Rudel's anti-tank cannon put paid to most of the T-34s before they had got within spitting distance of the Germans.

Hausser's motorised battalions thrust on northwards across the Psel and along the line of contact between Leibstandarte and Das Reich.

Totenkopf's hero now was Standartenfuehrer Karl Ullrich with 3rd Battalion, 6th SS-Panzer Grenadier Regiment. From the opposite bank rained down the full fury of Soviet artillery and mortar fire. Somehow, Ullrich sliced through it, his men hurtling towards the village of Krasnyy Oktabr. Here a small bridgehead was formed over the river and held against those merciless attacks of Soviet infantry and armour.

At the same time, Leibstandarte and Das Reich were also making for the village of Prokhorovka between the railway and the Psel.

Under the severest pressure now was General Katukov, Commander-in-Chief of Russia's reinforced Tank Army. His orders, issued by Army General Nikolai F. Vatutin and Military Council Member Nikita Khruschev had been explicit — '*On no account must the Germans break through to Oboyan.*' Oboyan was a small town, no great prize in itself, but a key Soviet defence area covering Kursk from the south.

Katukov was worried, deeply worried. Major-General

Shalin, his Chief-of-Staff, reported at the evening situation meeting: 'We are confronted by an unprecedented concentration of armour. It's the old tactic. But this time the armoured spearheads are led by Tigers, Panthers, and massive assault guns. The cannon of our T-34s can't pierce the Germans' frontal armour.'

Shalin went on: 'The other trouble is the ground support aircraft fitted with anti-tank artillery that the enemy uses. It's like hawks in a chicken yard. Time and again, armoured counter-attacks are shot up by the surprise intervention of these machines.'

One particular tank corps had lost no less than a dozen of its T-34s — knocked out by the flying tank-busters of Hans-Ulrich Rudel.

A Russian artillery observer reported: 'The attacking aircraft drops from some 2500 feet out of the sky and it does not pull out of the dive until it is at least within feet of the last tank. There is a crack of cannon, a flash. Then through the billowing smoke of the struck T-34, the pilot is climbing away. A moment later he dives in again, always from behind. His cannon knocks out tank after tank, invariably in the engine compartment, the most vulnerable part. Each hit results in an instant explosion.'

It was going to prove a monumental assignment for General Katukov. He needed help — and fast.

Early on 11 July, General Nikolai Rotmistrov's Fifth Guards Tank Army was ordered out of its staging area east of Kursk and sent racing south to smash SS-Panzer Corps.

Vatutin sweated. It was not enough. Armoured reserves of two tank corps were added to the fray. It failed to stop the onward hurtling advance of the Panzers of General Hoth. The terrible Prokhorovka offensive in the Kursk salient was about to begin.

16

Some 1,500 tanks and assault guns raced, fired, exploded, burnt, thundered and smoked on the minute sea of hills and valleys around Prokhorovka. Lieutenant-General Rotmistrov, viewing the battlefield from one of those hills, wrote:

'The tanks were moving across the steppe in small packs, under cover of patches of woodland and hedges. The bursts of gunfire merged into one continuous, mighty roar. The Soviet tanks thrust into German advanced formations at full speed and penetrated the German tank screen. The T-34s were knocking out Tigers at extremely close range, since their powerful guns and massive armour no longer gave them an advantage in close combat. The tanks of both sides were in closest possible contact.

'There was neither time nor room to disengage from the enemy and reform in battle order, or operate in formation. The shells fired at extremely close range, pierced not only the side armour but also the frontal armour of the fighting vehicles. At such range there was no protection in armour, and the length of the gun barrels was no longer decisive. Frequently, when a tank was hit, its ammunition and fuel blew up, and torn turrets were flung through the air over dozens of yards. At the same time over the battlefield furious aerial combats developed. Soviet as well as German airmen tried to help their ground forces to win the battle.'

To Rotmistrov, it seemed that the bombers, ground-support aircraft and fighters were permanently suspended in the sky above Prokhorovka with one aerial combat succeeding another. Soon the whole sky was shrouded by the thick black smoke of the burning wrecks, while on the black scorched earth the gutted tanks burnt like torches.

Which side was attacking and which defending? This was an academic question, the language of the school-room board-game, not the real world of the Kursk salient in 1943.

The 2nd Battalion, 18th Tank Brigade of 18th Tank Corps, attacking on the left bank of the Psel, encountered a clutch of Tigers.

The Germans opened fire on the Soviets. The Tigers' guns were lethal; it was vital for the Russians to close with the menace rapidly.

Captain Shripkin, the battalion commander, rapped out the order: *'Forward, follow me!'* The first shell of the commander's tank sliced into the side of the Tiger; there was a vast wall of flame as another Panzer took instant revenge. The severely wounded Shripkin was dragged from his T-34 by his driver and wireless operator. The trio took shelter in a shell crater. But here there was no rest. Another Tiger hurtled towards them.

Rotmistrov related:

'Aleksandr Nikolayev, the driver, leapt back into his damaged and already smouldering tank, started the engine and raced up to meet the enemy tank. Like a flaming ball of fire, the T-34 raced over the ground. The Tiger halted. But it was too late. The blazing tank rammed the German Panzer at full speed. The detonation made the ground shake.'

To Totenkopf was endlessly repeated the order: *Hold Hausser's flank!* For two days, the door was kept firmly slammed on the progress of the two Soviet corps, but for how long would the severely strained hinges be held in place? It was later reckoned that Totenkopf was outnumbered four-to-one in both tanks and infantry.

And what of the Luftwaffe? What of Rudel's tank-busters? In that dreadful reek it was largely a matter of luck when it came to spotting the swastika identification panels on the armoured decks.

But they were there, the Stukas and the Henschel 129s, flying in like enormous black hawks, their cannon pounding. The Russian mobile flak opened up in full fury. Amid the black, it was possible at times to detect the dull white puffs of smoke. Then one of the hawks would break up, a wing splitting and falling, only to be followed by the rest plummeting into the mêlée of tanks below, exploding in a single giant fireball.

The tank-busters kept on coming. The hits on the T-34s were followed by the explosion of the ammunition racks and the thick black smoke belching from the engine cowling. There was a stench of dust and oil and the terrible screams of the trapped Soviet tank crews.

By 15 July, it was reckoned that Totenkopf had lost over half its tanks and vehicles; casualties among the combat units had been horrific.

By then Hitler had summoned his Feldmarschalls to his East Prussian HQ and told them bluntly: 'I am obliged to postpone Zitadelle.'

Like a magnificent thoroughbred whose muscles and sinews had been savaged, ripped and torn, 3rd SS-Panzer Division Totenkopf could only lie battered, bleeding and exhausted, praying that it would be left alone for a while. True, a few extra tanks and assault guns were available, but their combat potential was pathetic. Time was needed for rest and refitting, but even that would have availed Hitler little. The throat of the German armed forces had been hacked and bludgeoned; the war was lost after Kursk in July 1943.

Still, Manstein had protested. His one army group, he believed, should continue to slog it out. This was doubly important since the enemy was already committing fresh mobile reserves which should be annihilated.

Hitler, though, was adamant. And not just because of the Russian front. The Western Allies had already landed in Sicily. Forces were needed for Italy, where resistance had crumbled. There was sure to be trouble in the Balkans. Forces would have to be syphoned off from the Russian front.

Those who attended Hitler's long, sadly irrelevant ramblings on the course of the war confirmed what Guderian had suspected earlier. The Fuehrer had lost heart, at any rate in the Russian campaign.

Zitadelle had been, by any reckoning, an appalling disaster. Guderian wondered desperately if there was not some way of making the Fuehrer see sense. The General went to Headquarters intent on speaking his mind:

'I went to see Jodl to whom I submitted my proposals for a reorganisation of the Supreme Command: the Chief of the Armed Forces General Staff would control the actual conduct of operations, while Hitler would be limited to his proper field of activities, supreme control of the political situation and of the highest war strategy.

'After I had expounded my ideas at length and in detail Jodl replied laconically: "Do you know of a better supreme commander than Adolf Hitler?" His expression had remained impassive as he said this and his whole manner was one of icy disapproval. In view of his attitude I put my papers back in my briefcase and left the room.'

Four days after his termination of Zitadelle, the Fuehrer announced that Hausser's SS-Panzer Corps would be snatched from the east and sent to Italy.

For a short time, shattered and devastated Kharkov seemed a luxurious centre of convalescence for the men of Totenkopf, reduced to physical and mental zombies by the tank massacre of Prokhorovka.

The prospect of Italy seemed almost seductive. General Rodion I. Malinovsky, however, had not yet done with the men of the Death's Head.

A thunderous artillery salvo reverberated over Moscow. An air almost of gaiety seemed to grip the Soviet capital.

194

Stalin had ordered a day of victory celebrations. Two strategic centres of the Ukraine had been recaptured from the Germans — Belgorod and Orel were once again in Soviet hands.

With their loss, Kharkov was again under threat. Hitler's reaction had been predictable: '*Kharkov must be held at all costs.*'

Totenkopf was back in a 'fire brigade' role. Manstein ordered the division, together with SS-Das Reich, to rush to the defence of the area west of Kharkov.

The division dug in south of the town of Akhtyrka. Now it was braced for the armoured Soviet avalanche descending from the north and east. The Russians were all set to break through to the south-west towards the Dnieper.

In Kharkov itself, the situation had become virtually untenable.

On 12 August, the Russians attacked the German front east and south-east of the town. The danger which then resulted was of nightmarish familiarity: total encirclement, the predicament of Stalingrad.

Manstein was blunt: 'The army group had no intention of sacrificing an army for Kharkov.'

In terms of sheer mathematics it looked impossible, anyway. Any offensive would have to be undertaken by six mauled divisions.

General Otto Woehler, Manstein's one-time Chief-of-Staff and now in charge of the Eighth Army (formerly Army Detachment Kempf) was ordered to rebuild the shattered German front west of Kharkov. It seemed a hopeless task, but the fortunes in this unusual war were totally unpredictable. What happened at the little village of Akhtyrka outside Kharkov proved that the Germans, shattered at Kursk and barely able to hold Kharkov, had never ceased to astonish the Russians.

Stalin had been becoming increasingly impatient over Kharkov. An impatient Stalin was a dangerous man. Commanders who carried out his orders with less than the required despatch had a habit of being relieved of their commands and disappearing.

General Rotmistrov and his Fifth Guards Tank Army had no wish to end their days in the bleak reaches of Siberia. On the morning of 19 August, the tanks rumbled through the vast fields of sunflowers lying under the blistering sun. On the German side, General Raus was content to watch the German progress for the moment. His anti-tank and assault guns and 8.8 flak battle groups would have their work to do soon enough. Totenkopf and Das Reich, buttressed by their Panthers, Tigers and assault guns, would be there too.

For some hours, as at Kursk, it was impossible to be sure which side was getting the worst of it. Only after three hours was Raus able to gain any reliable figures. But it became clear that he had won the duel: eighty gutted T-34s lay on the battlefield. A mere three Russian tanks had got through to the edge of Kharkov, and they had soon been destroyed.

But losses had been high. The 39th Panzer Grenadier Regiment of 3rd Panzer Division, for example, was down to the strength of two rifle companies. Sixth Panzer Division was left with only fifteen tanks, while one of the Panzer battalions could summon just nine Tigers.

Kharkov remained obstinately in German hands.

Not for the first time, Manstein had good cause to praise Totenkopf. It and Das Reich had given him a much needed breathing spell. There was a chance that the Germans' Eighth Army could be redeployed; the Russians had not reached the Dnieper and they had not taken Kharkov.

Kharkov! The very name appeared almost as big an obsession with Hitler as with Stalin. The SS divisions, he argued, had saved the city before. They could do it again. Only the Waffen-SS, the Fuehrer went on, had the necessary ruthlessness and determination to hold it.

With a feeling of despair, Manstein recognised that Hitler's understanding of the military implications of what was happening on the eastern front had become severely blunted.

Hitler began to view Kharkov purely in prestige terms.

He implored the Feldmarschall: 'The fall of the city will have serious political consequences. I need the support of the Turks and Bulgarians. If we abandon Kharkov we'll lose face in Ankara and Sofia.'

As for Stalin, he had now begun to think beyond Kharkov. He still wanted the city, certainly. But the aim was to knife through to the Dnieper, chasing the Germans all the way.

There was a series of lengthy, abortive meetings between Hitler and Manstein. Still the Fuehrer temporised; it was not until 15 September that he agreed reluctantly to the withdrawal of Fourth Panzer and Eighth Armies.

Manstein turned yet again to the resources of the SS. Totenkopf and Das Reich were to protect the rear of Eighth Army in its headlong rush for the Dnieper.

By now, the lease of the long hot summer was drawing to an end. In this daunting land of violent seasonal contrasts, the months of the sun abruptly vanished. The rain cascaded as if tipped from giant buckets. Dust became mud; mud in its turn became impassable swamps that sucked equally at men and material.

For General Woehler life was one long nightmare. Progress, due to the appalling weather, was at the pace of a snail. There was harrying from the Russians and there was the inevitable snarl-up of vehicles. In Army Group South's sector there were only six bridges; the entire group would have to cross them, to say nothing of two hundred thousand wounded.

For the officers of Totenkopf, the senior heirs of Theodor Eicke's iron-hard élite formation, this sort of fighting was small beer indeed; which only made more bitter their dawning realisation that victory was hopeless.

The defensive barrage of the German artillery failed to stop Rotmistrov's tanks. But behind the fields with their tall sunflowers, the forces of General Raus were spread out in a chequer-board pattern. The Russians stumbled directly into the fresh defensive network. A short time before, the Panzers had faced the same situation at Kursk and got the worst of it. Now it was the Russians' turn. The Panzers, Tigers and assault guns charged at the Russian might and won the day.

There could be no argument that the statistics were impressive: 184 T-34s had been knocked out.

Impressive? Perhaps. But hardly significant. Kharkov still loomed. Three bloody battles had already waged there. Its loss had been a stupefying blow for the Russians. Only in a personal dictatorship of such consummate ruthlessness could a head of state survive such a loss.

Kharkov *had* to be Russian again. As for General Rotmistrov, he had 160 tanks in reserve.

The battle died with the day and for a few hours there was an uneasy silence over the field of sunflowers.

Rotmistrov waited for the welcome curtain of night. At midnight, the clatter of tank tracks fractured the calm; the Panthers and T-34s hurtled at one another. Rotmistrov kept going, only to run into further opposition from this vast mechanised armada.

The early days of October 1943 produced a fresh Soviet hero in Marshal Ivan S. Konev. This veteran of the Tsarist army had been on a winning streak previously in the war. During the Soviet offensive around Moscow in December 1941, he had commanded the Kalinin Front (Army Group) in the decisive struggle for the northern front, and by the start of 1942 had forced the invaders back over one hundred miles.

Now the great offensives of 1943 were to give him a new role. On 15 October, his newly organised Soviet Second Ukrainian Front struck out of the Kremenchug bridgehead. Here was the gigantic muscle of no less than six armies, punching a gap in the German front between the right flank of Woehler's Eighth Army and General Hans Valentin Hube's First Panzer Army.

Konev charged into the hinterland west of the Dnieper. His long armoured columns then wheeled south, roaring straight for Krivoi Rog, the mining centre for Ukrainian iron ore.

The prize was considerable. Here was the communications, supply and rail centre for Army Group South.

The prize was more, much more, than simply the material which Manstein's group could offer. For this was also the area of Zaporozhye and Nikopol, with their precious hoards of copper and nickel so vital for armaments. And far beyond, beckoned the oilfields of Rumania.

Manstein's overall plan of a strong counter-attack to halt Konev had, for the moment, to be set aside. The implications of losing Krivoi Rog were almost too appalling to contemplate.

The resources at his disposal were decidedly patchy in quality. There was General Ferdinand Schoerner's 40th Panzer Corps — Totenkopf Division together with 14th and 24th Panzer Divisions. There was also the 9th and 11th Panzers and the 16th Panzer Grenadier Division.

It was certainly daunting on paper. The truth was these were reserves cobbled together for a seemingly hopeless task. What Manstein in fact had was six weakened armoured formations expected to do battle with six Russian armies.

Man of the hour for Totenkopf was SS-Oberfuehrer Hellmuth Becker, who was eventually to become the division's final commander after Max Simon and his immediate successor, SS-Brigadefuehrer Hermann Priess had gone on to other commands. Becker was an early protégé of Theodor Eicke. A fighter of ruthlessness and courage, he now launched into Konev's force in the right flank from positions north of Krivoi Rog.

The Russians hung on for four grim months. The cost to Konev when it was all over was 10,000 lives, more than 300 tanks and 5,000 prisoners. In terms of advance for the Russians it was a severe setback — an ignominous retreat which threw them back half the distance to the Dnieper. Manstein's front was stabilised yet again.

But the Feldmarschall was under no illusions, and later wrote:

'With the odds still as much against us as ever . . .our forces had not been sufficient to throw the enemy back on the northern bank of the Dnieper.'

Veteran members of the division must have been struck more than once by the irony of the situation when they handled the very best equipment which was now supplied to them without stint. With the situation on the front so desperate, it was no longer necessary, as in the days of Eicke, quite literally to beg, borrow or steal what was needed. Totenkopf Division was to end 1943 as easily the strongest of the SS formations in the First Panzer Army.

The tank arm, admittedly, was weak — something like forty per cent effective. But, considering the bitterness of the fighting, it was a highly respectable showing.

The tank men of Totenkopf were veterans now and they dealt with the T-34s in classic style. The technique was to allow the tanks to roll over the forward positions, then methodical machine-gun fire would chop down the following infantry.

The unaccompanied T-34s were tackled next. Finally, entrenched heavy guns and artillery in the third line put paid to stray tanks which had somehow managed to get through the net.

It was perhaps understandable that when the post-war memoirs came to be written, surviving Totenkopf members felt bitter that sparse mention — with honourable exceptions such as Feldmarschall von Manstein — at best gave them scant acknowledgement for the victories or, at worst, ignored them altogether.

General Woehler, the Commander of Eighth Army, was, compared with his fellows, remarkably generous. In a despatch, he commended an SS-Panzer division for having 'stood like a rock in the army [*Wie ein Fels im Heer*], while the enemy broke through in neighbouring sectors'. On another occasion he described Totenkopf as 'a lightning sword of retribution' which fulfilled its tasks 'with unshakeable fortitude [*unerschuetterlicher Kampfkraft*]'.

Such generosity, however, could not alter the cold fact that the situation worsened throughout the autumn and winter of 1943 along the eastern front. Hitler was forced to rush the Leibstandarte Division back to Russia from

Italy — plus the cream of the new tanks. Each month was dreary and disaster-filled, culminating in the decisive blow of the great winter offensive.

On 13 December, Russian forces were unleashed from the Nevel salient towards the south-west, overwhelming Army Group Centre. Prizes such as Zhitomir and Korosten were regained, and soon the pre-war Polish frontiers were in Russian hands. On 14 January 1944, the long cruel agony of Leningrad was over. The Red Army struck at Army Group Centre there; the city that Hitler had regarded as 'the cradle of Bolshevism' was encircled.

Stalingrad, Kharkov — and now, at the start of 1944, Kirovograd — was Hitler's obsession. It must be held to prevent the Russians penetrating the Rumanian frontier.

Two mechanised corps had already broken through. It was a job for the 'fire brigade' — or, more specifically, Grossdeutschland Division, buttressed by Totenkopf's Panzers, to stop them. The Soviet corps had been badly mauled, but they were by no means out of action. They would keep going.

In Kirovograd itself, three German divisions encircled the town. Hitler's orders, of course, could be predicted. '*Kirovograd is to be defended as a fortress,*' intoned the Fuehrer. '*It is to be held until the very end.*'

General Woehler's intention was to use Totenkopf to cover the planned withdrawal of Eighth Army to a new defensive line on the River Bug. Before that happened, the southern flank of the Soviet forces had to be smashed. They must not be allowed to envelop Kirovograd.

A series of quick sharp engagements took the heat off the threatened town. The three embattled divisions withdrew. It became obvious even to Hitler that the holding of a continuous front on the Bug was impossible. The withdrawal continued. Now the order to Totenkopf was: '*Hold the Dniester line*' — the river was the border between Rumania and the Soviet Union.

But the front of Malinovsky, now promoted to Marshal, and General Fyodor I. Tolbukhin, future Marshal of the Soviet Union, were too powerful. All Totenkopf could do now — all *anyone* could do — was to blunt the Russian attacks as best they could while withdrawing.

Summer had come again by the time the division was entrenched in the foothills of the Carpathians. The deep mud of the spring thaw had been cursed over the last two years. But now the mud was actually welcomed by the two sides, each virtually suffocated under a blanket of fatigue.

17

The one individual who had no doubt about what Stalin would do next — and was deaf to any proposed alternatives — was, predictably, Adolf Hitler.

There was yet another obsession to follow. Kirovograd. This time it was Galicia. There, the supreme warlord argued, Stalin had a great strategic opportunity to advance towards Warsaw and the Vistula and slam into the rear of Army Group Centre. The Russians, so went Hitler's reasoning, would strike north between the Pripet Marshes and the Carpathians. Their destination would be Koenigsberg. From there they would cross the Vistula into Poland.

Army Group Northern Ukraine must therefore be stiffened to meet this new menace. Such reasoning left one detail out of the reckoning — this could only be done at the expense of weakening Army Group Centre.

Yet all intelligence reports conspired to prove the Fuehrer wrong. Troop build-ups, such reports suggested, were in front of Army Group Centre, situated well to the north in the area of Minsk. Hitler would have none of it, dismissing each confirmation as mere scare tactics by the Russians. 'These are military feints,' he assured his equally mesmerised senior colleagues.

Their sadly misguided faith in their Fuehrer was

echoed by Feldmarschall Keitel, the Chief of the Wehrmacht who, on 20 June 1944, delivered a lecture on the overall military situation.

Keitel argued that, since invasion forces had already landed in Normandy, the Russians would wait until the western powers had achieved some success before taking a major initiative.

Just forty-eight hours after Keitel had spoken, the Soviets attacked. But not in Galicia.

Shrewdly, Stalin had chosen 22 June 1944 for his assault. By opting for the third anniversary of the German attack on the Soviet Union, the Russians started with a considerable psychological advantage. The choice of such a date would boost Russian morale and deflate that of the severely beleaguered Germans.

And what of Totenkopf? By some miracle, Himmler had found a way yet again of strengthening the division's desperately mauled forces. Back in October 1943, Himmler had raised two SS-Panzer Grenadier Divisions, Goetz von Berlichingen and Reichsfuehrer-SS. The latter had proved itself in battle under Max Simon, the former Totenkopf commander. Himmler now plundered it for new recruits to Totenkopf and despatched fresh consignments of tanks, assault guns, artillery pieces and vehicles.

They were needed with a vengeance! In vain, General Woehler, the Commander of Eighth Army, had planned to pull the division out of the front line and send it into reserve for a period of rest and recuperation. But the situation on the western front allowed for no such thing. Once again, there was a 'fire brigade' role for the crack SS division.

It was rushed north to bolster Army Group Centre; the situation it encountered scarcely required anything approaching the arts of war. Here was sublime chaos — planned by the Russians with cold-blooded, almost mathematical exactitude.

The groundwork had been the responsibility of the partisans. During the night of 19-20 June, they succeeded in turning the area of the Dnieper west of Minsk into a minor inferno. Railway lines were wrecked by more than ten thousand explosions. Principal bridges were blown up; supply columns halted. The Germans might have wanted to leave in a hurry but the cold truth was that they were not being allowed to.

Stalin went even further. Partisans were ordered to go for the jugular of the German supply system. Telephone cables along the railways were severed. Hot on this highly successful paralysis of essential communications, the Russians struck. Their assault into Army Group Centre destroyed a vast front of two hundred miles.

A terrifying hole had been punched between Ostrov, which was on the former Soviet-Lithuanian frontier, and Kovel on the south-western edge of the Pripet Marshes.

The resources of Totenkopf were mustered to bolster General Busch's Fourth Army, struggling with the sweepings of two infantry divisions. For Busch, it was not simply a question of fighting. He would have welcomed that. Instead, his main preoccupation was finding ways to get his forces to move at all; increasingly, he found himself bogged down in the tortuous rail-bottlenecks behind what was left of Army Group Centre's front.

Although he had little cause for it, Hitler displayed an almost bouncy optimism. He told his staff: 'One man will save the day — Model, my little magician.'

It was an understandable choice. The ruthless, aggressive Model had brought off any number of defensive triumphs when the situation had seemed beyond hope.

But now the plight of the German Army was more dire than anything even he had previously experienced. Thirty divisions had been destroyed; this amounted virtually to the whole of Army Group Centre. Fourth Army had been severely crippled, along with the bulk of Ninth Army and Third Panzer Army. In these unequal battles, twenty-one generals had been taken prisoner and more than ten killed. Hitler had totally misinterpreted the intentions and potential of the enemy. Reserves had been lamentably inadequate; there had been virtually no Luftwaffe support.

The cold truth was that the Red Army was now in a position to ram the German centre as far back as the Vistula and the frontier of East Prussia. German troops were threatened in the Balkan states.

Moreover, Hitler's opponents were not only the Russians. At one o'clock on the morning of 21 July 1944, the German people heard the solemn tones of Hans Fritzsche, the Nazi's chief radio spokesman, announce over the air: *'The Fuehrer speaks.'*

Then had come the harsh, slightly quavering tones of Adolf Hitler himself. The Fuehrer related what had happened on 20 July at a staff conference at Rastenburg:

'A very small clique of ambitious, dishonourable and criminally stupid officers had formed a plot to remove me and at the same time overturn the High Command of the German armed forces.

'A bomb planted by Oberst von Stauffenberg exploded two metres to my right. It very seriously wounded a number of faithful members of my staff. One of them has died. I myself am absolutely unhurt, except for very minor scratches, bruises and burns. I regard this as a confirmation of the decree of Providence that I should continue to pursue the goal of my life, as I have done up to now. . .'

The officers responsible for the assassination attempt believed that killing Hitler was the only way to save the honour of Germany.

The time-bomb at Rastenburg had injured all nineteen of the officers at the afternoon situation conference. Hitler had escaped with minor burns, bruises and an ear injury. In the first hours after the explosion, a widespread conspiracy against the Fuehrer centred largely in the army and reaching into the very highest echelons of command had been revealed. For Himmler and his SS, only too conscious of being hated and despised over the years, it was a luxurious opportunity for revenge.

The conspiracy was put down with exemplary ferocity.

The arrests and drum-head trials and executions by hanging from meathooks went ahead immediately. New men of unquestionable loyalty were placed in key posts. As far as the eastern front was concerned, the most significant appointment was of General Guderian as Acting Chief of Staff.

One of Guderian's first moves was to promise rein-forcements for each army group. Guderian attempted to inject a new spirit into the appallingly shattered Wehrmacht, by inserting into the objective the aphorism *'The thrust is the best parry.'*

It was all fine window-dressing. After reading the directive, Model's Chief of Staff told his superior that it would be at least a week before the army groups would get any effective reinforcements and a lot could happen in the meantime.

Army Group Centre was reorganised as far as possible; the best available divisions, though, could do little but act as breakwaters for the surging Red tide. Totenkopf was raced to the city of Grodno, which Model saw as being potentially the biggest breakwater of all. It lay right on the route to East Prussia. Furthermore, the loss of the city would open up a hole between the right flank of Fourth Army to the north and the left wing of what remained of Second Army to the south.

But seemingly nothing could stop the Russians during this long hot summer. There was the scent of victory in the air for Stalin fighting his 'great patriotic war'. In the Baltic, Lithuania had fallen. The Germans had made every effort to hold the capital, Vilna, the key railway junction on the distant approaches to East Prussia which beckoned tantalisingly. Again, this was partly a partisan victory: eleven Lithuanian partisan detachments entered Vilna with the Red Army.

And for eleven days, Totenkopf Division, out-numbered seven-to-one in men and ten-to-one in armour, stood firm. Model had attended a situation conference with Guderian; he had left it with the words of his superior ringing in his ears. Guderian had demanded: 'We must take the offensive everywhere! To retreat any further is intolerable!' Intolerable or not, it proved unavoidable. Model gave reluctant permission for the men of the Death's Head to withdraw. The Red Flag was hauled in triumph over Grodno.

Faith was pinned now in Siedlce, an important Polish road and rail junction eminently useful to the fleeing Germans.

The plan was for the Russian 11th Tank Corps to rush the city. The promise of victory was strong. At dawn on 25 July, the tanks of the Red Army rumbled through the suburbs. They were spurred on their way by a fresh declaration from Stalin, who had ordered the Stavka to recast completely its indoctrination programme for the troops. One theme was hammered time and again: every inch on the eastern front was to be recaptured.

From now on, the Soviet forces were fighting on foreign soil, but it made no difference. The new theme, in a word, was *Vengeance*! It followed the Russian soldier everywhere. He confronted it at meetings, in slogans, on signs posted along the road and in a string of articles and leaflets. Lecturers recounted stories of crimes committed by the SS against Russian women and children; there were tales of German looting and destruction in the Soviet Union. Troops were encouraged to relate what had happened in their own families. The object was to give each man the feeling that his was a personal score to settle.

A good deal of the propaganda proved unnecessary; the Germans had condemned themselves. The left-flank armies of Marshal Konstantin K. Rokossovsky — who had been responsible for the encirclement and destruction of large forces at Stalingrad and who had accepted the surrender of Feldmarschall Paulus — on the way to Vistula and up to Warsaw had stumbled across unimagined horrors.

There had been the ghastly 'death factory' at Maidanek, just to the west of Lublin, where a million died. Then had come the nightmare of Auschwitz-Birkenau.

Fuelled by cold fury, the Russians prepared to wrench their enemies out of Siedlce.

But the Germans had every intention of holding the town. Their units swept in immediately from the north and north-east, orchestrated by the Luftwaffe. Now the Germans dared to hope; the Soviet 11th Corps was forced on the defensive.

Ninth Army was given 3rd SS-Panzer Division Totenkopf, the Hermann Goering Division and two infantry divisions.

For a while, the Russians got the worst of it. The commanders of 11th Corps and 2nd Guards Cavalry Corps felt the chill winds of Siberia on their faces.

The Soviet forces were pulled out and regrouped for a concentric attack the next day which would entail surrounding Siedlce completely and then storming it. The plan failed. The town had been cleared, certainly. But Totenkopf and its comrades were still there.

Only on 31 July, after virtually pulverising the town out of existence, did the Soviets win the day and the SS abandon their defences at Siedlce.

Totenkopf Division was back in its now sadly familiar role: keeping the escape route open towards Moscow and delivering kicks wherever possible at the pursuing Soviet Second Tank Army. Yet Model's debt to Totenkopf was considerable. The division shielded thousands of fleeing Germans. They could so easily have turned into a rabble; now they were being halted and reorganised along the Vistula by Ninth Army.

Something of the success of the forces seeped through to Warsaw. For five long years, the jackboot had relentlessly ground the Poles into the dust. The bid for freedom when it came was violent and spectacular and ultimately fruitless. On 1 August 1944 the fifty-thousand-strong Polish underground forces (the Home Army — *Armia Krajova*) rose but were put down with ferocity by the Germans.

News of the quelling of Warsaw did have one effect on Totenkopf fighting in Russia. It had been a German success; there were few enough of those these days. The men of the Death's Head dared to hope again.

Some of the optimism even affected the gloomy and sardonic Model, increasingly conscious that his much vaunted reputation for producing miracles was severely under strain.

Rushed into existence was 4th SS-Panzer Corps under SS-Gruppenfuehrer Herbert Gille, forthwith saddled with probably the most unenviable job in the entire Waffen-SS.

Corps were accustomed to have SS-Panzer or Panzer Grenadier divisions built into their resources. But that was a luxury which circumstances no longer permitted. The constant shifting of the élite SS divisions from one trouble-spot to another made full strength out of the question. No corps had any divine right to one SS division. These were moved from corps to corps to deal with the by now monotonous series of crises.

Hitler continued to insist to Guderian, Model and others that he alone knew precisely what the Stavka would do next. No one dared stand up to the Fuehrer or be so unwise as to whisper *Galicia*.

Ironically, to the astonishment of his immediate circle, the supreme war-lord turned out this time to be right.

Hitler reasoned that the Russians would try again for a major thrust across the Vistula to envelop Warsaw. This needed no strategic genius, but where Hitler scored was in guessing just where such a crossing would be. He opted for the west, so when in fact the Soviets did attack in this theatre on 14 August, the SS divisions were well prepared. For an entire week, Totenkopf and Viking were able to repulse a combined enemy force of fifteen rifle divisions and two armoured brigades. Fiercest fighting was in the Wolomin sector, where the Russians threw in eight rifle divisions, a motorised rifle brigade and swarms of fighters. The Red Army was like one gigantic bulldozer which shoved the Panzer Corps slowly west towards Warsaw and the Vistula. Indeed, the Soviet spearhead actually reached the Warsaw suburb of Praga. There they encountered the legions of the SS-Grenadiers, men grey and gaunt with fatigue but very far from beaten.

The bulldozer suddenly came up against what seemed to be a wall of obstinately impenetrable steel. Hitler felt triumphant and did not hesitate to say so. He proclaimed: 'The front is stabilised. In my opinion we will be able to set things right in the east.'

The Soviet forces had advanced an incredible one hundred and fifty miles. They had done it, furthermore, at speed — and it was this which, for the moment at least, was to prove their undoing. They had, not for the first time, run ahead of their supplies. In this sector, they no longer represented a solid front. They could be dammed and in places diverted.

But heralding this as a major victory and a turning of the tide was yet another symptom of the delusions to which Hitler was becoming progressively subject.

Elsewhere the day of collapse, the end of the 'Thousand-Year Reich', could not be far off. There had been the Allied landings in Normandy and southern France. The American, Canadian and British forces were at the very frontiers of Germany. Rome had fallen, and the German forces had been routed in the direction of the Apennines. Rumania had gone. Greece had gone. Yugoslavia and Hungary were mere havens for the vanquished.

An ominous lull settled during October around Warsaw. Fourth SS-Panzer Corps withered under yet another Russian offensive and, at the end of it, Gille found himself at the join of the Bug and Vistula rivers.

Vast stretches of wartime Europe were by now sullen monuments to Hitler's nihilism. Yet, he insisted, everyone would fight to the end, to the very destruction of Germany itself.

The men of Totenkopf were not to be exempt. Hitler was to find more work for them.

But first there was to be a bizarre interlude.

18

The certainty of total defeat lowered over the battle–fields. By the autumn of 1944 they shook under the march of Hitler's enemies, who had advanced to the Rhineland border, to the very threshold of East Prussia.

There was scarcely a German soldier, SS or Wehrmacht, who did not sense the truth. Anyone who was deaf to the clash of arms on the ground had only to listen to the Allied bombers in the air. Annihilation was no longer in question. Which of the invaders would get to Berlin first? That was the sole doubt.

But Adolf Hitler, still wrapped in a thick cocoon of delusion, refused to acknowledge the signs and screamed *Feigling* at even the most timorous of his critics. Only a coward, the Fuehrer maintained, could fail to recognise the great opportunities within Germany's grasp.

The ageing, stooping, shaking figure clung tenaciously to the reassuring props of situation maps and coloured pencils. Then the eyes would light up with their old fire. The hoarse voice would gain in strength, and even intimates were caught off-balance by the man's still formidable reserves of power.

Hitler asserted: 'One more bold counter-offensive. That's all that's needed.'

To the dismay of Guderian, Hitler opted for an attack in the west. Guderian wrote:

'A sensible commander would. . .have remembered the looming dangers on the eastern front which could only be countered by a timely breaking-off of the operations in the west and that was already, from the long view, a failure.'

211

It most certainly was. Hitler had appeared to lose interest and heart in grappling with the Russians. He had argued that victory would come with a bold counter-stroke to capture Antwerp, split the Anglo-American forces and lead to another greater Dunkirk.

Hitler had personally drawn up a plan for an attack from the Ardennes. This, the classic invasion route from Germany to the west, was the area which had led to such magnificent triumphs in 1940. The result, the so-called Battle of the Bulge, was to turn into a crushing failure. Losses both for German and American forces were to be horrific; 100,000 Germans were to be killed, wounded or captured and the Americans were to lose 76,000.

In the meantime, there was the situation in the east. Hitler became mesmerised by Hungary. Here was the site for the next great offensive by the forces of the Third Reich. Here was fresh work for the SS divisions.

Hitler nursed a personal grudge against Hungary, or more specifically, its Regent, Admiral Miklos Horthy. After service in the Austro-Hungarian Navy during World War I, Horthy had become leader of the White — anti-Communist — regime in Hungary and in 1920 was appointed Regent. Nazi Germany had courted Hungary assiduously; the country had been supported in its terri-torial ambitions.

Horthy was a gentleman of the old school whose small talk consisted of hunting and horses. Hitler had a minimum of small talk; such gossip as there was over mint tea certainly did not dwell on such generalities as sport. That sort of world made the Fuehrer feel inferior.

But boredom was a small price to pay for Hungary's support which had certainly been needed for the suc-cessful prosecution of the war in the east. Hitler had reacted with a certain sardonic amusement to a secret letter from Horthy which had put forward the suggestion of a German attack on Russia. At that point, Barbarossa had been but two months away.

Never mind, there was an extremely flattering wel-come for the Regent when he visited Hitler on 24 April 1941. The Fuehrer was gracious enough to acknowledge

Horthy's considerable bravery as a sailor with the Austro-Hungarian Navy, but it was the man's political acquiescence that Hitler was seeking.

Three years later, matters were very different. The Horthy whom Hitler confronted on 19 March 1944 was not a man to be flattered or patronised. Not to put too fine a point on it, he had become dangerous.

Horthy refused point-blank to recognise the new puppet government which Hitler had insisted on, following the Duce's dismissal in Rome. Furthermore, Horthy demanded the return of nine Hungarian divisions on the Russian front. Hitler also had evidence that the Hungarian government was sabotaging German military trains travelling through the country.

But there was worse, far worse. There were rumours that Horthy was trying to negotiate a peace treaty with the Soviet Union.

There could be no time for diplomatic niceties. Horthy must be got rid of and troops sent into Hungary. Among them would be SS troops.

Above all, there would be 3rd SS-Panzer Division Totenkopf.

It was true that Hitler's faith in the legacy of Theodor Eicke had been severely dented by the final loss of Kharkov, but he had by no means lost confidence in Totenkopf or the essential dependability of Leibstandarte and Das Reich.

When the supreme melodramatic gesture was called for, few figures were better suited than Hitler's fellow Austrian, Sturmbannfuehrer Otto Skorzeny, an enthusiastic thug who had already distinguished himself with a daring commando and glider raid that in September 1943 had snatched the deposed Mussolini from a mountaintop prison.

Although Skorzeny had a job in the Reich Security Office (RSHA — Reichssicherheitshauptamt) which controlled the Gestapo, Himmler had no love for this unscrupulous freebooter who was nicknamed 'Scarface'. Skorzeny was a renowned womaniser, drinker and (the Reichsfuehrer-SS shuddered) heavy smoker.

Himmler exploded: 'The man is nothing but a gangster.'

Hitler agreed. But he saw only the man's propensity for ruthless action. It was to Skorzeny that he turned for the successful prosecution of an extraordinary Hungarian adventure.

Stuck away with Heydrich's thugs, Skorzeny had been largely isolated from the real world. He knew that Germany's plight was dire, certainly. But the appalling truth only came home to him when on 18 September he received the summons to the Wolfsschanze from General Jodl.

There would, Jodl intimated pompously, be discussions on grand strategy. These would broaden Skorzeny's mind for the operation in which the Fuehrer wished to interest him.

Grand strategy! The reports from the front spelt out the relevance of *that*. The situation in the west was black. As for the Russian front, it was catastrophic. Finland had just gone. The Baltic states had been eliminated. Army Group Centre? Its effectiveness could justifiably be likened to a deflated paper bag. The Russians had punched through four hundred miles of it in a month. Rumania? The oilfields could be forgotten. Bulgaria was as good as lost. In Yugoslavia, Tito's partisans had joined hands with the Reds.

And yet, Skorzeny reflected, the charade at Wolfsschanze was played out twice daily. There was the long table in the map-room with the stool that Hitler scarcely ever used. There were the arrays of freshly sharpened coloured pencils, clutched by the supreme commander, who called on his slender reserves and switched his thinning forces.

But it was the talk of the generals that made Skorzeny's blood run cold. There was airy mention of infantry divisions and army corps. There was an almost mystical dependence on flags pinned on situation maps. These represented only a few hundred men, when they should have spelt manpower in thousands.

Occasionally, there were diversions. Hitler would burst into one of his screaming tantrums. The coloured pencils would be cast to the floor. Then would come the accusations of treachery. The biggest row developed when Hitler discovered that strenuous efforts had been made to keep news of the Warsaw Uprising from him, at a time when it looked as if the Poles were winning. But Hitler had found out and raised a storm.

So this was the power-house of the greatest military machine the world had ever known! After a number of these farces, with their revelations of the Fuehrer's rampant instability, Skorzeny began to wonder what on earth he was doing there.

At last, one evening Hitler gave him a sign to stay on after the briefing. Keitel, Jodl, Ribbentrop and Himmler settled uneasily into armchairs. Hitler began, predictably enough, with a lecture incorporating a diatribe.

'Gentleman, I have news for you. I thought it impossible that anyone could surpass the generals when it came to stupidity. I was wrong. The diplomats have gone one better. They have been unable to save Hungary from going over to the other side.

'She was my last remaining ally. These so-called diplomats can be proud of themselves. They have probably lost me the war.'

The mood changed. Hungary might yet be saved. It was a vital source of grain, of oil and bauxite. But, more to the point, if it fell that would be the end of seventy divisions. They would be cut off from the main battle-front. The path would be open to the relief of Italy and Greece. Occupied Europe would follow. Within a month, there would be nothing to do but slit one's throat.

Hitler proclaimed: 'The only hope is in the SS. The fighting divisions can hold the Russians there.

'But before that can be done, the SS has yet another role. And that brings me to you, Skorzeny.'

So that was it! A one-man 'fire brigade' for the SS divisions!

But *Hungary*? Why should the Fuehrer be so worried about Hungary? Her armies were fighting bitterly in the

Carpathians, buttressed by a million Germans. Between them they held a mountain chain which had kept out invaders down the centuries. Why should Hungary fall?

Hitler seemed to read his thoughts. He explained: 'Germany is being betrayed. Admiral Horthy is a traitor who has been trafficking with the enemy.

'I happen to know that he went first to the British. They had no interest in Hungary, particularly as the Red Army was threatening the country. He was told to try Moscow.

'If he succeeds in throwing them Budapest, that seals the doom of Vienna and Berlin.'

The clutch of sycophants in their armchairs would never have dreamed of approaching the map-table without permission. Skorzeny had no such inhibitions. He strode across and leant over the detailed display of southern Europe. There was an arc of flags stuck there, but they were Russian, not German. Each one stood for a Russian army. They were clustered like flies beside the horseshoe contours representing the country's eastern border.

One hundred and twenty enemy divisions along the Carpathians. One hundred and twenty divisions which in a vast tidal wave could surge over the Danubian plain. The Germans would be trounced where they stood.

Hitler's voice broke in on Skorzeny's thoughts: 'You, Skorzeny, will deal with this Admiral Horthy.'

The Mussolini affair had entailed snatching the Duce from a remote Alpine peak. This time the job would have to be right in the heart of Budapest, at Castle Hill. Here, the Regent would be snatched and his government overturned.

Hitler added: 'Don't imagine that you can just walk in there and arrest him. Horthy has been suspicious ever since that business with Mussolini. He is heavily guarded.

'No half measures will do. The castle must be taken by storm.'

General Jodl was speaking now. 'The Fuehrer is in favour of an airborne attack. For this the General Staff will furnish a glider squadron, two paratroop battalions and a crack battalion of officer cadets.

'You will be given a special plane of the Fuehrer's Squadron.'

Skorzeny was disconcerted by a sudden switch in Hitler's mood. He no longer seemed interested in any further discussion. There was a far-away look in those piercing eyes, which were now scanning the maps. Almost absently, Hitler handed Skorzeny a large crackling sheet of Third Reich official stationery bearing the eagle and the Swastika in gilt relief in the left-hand corner. There was the legend *Fuehrer and Chancellor of the Reich*.

The order was in Hitler's lurching, spidery hand. Skorzeny made out:

'Sturmbannfuehrer Skorzeny of the Reserve Corps has been charged directly by myself to execute personal and confidential orders of the highest importance. I request all military and civilian services to bring all possible help to Sturmbannfuehrer Skorzeny and to comply with all his wishes.'

Skorzeny barely had time to take in this all-embracing *Befehl* before he was hustled out of the Wolfsschanze — which seemed to suggest that Hitler had endured his presence long enough.

It was only then that the magnitude of his task hit Skorzeny. With the Mussolini rescue, he had been faced with a broken, dispirited man guarded by a knot of fellow Italians of dubious loyalty. But *this*!

Admiral Horthy ruled the eastern marches of the former Austro-Hungarian empire as the heir to the Hapsburgs. Horthy, it was said, coveted the Iron Crown of Hungary.

Skorzeny was not over-awed by titles, royal or otherwise. It was the power involved in Horthy's position which interested him. And that power was considerable. It enabled Horthy to be protected like a medieval monarch. Ministers, guards and troops cocooned him on

217

the heights of Castle Hill which dominated all Budapest.

With a grim smile, Otto Skorzeny remembered how in his student days he had pottered around the ramparts of the castle, guidebook in hand.

Now he was going back. And, what was more, he would take a guidebook with him.

19

Clad in an expensive business-suit, Dr Solar Wolff, representative of a firm of machine-tool makers from Cologne, stepped off the airliner at Budapest airport and was wafted through the streets to the discreet private house where rooms had been booked for him.

Dr Wolff was by no means averse to the sort of hotel luxury currently being enjoyed by senior German officers, but he felt this might make him unduly conspicuous. It would be embarrassing if some friendly colleague suddenly appeared and insisted on pumping the hand of Otto Skorzeny.

Dr Wolff's business in the matter of machine-tools was despatched remarkably quickly. Now was the time to go out with guidebook in hand and explore old haunts. The air was particularly pleasant on the summit of Castle Hill, known as the Burgberg.

It was not just the castle which interested the amiable doctor. He seemed equally entranced by the houses, embassies, ministries and garrison quarters for troops. The latter stood out, which was understandable since extensive quarters were needed to house the soldiers who stuffed the streets, and sentries who manned the well-sited guns.

The visitor from Germany took in the castle itself, which overhung the Danube. The standard of the Hungarian Hapsburgs flew from it; the Regent was at home.

Dr Wolff continued to smile at everyone in friendly fashion as he scaled the Burgberg. Inwardly, though, Sturmbannfuehrer Otto Skorzeny was prey to the most gloomy thoughts.

It was only too clear that an assault force would be butchered on its way up. Siege artillery? Hungarians firing on Germans? That could benefit no one but the Russians. Airborne troops? They were all very well in theory, but where could they land? The only possible open space turned out to be ringed with buildings. Sustained fire from these could wipe the lot out before they managed to shed their parachutes. Skorzeny noticed from his guidebook that this open space was known as 'The Field of Blood'. How appropriate!

He decided to leave the matter of the assault method for the moment and concentrate instead on the activities of Admiral Horthy.

The first thing he learnt was that the Regent lived, not in the castle, but in a well guarded and luxurious government building known as the Citadel. Not that this made much difference: an aerial assault was plainly out of the question.

But would Hitler see it that way? The Fuehrer was anxious to get the whole business over swiftly so that his SS divisions could snatch their glory.

Skorzeny returned to his rooms and immediately began secret discussions with those in the know — German diplomats from Castle Hill, military and intelligence chiefs, and Hungarian spies in the pay of the Nazis. He urged them: 'If any order comes to attack the Burgberg and occupy the Citadel we've got to resist it. The result would be a massacre.'

Hitler, it soon turned out, was thinking on even less subtle lines. The Fuehrer promptly sent to Budapest what he plainly regarded as a rare present for Skorzeny — SS-Obergruppenfuehrer Erich von dem Bach-Zelewski. The Obergruppenfuehrer, not without justification, considered himself to be an expert in anti-partisan operations. He had been particularly admired by Hitler for his brutally effective handling of the Warsaw Uprising. He brought with him a giant 650 mm mortar.

With a schoolboy enthusiasm, Bach-Zelewski told Skorzeny: 'With what I've got, I could blow the Citadel off the hill.'

It was an awkward predicament for Skorzeny. He was, after all, in the presence of a senior officer. But he nevertheless insisted: 'Only as a last resort.'

The use of such a weapon would be sheer madness; it would let the Russians in. The SS divisions would be at the mercy of the Russian Fortieth Army, the Seventh Guards Army, and the Twenty-seventh Army, which were poised to attack from the Debrecen area. This took no account of the Soviet Sixth Tank Army already fighting German and Hungarian troops in the Turda region. From the town of Arad, the Fifty-third Army of General I.M. Managarov was also advancing. The defection of any Hungarian troops would spell the end.

To the cynical Skorzeny it did not seem in the long run to make much difference whether the Regent signed an agreement with the Allies, or the Russians took over Hungary. The result would be the same for Germany, but it was clearly necessary to see this farce through to the end. Hitler seemed determined that his precious SS divisions should have their moment of glory when it came to the scrap.

Events appeared to be moving fast. On 22 September, Colonel-General Nadai, a representative of the Hungarian government, flew to Naples. The object was a meeting with the British and American representatives. It was obvious what had been discussed. Hungary would be occupied by Britain and the United States and then turned over to the Russians.

As it turned out, the meeting ended in failure. Not that this was much consolation to Hitler. A few days later, a delegation of Hungarians flew to Moscow to see if they could come to an accommodation with Stalin.

Such a mission looked like succeeding, particularly when Skorzeny managed to lay hands on a copy of a letter sent to General Bela Miklos, commander of the First Hungarian Army. It was from Hungarian prisoners of war in the Soviet Union. It urged Miklos:

'Abandon the Germans! Join with the Soviet Union in attacking the Wehrmacht. The defeat of Nazi Germany, militarily and politically, is only a matter of time. Every other satellite except Hungary has already broken with Hitler.'

The news from the south-eastern front was grim confirmation. Hitler had pinned faith in thirty Rumanian and Bulgarian divisions. He could do so no longer; they had turned against him. If the Hungarian armies changed sides, then the front would collapse beyond a doubt.

Something, no matter how desperate, had to be done.

One thing particularly puzzled Skorzeny. Subtlety was not his strong point. He expected men to behave consistently, and when they failed he was worried. Admiral Horthy, Regent of Hungary, worried him mightily. After all, here was an autocrat who had seized power from the *Communists* in 1919. He had ruled his country with a rod of iron ever since. Why on earth, then, was he so keen to sell out to Stalin, of all people?

Skorzeny decided to find out all he could about the enigmatic Regent. The source of his information was Edmund Veesenmayer, the Reich's plenipotentiary in Hungary and one of Foreign Minister Ribbentrop's most ardent lapdogs.

Veesenmayer told Skorzeny: 'You shouldn't be paying so much attention to the old man. The key could well be his son Nicholas.'

Skorzeny was taken aback. Nicholas or, as he was generally know, Miki? The son was in his thirties and generally regarded as a playboy leaping nimbly between the bars and beds of high-society Budapest. It was agreed that as far as politics were concerned, he was a mere innocent.

Veesenmayer commented grimly: 'As such, he's perfect prey for the Russians. Our information is that he has been told that his father's dynasty could survive perfectly well inside a Russian bear-hug. What we don't know is whether or not he has risen to the bait.'

All too soon there were signs that he had done precisely that. There was news of a meeting between Miki and representatives of the Yugoslav partisan chief Tito. The role of the latter, it was widely believed, was as a go-between for Stalin.

It still seemed incredible to Skorzeny when he recalled the young, dark-haired and almost ludicrously handsome Miki. Then he remembered that Horthy's oldest son Istvan had been killed when his aircraft was shot down on the Russian front. After that, the Admiral had transferred all his affection to the younger boy. And there was evidence from Ribbentrop's men of previous meetings with Tito.

The son! Why bother with snatching the father when an adored boy was to hand? A single hint that the precious Miki was undergoing the fond attentions of the Gestapo might very well be enough to bring this tiresome Regent round to the Fuehrer's way of thinking.

It was worth a try.

If Skorzeny had not been in possession of definite proof of the meetings with Tito, he might still have hesitated to believe in treachery by Miki Horthy, who presumably had his followers. Hungarians and Germans continued to meet daily on the Burgberg. The German Embassy occupied a place of honour among the government palaces; the glittering dinners with their fulsome assurances of German victory continued. The railway yards at Budapest were still noisy with German rolling-stock trundling up to the Carpathians to feed the divisions.

Yet Skorzeny had to acknowledge that behind the face of public friendship, the Hungarians were preparing to sell out.

Very well then. If anyone still doubted Miki Horthy's links with Tito, there was only one way to convince them. The 'crown prince' must be caught red-handed and his treachery exposed.

Skorzeny got wind of a meeting proposed for Sunday,

18 October. Its location was the second floor of a building near the Danube. It seemed logical that Miki Horthy would be well protected; it would be useful to have some muscle about.

Skorzeny stationed his officers in a rented apartment on the third floor of the building. Others were positioned within a comfortable distance of the front entrance. A passer-by might wonder why there were some men patrolling in the uniform of the German Army Feld-gendarmen (Military Police), but apart from that, everything appeared normal.

There was nothing suspicious either about the Mercedes which drove past the building with a respectable civilian businessman at the wheel. The businessman carried proof that he was Dr Solar Wolff from Cologne and had a perfectly innocuous dinner date ahead of him.

Skorzeny reflected that it was indeed comforting to have a good cover story when before you was parked a suspicious-looking truck with a heavy canvas cover tied securely in place. Suddenly, it became desperately important to find out what was behind that tarpaulin.

Dr Wolff appeared to be having trouble with the Mercedes, which had stalled. Cursing, he managed to restart it and propel it slowly to a parking place. Then he climbed out of the driving-seat, wandered round to the front and lifted the bonnet.

He did not dare chance even a single look at the building. But he did risk a glance at the truck. It was worth it. The sound of the bonnet being lifted had been too much for the soldiers stuffed in the truck. Skorzeny caught a brief sight of them — and their machine-guns — before the canvas was replaced. Evidently, they were satisfied that he was merely some stupid civilian in difficulty with his car.

He continued tinkering with the car, at the same time taking in the other Hungarian troops trying to look inconspicuous further up the street.

Incredibly, he had been outside the building less than five minutes. Now the seconds were ticking away to the scheduled time for the attack.

Skorzeny tried to envisage what was going on inside the building. In the minutes before the attack, the commandos in the apartment above Horthy and the Yugoslavs had been instructed to make their way as quietly as possible to the secret meeting-place.

The driver of the Mercedes shut the bonnet, but instead of going back to his seat he began walking towards the building. As he did so, a number of commandos playing at being Feldgendarmen walked towards him.

But the Hungarians in the truck were already suspicious and they had thrown back the tarpaulin and were standing with their weapons at the ready. The ensuing fire felled one of the commandos.

That inevitably attracted the attention of the Hungarians further down the street. Skorzeny put his whistle to his mouth and blew furiously; it was the signal for the other commandos to join the action.

The firepower increased in fury. Nobody relished a clash more than Skorzeny but he had no intention of being mown down before the day's business had even begun. He darted back behind the Mercedes, later recalling that the sounds of bullets piercing doors and shattering the windscreen were among the most unpleasant of his life.

He risked putting his head up once and was rewarded with the sight of three Germans attempting to despatch the Hungarians' truck with pistol shots. Pistols against machine-guns! Something dramatic would have to happen before long.

The Hungarians had left the truck by now, but instead of storming the building they headed for next door. That too was full of Hungarian troops, extra forces Skorzeny had not reckoned on.

Plainly, Miki Horthy was not such a nonentity after all.

Skorzeny stood up, conscious that one of his commandos was lying next to him. He snatched a grenade from the man, hurled it towards the Hungarians and yelled: 'Don't let them get into the open.'

Skorzeny's aim was just about perfect. The portal of the building was of solid marble. Down it crashed, slicing into the Hungarian troops below. Brickbats and solid concrete did everything that could be expected of them.

A knot of prisoners was struggling downstairs. The Germans on the top floor had done their work well. One of them told Skorzeny breathlessly: 'We stormed in and nabbed the lot.'

Miki Horthy was beside himself with rage, screaming vengeance.

There had, Skorzeny reasoned, been quite enough noise already. Any more commotion could alert other Hungarian troops, and the mission might yet fail. It was vital to remove the enraged young Horthy from the scene.

Skorzeny glanced into the hall of the apartment. The very thing! A heavy Persian rug was snatched up, a rope tugged from a curtain. In no time at all, Miki Horthy, son of the Regent of Hungary, the would-be saviour of his country from the Nazi menace, was trussed up like a chicken and slung into a lorry.

Skorzeny shouted: 'Get to the airport — and fast — I'll follow.' He turned to the rest of the troops, nodding his thanks with a wide grin. 'Sorry, boys, no more shooting.'

It proved a tough job keeping up with the lorry containing Miki. Skorzeny was fearful that the speed of both vehicles was attracting undue attention.

He was right. Suddenly, a company of Hungarian troops was making its way towards them at the double. Skorzeny also noted that three other companies were in line behind him. These must be more of Horthy's reinforcements. What had kept them?

There was no time to ponder that now. It would look odd, arguing with a Hungarian commander while wearing civilian clothes, but the risk must be taken. The Hungarians had to be prevented at all costs from getting to the scene of the shooting. Skorzeny's remaining commandos ran the risk of being annihilated.

He told the baffled commander: 'There's been some

quite heavy shooting going on and a lot of confusion. I think you had better check before going any further.'

The Hungarian commander was puzzled. With puzzlement came hesitation. Skorzeny pushed his luck right to the edge: 'I suggest you telephone headquarters for further orders.'

As the officer walked off, Skorzeny shot the Mercedes forward. Then his stomach was lurching anew. Where was the truck with Miki Horthy? Skorzeny kept going in what he thought was the direction of the airport. To his intense relief, he spotted his quarry ahead.

There was fresh anxiety as the carpet was hauled towards the aircraft. Not unnaturally, its prisoner was struggling furiously. It only needed some zealous airport official to start asking questions for the whole thing to be ruined.

But eventually the cargo was in place and Skorzeny ordered: 'Get him to Vienna as fast as possible.'

He went back to the Mercedes, suddenly drained of all energy and all interest. The Fuehrer wanted a Hungary loyal to Germany so that together they could beat the Soviets with the aid of his pet Waffen-SS divisions.

Only time would tell if this Hollywood-style caper — it had been code-named 'Operation Mickey Mouse' — had been anything like successful.

At German Army headquarters Skorzeny allowed himself the luxury of a bath and a rest, but he kept his ear firmly cocked for the telephone. An embassy contact was to ring him at the first sign of any developments, good or bad.

Eventually, the instrument jangled. The informant said: 'It's impossible to move from here. The hill is ringed with troops, barricaded and mined. The military attaché tried to get down to the town and was turned back. He was told Germany was guilty of an "unfriendly act".'

Skorzeny cursed. So the old man had not caved in; all that had happened was that the hive of bees had been turned over and was buzzing furiously. It was not his fault. He had carried out the suggestions of Ribbentrop's sidekicks. The politicians, as usual, had miscalculated. Well, what now?

Skorzeny switched on the radio. At 2 p.m., Admiral Horthy himself was on the air, delivering a long, rambling tirade against the Germans who had kidnapped his son. Then with the air of a man who has got a long-standing grudge off his chest, Horthy went on to announce in measured terms:

'It is clear today that Germany has lost the war. . . Hungary had accordingly concluded a preliminary armistice with Russia and will cease all hostilities against her. I have issued the corresponding orders to the military command.'

One phrase struck Skorzeny as odd. What was meant by 'a preliminary armistice'? Either there was an armistice or there was not; a qualification was obvious nonsense. A quick check was made: no signals had been sent by the Hungarian War Office to the Russians. A radio statement was not an order. Confused at the lack of direction, the Hungarian forces were slow to lay down their arms, even after General Miklos, Horthy's Commander-in-Chief, had successfully crossed into the Soviet lines.

Skorzeny's instinct was to press the advantage immediately. He saw the solution in characteristically lurid terms; the Burgberg must be stormed at once. German officers were sent to countermand Horthy's orders to surrender. The Hungarians were now in a state of utter bewilderment and it was a fairly simple matter for Army Group South to take over all Hungarian troop operations. Hitler declared: 'The Regent must be made to change his mind. It is up to you Skorzeny to handle the matter immediately.'

At this point Skorzeny found himself with a rival. The tireless Bach-Zelewski was keen to grab for himself any glory that was going. Surely now was a first-rate opportunity for using his pet mortar. He urged: 'Give me a free hand and I'll blast the castle to powder.'

Still Skorzeny held firm. He snapped: 'Can't you see that is just the way to send Hungary straight into the Soviet camp? We want to seduce her back, not force her so crudely.'

The SS freebooter decided to try the kid-glove approach. At least at first. A messenger was despatched to Admiral Horthy. The Regent was told that if he resigned and transferred power legally to Ferenc Szalasi, the Hungarian Fascist leader, and agreed to go into exile, Miki would be returned to him and he would be given refuge in Austria. If he refused, then the Citadel on the Burgberg would be attacked at six o'clock the following morning.

Nothing as unsubtle as a head-on assault was contemplated. One group of forces would gradually surround the hill as if the intention was merely a bloodless siege. Two battalions would move in along the western slopes. Horthy would be mystified as to just where the main attack was intended.

As for that, Skorzeny himself would be where he was happiest — in the lead and in the thick of it. The assault would have a suitably lurid code-name, 'Bazooka'.

There were those who doubted that Skorzeny's talent for boy-scout melodrama was exactly what was wanted to bring the Hungarians to heel. Predictably, Bach-Zelewski saw his own place in the limelight ebbing away.

Arguments for and against Bazooka were interrupted by an approach from a Hungarian intermediary. The man's tone was reasonable. Simply because Hungary was seeking a peaceful accommodation with Russia, there was no need for relations with Germany to become overstrained.

Skorzeny was icy. 'Why,' he asked, 'are our diplomats penned up on the Burgberg? Why can't they come down into the town? Don't you respect diplomatic privilege?'

It was nothing short of monstrous, isolating an ambassador and his staff by force. There was a reasonable case, surely, for at least clearing the mines from Vienna Road, which the German ambassador used.

Skorzeny pressed on. 'It is clearly ridiculous to mine and barricade a road always protected by crossfire. The garrison is bristling with guns. There must be a give-and-take in this business.'

The Hungarian wavered. Now he could think of nothing more to say beyond a placatory comment that nobody wanted to fall foul of the Germans, provided they kept the peace.

What in fact the Hungarian did not know — could not know — was that whether or not the relevant road was mined scarcely mattered. Goliath tanks, newly arrived from the Reich, would spearhead the drive up the road. They had the supreme advantage of being remote-controlled vehicles ideal for exploding mines ahead of advancing troops. On the other hand, it would be a shame to waste these brilliant examples of German technology on unmined roads!

The envoy departed unhappily. Skorzeny began planning the order of march on Vienna Road.

He, of course, would lead the drive up the hill himself in a small truck. The Goliaths would be positioned along with regular tanks at an interval behind the truck. The rest of the commandos would follow the tanks.

There was a strong risk, of course. By keeping the Goliaths behind there was every likelihood of the first Hungarian machine-gun nest slaughtering Skorzeny and everyone in the truck.

Skorzeny's argument to his critics was: 'Horthy is still wavering. If he fires on German troops that is the end of Hitler's support. He can still save face if he wants to change his mind about deserting to the Russians.

'I believe he is still bluffing and hasn't finally made up his mind.'

It was an appalling risk. Even if the Germans were allowed to travel unimpeded along Vienna Road they could still be led into a trap. And, of course, there was no guarantee that the mines had been removed.

Nevertheless, it was a gamble that Skorzeny felt worth taking. At just before six o'clock, the snarl of tank engines sliced into the morning air. Skorzeny, in full SS uniform, stood upright in the truck.

He raised his hand and swept it forward. Bazooka was under way.

Mines presented the main hazard on that first lap where the road soared to the Vienna Gate. Any moment, Skorzeny braced himself for the sort of explosion which, he had heard, did not always lead to a quick death. Men could either be blown to pieces immediately or propelled into the air as if from a giant fist. Then their still-conscious bodies would crash to earth, their spinal columns cracked like snapped matches.

Fifty yards, one hundred yards. He stood defiant, ramrod to attention, rather as a brave man might face a firing-squad. Nothing happened. The mines had been removed. Ahead lay the barricades.

The Hungarian sentries moved into the middle of the road and Skorzeny knew that the test had come. Maybe it would be sensible to drop speed just a little. And there would be no harm in politeness. He saluted and flashed a friendly smile. The mesmerised Hungarians returned the greeting.

The roar behind Skorzeny seemed deafening. An age appeared to stretch by before the entire column was through. Every minute of it, Skorzeny had the fear that the Hungarians might change their minds, that there might be telephone instructions.

He concentrated on the clear road ahead. Soon the whole contingent was climbing; below them lay the roofs and tree-tops of sleeping Budapest.

Soon the dour squat shape of the castle barracks was in view.

This was tempting fate with a vengeance. Here were sand-bagged emplacements and men with machine-guns at the ready. They only had to fire once for upwards of a thousand troops to come tumbling out of the barracks and bring the whole elaborate charade to an end.

With supreme insouciance, Skorzeny threw another smart salute. There was no shooting. Clearly, the guards recognised that troops allowed through the Vienna Gate were on lawful business.

The need for bluff was over now. The truck was roaring at speed, catapulting along the mile-long avenue which led past the German Embassy. Half the column was stuck with Skorzeny. The rest peeled off to take a second avenue leading to the Citadel. The Ministry of War, crammed with a thousand more men, was behind Skorzeny. He was more worried about the yawning gap represented by the square in front of the Citadel. This was the worst position of all; not a vestige of cover and, what was more, three heavy Hungarian tanks. The guns turned upwards at the first sight of Skorzeny's tornado.

Instructions given to the raiders at preliminary briefings had been clear; no matter what, keep going. The truck swerved and weaved to make a harder target. Behind it, a Panther crashed through the rampart of building-blocks which had been assembled hastily at the Citadel's entrance.

Six succeeding tanks faced an additional hazard: six anti-tank guns guarded the palace. They were ignored. Skorzeny leapt from the truck, streaking towards an archway into the building. At that moment, the alarm screeched, alerting the colonel of the guard, who leapt forward, pistol at the ready.

The weapon was smashed out of the man's hand and he was thrust aside. To a second officer, Skorzeny shouted: 'Come with me. This is an emergency. I have to see the Commandant at once.'

The officer shrugged. No member of the Admiral's entourage seemed capable of giving a coherent order any longer, but this one at least was clear. The Hungarian led the way up a marble staircase, followed by Skorzeny.

Never before in his career had the Commandant spent so bewildering a few minutes. First his peace had been shattered by the roar of trucks in the square below. How they had managed to get so far unchallenged was a mystery. He had no time to reason it out because the door had been flung open to frame a gigantic SS man whose face was bisected by a livid scar which gave him a dauntingly piratical appearance. Like a man in a dream, the Commandant allowed his own pistol to be taken from him and flung into the courtyard below.

The SS-Sturmbannfuehrer was speaking in German, which was flattering because it assumed the other man was educated enough to understand him. The tone was courteous but firm. Skorzeny said: 'You must understand that the whole of the Burgberg is now in German hands. I have enough men to withstand any assault from Vienna Road. Further bloodshed will do no one any good. Please order me to call off my men.'

Nothing altered the tone of sweet reasonableness, but Skorzeny raised his pistol a few inches. The Commandant contented himself with a rueful nod. Skorzeny instructed an aide: 'The firing is to cease immediately.'

The pistol was returned to its holster. Skorzeny stepped forward and shook the disconsolate Commandant's hand vigorously. He assured him: 'It's a humane decision. I would like, if I may, to borrow two of your officers.'

Skorzeny framed the request as if asking a favour. It was tactful, but it did not deceive the Commandant for one moment. He knew that he had received an order, and one that should be obeyed quickly.

Two Hungarian majors were summoned. Skorzeny explained: 'You are my liaison officers from now on. I would like you to go down into the courtyard and pile up your soldiers' arms.'

Was there any way in which magnanimity could be extended? There was. Skorzeny added: 'Officers may, of course, keep their revolvers.'

He turned back to the Commandant. In the same vein, he added: 'It is necessary, you understand, for me to speak to the Regent. Could you take me to his quarters, please?'

It might have been imagination, but Skorzeny fancied that a ghost of a smile flitted across the Commandant's face. Nevertheless, the latter looked impassive as he led his giant visitor down the corridor to the Regent's apartment and opened the door.

The room was empty.

The Commandant said gravely: 'I must inform you

that the Regent left the Citadel a few minutes before six this morning. He has placed himself under the protection of Gruppenfuehrer Pfeffer-Wildenbruch in this city.'

Skorzeny heaved a sigh of relief. At least the Admiral was, so to speak, still in the family. Gruppenfuehrer Karl Pfeffer-Wildenbruch was the Waffen-SS Commander in Budapest. What to do now? Skorzeny, after telephoning the SS headquarters and verifying that the Regent was indeed there, telexed Hitler at the Wolfsschanze.

The reply was: *'Skorzeny will take up residence in the Citadel and command the Regent's residence until further notice.'*

It provided a relaxing interlude, but plainly one that could not last. Skorzeny allowed himself three days' rest before driving back along Vienna Road to be presented formally to the vanquished admiral at the house of Gruppenfuehrer Pfeffer-Wildenbruch. There it was explained to Horthy that Hitler had ordered him to be sent under safe conduct with 'guest of honour' status to Hirschberg Castle in Bavaria. It was, Skorzeny explained blandly, a very secure castle indeed.

On his last drive through his capital, Horthy received scarcely a sign of recognition. He left behind him a pro-German puppet government — and, of paramount importance to Hitler, Hungarian military forces still fighting side by side with the Germans.

Otto Skorzeny had secured Hungary for Adolf Hitler. It was to be saved, the Fuehrer had convinced himself, by his SS divisions.

Skorzeny had paved the way for the last offensive of 3rd SS-Panzer Division Totenkopf.

20

Hungarians, vainly hoping to snatch a little seasonal relief from a bewildering war which so divided their loyalties, crowded the streets of Buda, in the western part of the city.

It was Christmas Eve 1944, but it was not bright lights or gaily decorated shops that held the attention.

That was focussed on tanks. And not Hitler's, either. They bore a red star on their turrets. The Russians had arrived!

The puppet regime installed by Hitler under the direction of Ferenc Szalasi, a former major of the Hungarian general staff, proved totally unable to stabilise the country. To stem the Russian steamroller proved impossible, given the puny strength of the German forces.

The Christmas shoppers in Buda had scattered in panic at the first sight of the tanks.

Soon trapped in the city were fifty thousand men of the 9th SS-Corps, including 8th SS-Kavallerie Division Florian Geyer and 22nd SS-Freiwilligen-Kavallerie Division, under the command of Obergruppenfuehrer Pfeffer-Wildenbruch.

This seasoned veteran of the very first armed SS divisions back in the miracle days of 1939 now had the sole responsibility of keeping the T-34s from rumbling across the Danube.

In the western part of the city, the men of the SS-Totenkopf and their comrades in Viking were poised to break through. It was a crucial operation for unhappy Herbert Gille with his command of 4th SS-Panzer Corps.

Gille had been yanked at speed out of the fighting in

Warsaw. Then had come the speedy shuttle by train —
through Prague, Vienna and Bratislava to Komarno in
western Hungary.

By 11 February 1945, Pfeffer-Wildenbruch knew that
the relief offensive had crumbled. Unless he moved fast,
the sure result was destruction.

He evolved a plan to smash through the Red ring of
steel gripping the city. It was hasty improvisation; there
had been no time for planning, no time for security.

The Russians opened up with their rocket artillery; the
infantry moved in for the slaughter. Within minutes, most
members of the breakout force were dead. The Hungarians began deserting in droves to the Russians — they had
little choice. As for the men of the SS, they received the
sort of treatment which they had meted out to others.
Many prisoners were stripped naked in the freezing cold
and shot.

Pfeffer-Wildenbruch was captured. Of his 70,000 men,
a mere 785 reached the German lines. The Russians were
masters of Budapest.

Yet Hitler refused to give up. The year was still young,
he proclaimed, there could be a complete reversal of
Germany's sagging fortunes.

But what of SS-Totenkopf Division? The luckless Gille
had advanced a few miles; then came the full fury of an
assault by Soviet Fourth Guards and Sixth Guards Tank
Armies. Advance, when such a thing was impossible,
amounted to little more than a mile a day. Eventually, the
losses were so severe that the relief attempt was postponed.

In the Ardennes the situation was hopeless and Hitler
knew it. Pride and optimism however had prevented him
from admitting it until 8 January 1945. He pulled Sixth
Panzer Army out of the offensive. Its four Panzer divisions and 1st and 2nd Panzer Corps were to be refitted.

Hitler had returned by now to Berlin from Adlerhorst,
the western headquarters at Bad Nauheim, from where
he had directed the operations in the Ardennes.

In vain Guderian entreated Hitler to forget Hungary
and transfer forces from the west to smash the Red army

on the Oder. But Hitler desperately wanted a prestige victory, and his frank acknowledgement of this made Guderian and other senior officers sweat.

Was the Fuehrer bent on yet another obstinate adventure which would finish them all?

It seemed so. The Fuehrer remained mesmerised by Hungary. Guderian protested vehemently. It was no use. Hitler, as his premier tank theorist put it, 'reaffirmed his intention to attack in Hungary, to throw the Russians back across the Danube and to relieve Budapest.'

. It was not merely a question of Hungary being the latest in the woefully long list of Adolf Hitler's obsessions. He was forced to mount an offensive there along the Oder by the sheer pressure of events which he could not wish out of existence.

By January 1945, Allied bombings had destroyed by far the greater part of Germany's synthetic oil plants. All that remained for the fuel-starved Wehrmacht were the wells at Zisterdorf in Austria and around Lake Balaton in Hungary. By the start of 1945, supplies of motor fuel were 28 per cent down on the previous August. Aviation fuel supplies had dwindled by a horrific 94 per cent.

Throughout the campaign in the east and latterly in the Ardennes, Hitler had pinned his faith on the always dependable Waffen-SS. But now, it seemed, even the black-and-silver paladins of the Thousand-Year Reich could do little for him. It was all very well for Himmler to comment grandly: 'So far the Waffen-SS has never under any circumstances caused disappointment and it will not — even under the most severe hardships to come — disappoint in the future.'

But the resources were not there; and Hitler suspected that even the will to fight had become gradually dissipated, probably from the time of the major débâcle at Kursk.

Still there were false dawns; any recovery was comparable to that of a dying man who, to the astonishment of those around his deathbed, suddenly exhibits symptoms of recovery, only to relapse within hours.

There had been one such moment back on 11 January

which had led to an over-enthusiastic Hitler awarding Pfeffer-Wildenbruch the Knight's Cross.

Army Group South had lain in a vast arc west of the Danube with its boundaries extending from the Drau River to Lake Balaton. Then the lines had swung westwards to the Vertes mountains and on to a bridgehead which the Red Army had established on the Danube's northern bank at Gran. Pfeffer-Wildenbruch's corps had, in five days, marched seventy miles over mountain roads and through snowdrifts to Lake Balaton's northern tip.

A fast push to Budapest had looked so possible then!

But now? There was Totenkopf and Viking, of course. but reports were soon reaching the Fuehrer that Obergruppenfuehrer Gille lacked the necessary experience to sustain a large-scale offensive. Even worse, there were signs that the man was in danger of losing his nerve.

In an act of defeatism completely out of character in a Totenkopf man, he had tried to persuade General Otto Woehler, the commander of Army Group South, to call off further attacks. From Russian prisoners he had learnt that the Russians had three thousand armoured vehicles in reserve. Totenkopf and Viking would be massacred by such a force; Woehler shrugged. He was a realist. He knew the war was lost, anyway. Let the SS obey orders for a change, even if it was for a suicide mission.

Gille was plainly no good. What Hitler needed was something infinitely more formidable. And he needed it fast.

If there was any figure left in the Waffen-SS comparable in stature to the late Theodor Eicke, it was another buccaneering veteran from the early days of street struggle, the charismatic Josef Dietrich, known affectionately by his men and friends as 'Sepp'.

Hitler had good reason to be grateful to Dietrich, the one-time tobacco factory foreman and petrol-pump attendant who had been instrumental in putting a bullet through Ernst Roehm.

Back in 1931 Dietrich had become an SS-Gruppenfuehrer and was given command of that most élite of SS formations, the Leibstandarte-SS Adolf Hitler, whose task was to act as personal bodyguard to the Fuehrer.

With the onset of war, Dietrich progressed to become one of the most highly decorated commanders of the German armed forces. From then on, awards came thick and fast: Knight's Cross in 1940, followed by the Oak Leaves in December of the following year. Those honours had been followed by the addition of Swords in March 1943, and finally Dietrich had joined the highly select group garlanded with Diamonds to the Knight's Cross.

Dietrich's degree of education and culture was roughly comparable to that of Theodor Eicke; in other words, he scarcely possessed any at all.

His beer-inflated frame was certainly substantial enough for a man bearing the imposing titles of Oberst-Gruppenfuehrer und Panzer Generaloberst der Waffen-SS. Dietrich, whose Sixth Panzer Army was ultimately to swallow Totenkopf for the fighting in Hungary, was essentially a soldier's soldier. Hitler proclaimed: 'I have always given him the opportunity to intervene in sore spots. He is a man who is simultaneously cunning, energetic and brutal. . .And what care he takes of his troops!'

It was to this former brawler of the Munich beer halls, who had started his military career as a trooper in 1st Uhlans under the Kaiser and ended it as commander of Sixth Panzer Army under Hitler, that the call came to plug the front in Hungary and, briefly, plot the destiny of Totenkopf.

These were indeed sorry days for the once so proud élite, young men with old faces who had been taught that the lands of the racially inferior Slavs were their own particular fiefdoms, almost of divine right. Totenkopf and Viking had dug in near Stuhlweissenburg, west of Budapest. Any attempt now to hold up the steamroller advance of the Soviet armies was fatuous. The scene was set for the death ride of 4th SS-Panzer Corps. The Soviet Twenty-sixth and Forty-sixth Armies sent the two German divisions reeling.

Though all reason told the commanders that resistance must ultimately be futile, they regrouped. They went on to slog it out under the cover of dense woods north of Lake Balaton.

Such glory as there was belonged entirely to Totenkopf, holding out against the probing attacks of the Soviets but wondering for just how long they could continue.

Hitler pinned his faith in Sepp Dietrich's Sixth SS-Panzer Army. The desperate shortage of fuel inevitably delayed Dietrich's arrival and the last of the divisions did not arrive from their whipping in the Ardennes until March.

Dietrich found awaiting him a plan with the grotesquely optimistic cover name of 'Fruehlingserwachen' ('Spring Awakening'). On 25 February, Hitler had said: 'I want the best sort of attack to get a big fast gain. The Russians have got to be thrown out of the oilfields along Lake Balaton and back across the Danube.'

Hitler's entourage as usual listened spellbound to its Fuehrer. No one dared ask the questions obvious to anyone who knew the weaknesses of the SS forces. Even if the Russians could be flung back — and it was a brave assumption — what resources were available to prevent their inevitable return?

What was particularly worrying to Hitler's advisers was that he seemed deaf to the intelligence reports that told him monotonously that the main bulk of the fighting would take place over marsh territory; the Panzers would wallow in the slime.

Hitler had learnt nothing from the previous winter offensive, which had ripped such a gap in the German defences and all but destroyed Army Group South. Here was the new obsession: the gap must be sealed. The supreme war-lord was proposing to do nothing but throw his forces into a giant mincing machine.

This did not mean that Allied Intelligence, both east and west, was not worried about Hitler's plans for Hungary. It was widely known that formidable SS support was on the way, but nobody knew precisely where it would strike.

To the worn-out veterans of Army Group South, the arrival of Dietrich's forces was like something out of a dream. All the rumours were that Germany was finished, that her armour was so much ironmongery and that there was scarcely enough fuel available to cross the Reich from one end to the other. But now, intent on helping to hold the fragile line west of the Danube, were trainloads of crack forces armed to the teeth with the most sophisticated weaponry.

It was all in fact cosmetic. Fresh-faced young men and good equipment there certainly were. But not enough of them; above all, not enough seasoned fighting talent. Still shell-shocked from the Ardennes offensive, many of the replacements for Sixth SS-Panzer Army were sailors and airmen lacking experience in land warfare.

Himmler had been forced to lay aside those simple, sunny Aryan dreams of happier times, it was more important now to keep up the numbers; the Waffen-SS was recruiting foreign riff-raff of even worse calibre than that once complained of by Eicke.

For the last time in this war, the SS was to go on the attack. Together with the 1st Panzer Army, Dietrich's 6th SS had the task of launching an attack from Lake Balaton, pushing forward to the Danube south of Budapest. Once there, it would split the Russian front in two. After that Dietrich would cross the Danube in a drive east.

Totenkopf and Viking, buttressed by 16th Panzer Grenadier Division Reichsfuehrer-SS, were up front. Motor-boat assault units arrowed across the Drau river. Here they came up against the imposing steel of 3rd Bulgarian Division, which clung tenaciously to the river line. The main thrust now was between Lake Balaton and Lake Velence. By 9 March the position of the Germans — including 4th SS-Panzer Corps and SS-Totenkopf — was looking good. A healthy hole appeared in the Russian lines. There had been an advance of around twenty miles.

First SS-Panzer Corps had been busy forcing bridge-heads across the Sio canal. It was here Hitler rued that he had not listened to his own intelligence reports. Even to contemplate a Panzer thrust in such mud was suicidal; not only was there no advance but tanks could be picked off at leisure by the Russians.

One of Sepp Dietrich's brightest protégés, Obersturm-bannfuehrer Jochen Peiper, had on 3 March stared gloomily at the proposed jumping-off point at the canal where, just to add to the difficulties, the rain was bucketing.

Peiper, described as 'one of the most dashing German officers of the war', a hero of the tank battles in Greece, the Soviet Union and the Ardennes, knew that the Tigers which had performed miracles elsewhere could not possibly get through this vast morass of thick mud stretching eastwards as far as the eye could see.

Heavy with sarcasm, he barked into the telephone to 1st SS-Corps Headquarters: 'What is this? I have tanks not submarines. An attack is out of the question.'

Army Group South was inflexible. The attack would go ahead, even though Dietrich knew well enough that there could be no sustained advance.

Tigers were a sheer waste of time in such circumstances. For this sort of war what was needed was plain old-fashioned infantry. But this was 1945 and such a commodity was in short supply.

A lot of it was lost in Hungary around Lake Balaton, in the death-throes of Hitler's war in the east. By the end of the first day's fighting for the Sio canal the advance had amounted to precisely two miles.

Officers had protested to Dietrich about the lunacy of the whole adventure. All he could do was reply cynically: 'We have to attack. If our vehicles can't reach the starting line in time, then we'll have to do it on foot.'

There were isolated gains. The towns of Simontornya and Ozora were prizes near the canal that the Soviets desperately wanted to snatch. Dietrich spurred along his old Leibstandarte colleagues. They romped ahead to seize Simontornya and make the canal bridgehead a reality.

Totenkopf's running mates from SS-Viking were in deep trouble at the town of Stuhlweissenburg. The order was not simply predictable but nonsensical: '*Stuhlweissenburg must be held at all costs*.' To obey would at least have settled one issue once and for all: the fate of SS-Viking. It would have been wiped off the earth. The order was given to evacuate Stuhlweissenburg.

By mid-March the Soviet offensive had reached a new ferocity. Totenkopf had expected that. There was no back-up. Supplies had dwindled to a trickle; the forward Grenadiers were bereft of fuel, ammunition and spares. These, including the severe losses, had reduced the total strength of the Panzer Army to 185 vehicles.

The blackest day for Totenkopf was 13 March, when the offensive halted. Winter was reluctant to relinquish its hold on Hungary; melting snow turned the primitive roads and surrounding country into a vast sticky mudhole.

The Russians had paid dearly for their impatience during many campaigns on their own soil but now they had learnt their lesson. For three days, the men of 3rd Ukrainian Front fought defensively.

At the right moment, there was a sudden switch. The Russian Ninth Guards Tank Army became a gigantic steamroller. It literally crushed Totenkopf into the mud. This massive terrifying juggernaut was catapulted into the rear of the Panzer Corps west of Lake Balaton. By 17 March 1945, the Russians were swarming all along the line.

Dietrich, ever the realist, was forced to authorise a general retreat towards the Austrian frontier.

21

Viking Division had for all intents and purposes ceased to exist; its few stragglers threw in their miserable lot with the sweepings of Totenkopf. Stuhlweissenburg had been virtually the last straw. The attempt to hold up the advance of the Soviet armies had been futile.

Totenkopf withdrew slowly towards the main highway to Vienna and Bratislava. With the division (pretentious word!) went the rump of Sixth SS-Panzer Army.

Dietrich was ordered to regroup and stand before Vienna. Furthermore, the orders stated that the city in which a vagabond Adolf Hitler had starved in his youth as a failed dauber of picture postcards was to be defended to the proverbial last man and last round.

The exhausted men of Totenkopf, ahead of them nameless horrors in defeat, rubbed their red-rimmed eyes and wondered if they had not ended up in a lunatic asylum. The propaganda machine of Joseph Goebbels was still keeping up a mood of desperate optimism. Over the radio, a breathless news-reader was telling of the vast number of new launching platforms for the secret weapons which even now would change the course of the war.

The broadcast proclaimed:

'The first radio-controlled flying bombs, Daughter of the Rhine and Fire Lily, are poised to go into action on the eastern and western front.'

Then had come the voice of Goebbels. Germany was urged to hang on a little longer. The technicians needed time to complete the construction of these miracle weapons that could defeat both Russia and America and win the war.

Meanwhile, the Russians were at Nickeldorff, dangerously near to Vienna itself.

Sixty Soviet divisions, a single enormous nightmarish hammer, forced the SS to seek refuge in the built-up area. The inevitable happened. In the resulting confusion, Himmler's knights lost touch with the Wehrmacht troops of General Hermann Balck's Sixth Army on the right flank. An angry Balck stormed to General Otto Woehler, commander of Army Group South: 'If the Leibstandarte can't hold the ground, what do you expect us to do?'

In that one spiteful outburst, Balck brought to the surface the resentment which had always existed between the Wehrmacht and the SS. It found its way to Hitler. In a towering rage, he sent the following message to Dietrich:

'The Fuehrer believes that the troops have not fought as the situation demanded and orders that the SS Divisions Adolf Hitler (Leibstandarte), Das Reich, Totenkopf and Hohenstauffen be stripped of their armbands.'

Guderian was ordered to make for the crumbling southern front and see to it personally that the order was carried out.

Guderian was no spineless lackey in the manner of Hitler's immediate colleagues, Keitel and Jodl. He stood his ground. Coldly, he told Hitler: 'I would remind you that Reichsfuehrer-SS Himmler is solely responsible for Waffen-SS disciplinary matters.'

Later, a story went around that Dietrich had announced that he would rather kill himself than obey such an order and, for good measure, had forwarded his own medals to the Fuehrer inside a chamber-pot. If he had done so, it would have been totally in character. But Dietrich, despite the appalling insult, was mindful to the last of his oath to his Fuehrer.

Even at this late stage, he behaved like a soldier. Possibly, he reasoned, Hitler had been misinformed. Calumny had been poured into the Fuehrer's ears by Woehler. Dietrich summoned his Chief of Staff Kraemer and ordered an emissary to be sent to Hitler's HQ to explain how hopeless the odds had been in Hungary. The receipt of Hitler's order caused Dietrich to throw it on the table in front of his divisional commanders and proclaim bitterly: 'That's your reward for all you've done.'

Dietrich and most of his senior officers contemptuously ignored Hitler's order. It was an understandable piece of bravado, but it made not a jot of difference. What was the point of pride now? The Waffen-SS could not even be dignified with the name of an army. These were not proud, merciless Aryans, superbly tuned technicians of war, with a mission to annihilate the Slav subhumans. The ranks were filled with the very depths: airmen who no longer had aircraft to fly or to service, seamen from ships long abandoned, combed-out factory workers who had never handled anything more lethal than a broom.

In the southern suburbs of Vienna the 2nd Ukrainian Front converged on the city from the north and front.

Marshal Malinovsky had fumed with impatience ever since the SS had grouped on the River Raub in Hungary. There, despite the glutinous mud and the roads that were little more than a rusting desert of damaged vehicles, the Germans had fought with a desperation born of the knowledge that the inevitable outcome could not be delayed much longer.

Malinovsky issued the order that everything was to be flung into the advance regardless of casualties. To go for the jugular with total ruthlessness was a way of waging war that Hitler understood, and once it had worked wonderfully for him. But too much had happened since then; too many lives had been sacrificed at Moscow, Kharkov, Kursk and, above all, in the hell that had been Stalingrad.

But the prospect of defeat in Vienna was not what finally put paid to the Waffen-SS divisions. That was brought about by the collapse of discipline and morale. An Unterscharfuehrer of 3rd Anti-tank Battalion refused to obey a simple order to go out on patrol. He was shot forthwith.

There were days of futile, sporadic skirmishes; then the surviving units of Dietrich's SS-Panzer Army withdrew from Vienna and retired round Linz. On 13 April Linz fell to the Russians; Sixth Guard Tank Army deployed west of Vienna anticipating a German counterattack.

It never came.

Hitler, incredibly, still had time for a fresh obsession. Now it was Prague. That was where the Russians would strike next; Berlin was safe for the moment. Then it became clear that the Soviets were hell-bent on reaching the capital of the Reich. The Third Panzer Army of General Hasso-Eccard von Manteuffel had been sliced in half.

No matter! It must attack again the very next day. In a sudden frenzy of tactlessness, General Burgdof, one of the Fuehrer's military advisers, suggested that the job be given to the SS.

Furthermore, Obergruppenfuehrer Felix Steiner, who had been the first commander of SS-Viking, was suggested as an ideal leader.

But the very name of the SS, once uttered as a sacred incantation, had lost all its power.

Hitler exploded: 'These SS leaders are arrogant and dull and can't make up their minds. In no circumstances will I have Steiner as commander!'

Hitler was still brooding on what he was convinced was Dietrich's treachery in Hungary. The Praetorian Guard had been dismissed for the unforgivable crime of betraying its Fuehrer.

But seemingly not quite. Hitler soon realised that he badly needed friends, inside the army or out. Generaloberst Jodl sped to Steiner's headquarters. He learnt that some one thousand Hitler Jugend and five thousand Volkssturm had been posted to Steiner's group. With opportunism born of desperation, Jodl directed that they be mobilised for the attack.

In the past, the sacrifice of a few more lives would not particularly have bothered the SS. But Steiner had no stomach left.

He told Jodl coldly: 'What you propose is sheer murder. These men are totally untrained. The Russians would slaughter them. I won't do it!'

A fierce argument developed between the two. Feldmarschall Keitel was the next to try and persuade Steiner; what had things come to when a junior officer had practically to be begged to before he would go into battle? But Steiner would not be moved. He repeated: 'It's sheer murder. I won't do it. You can do what you like with me!'

Keitel gave it up. At last it dawned on even him that the days of the SS as the unquestioned lapdogs of Adolf Hitler were long past.

22

If there was one Allied general who aroused awe and consternation in the Wehrmacht it was General George Smith Patton Jnr — 'Blood and Guts' Patton. From North Africa to Czechoslovakia this ebullient California-born convert from cavalry to armour had waged war according to a philosophy which the disciples of Theodor Eicke and his successors understood only too well.

Patton, the man who used to practise his 'war face' before the mirror, proclaimed: 'War is very simple, direct and ruthless. It takes a simple, direct and ruthless man to wage war.'

By 1945, Patton had secured a permanent niche in American military history at Bastogne, the town in the Ardennes which was the scene of an epic stand by 101st Airborne Division during 'the Battle of the Bulge'. Here

Patton had disengaged three divisions, turned them ninety degrees and sent them speeding off across icy roads to the relief within three days of Bastogne.

In that final April, Patton was a triumphant conqueror. His army had pulverised the industrial city of Kassel on west Germany's Fulda River, and went on to overrun the district of Saxe-Coburg and Gotha, cross the River Mulde to Chemnitz and sweep on beyond Nuremberg to the south.

Some 180,000 Germans surrendered to the unstoppable Third Army which, complete with three corps, romped triumphantly south-east. The 12th Corps made for Linz along the north bank of the Danube. The 20th Corps had dug in below Neumark, crossing the Danube's southern back at Regensburg. The 3rd Corps, which had been transferred from First Army, rushed south over the Danube towards Salzburg. Here was the so-called redoubt area where Hitler had dreamed of a last stand in his native Austria.

The 3rd Corps had engaged with a fanatical sprinkling of Hitler Jugend, while 12th Corps had been strongly counter-attacked when entering Austria to the north of the Danube.

Patton seethed with rage when 20th Corps was ordered to stop at certain points to await the arrival of the Russians. This was not his style at all. More attractive was the idea of launching a three-pronged offensive, with 20th Corps advancing into Czechoslovakia towards Pilsen, 5th Corps descending from the north and 12th Corps attacking from the south. Such was the stuff of dreams; Patton was forbidden to do any such thing.

Anyway, there were other preoccupations such as coming across the bodies of SS and Wehrmacht deserters dangling from trees along the roads.

With uncharacteristic meekness, Das Reich Division surrendered eventually to British 6th Armoured Division. As for Totenkopf, its end came amid scenes of almost indescribable horror. A final twist to the story of the Death's Head Division had about it the trappings of rough justice.

Heinrich Himmler had put to good use the weeks of 1938 that he spent in Austria. He had reported to Eicke that there was a huge quarry at Mauthausen from which Vienna had secured paving stones since late imperial times.

By then, Eicke had become something of an expert in his sinister speciality as concentration camp supremo. He had established a permanent camp system based on four enormous centres within the borders of the Reich. These were at Dachau, Sachsenhausen, Buchenwald and a new camp exclusively for women at Lichtenburg.

The Anschluss had created a new opportunity; obviously a major concentration camp was needed within Austria when it was incorporated in the Reich. Initially, it would hold the hordes of Austrian political prisoners scooped up by the Gestapo.

Austria could not have boasted many prettier villages than Mauthausen, nuzzling peacefully on the Danube's north bank. The quarry nearby was admittedly less pleasing; never mind, Eicke under Himmler's instructions, forthwith pressed it into service for the Third Reich.

Nazi bureaucracy was shown to be at its most efficient. In the spring of 1938, the SS firm Deutsche Erd-und Steinwerke GMbH (GEST) had been established. Its main purpose had been to set up brickworks and to exploit quarries. Large brickworks had indeed appeared; they flourished at Sachsenhausen, Flossenberg — and, latterly, at Mauthausen near Linz.

Mauthausen was envisaged not simply as a repository for racial and political inferiors; its inmates, Himmler decided, would work for the greater prosperity of the German Reich. There was the National Socialist Building Programme under the tireless Albert Speer, for example.

Besotted by his Fuehrer's vision of the transformation of the cities of Berlin, Munich, Nuremberg and Hamburg, the opportunist Speer, propelled by Himmler, conceived the idea of exploiting concentration camp labour to achieve all this.

A space on the wooded hillside was levelled and enclosed with huge sloping granite walls, on which were placed wooden guardhouses. For reasons best known to himself, Himmler was anxious that they should be faithful replicas of those guardhouses found on the Great Wall of China. Inside the walls was a rectangular camp with broad alleyways and a paved parade ground. Such a mundane description leaves out what is essential about the history of Mauthausen: the filth, overcrowding, hunger, corpses and tortures which went on there until the war's dying breath.

Here, Brigadefuehrer Richard Gluecks, Eicke's successor as concentration camp chief, was responsible overall for the movement throughout the war of SS personnel of all ranks back and forth between the Totenkopf Division and the concentration camps.

Mauthausen's role originally had been to provide a pool of forced labour to transform German cities — a role which inevitably changed under the realities of war.

By the winter of 1944, with the situation in the Reich becoming progressively more desperate, the purpose for which Mauthausen had been set up had long been forgotten.

The camp was transformed into an extermination centre, largely for 'politicals'. Survivors questioned by members of the US 11th Armoured Division gave horrific details about the methods of extermination.

In addition to starvation, gassing and shooting, countless deaths happened through exposure.

In the last December of the war, an American was given a hot shower and then placed naked on a stone wall, where he froze to death. Injections of petrol were common; the corpses of men killed this way burned more easily in the camp crematorium.

The last Commandant of Mauthausen, Frank Ziereis, who had been severely wounded in a fierce gun battle with American troops in a wood near the Spital area, revealed before his death that the camp had been garrisoned by original members of the Totenkopfverbaende, reinforced latterly with transferred Wehrmacht and Luftwaffe personnel.

The criminality of members of the guard detail of Totenkopf was indisputable. Reinhard Heydrich had ordered them personally to shoot 320 Poles. Ziereis revealed: 'The prisoners were made to walk into an empty room in which a gramophone was playing very loudly. Behind a screen was a machine gun which opened fire immediately.'

And now the reign of the Totenkopf guards at Mauthausen was coming to an end. Unknowingly, these men were about to meet other fellow SS in circumstances of which Patton's men were to take full advantage.

Tired to the point of imbecility, Hellmuth Becker, Totenkopf's last commander, had wandered purposelessly with his men between Russian and American lines, north of the Danube between Stockerau and Krems. On two occasions, the divisional commander staggered over to the Russian lines brandishing a white flag to negotiate a surrender. The second time he did not come back.

To the survivors, the message was clear. Whatever else happened, they must at all costs avoid falling into the hands of the Russians. The SS men therefore marched westwards to the demarcation line between the Russians and the Americans.

At first, the Americans refused to accept them. Then someone had an inspiration. Mauthausen was nearby. The order was given to the new prisoners: 'There are Totenkopf men among the guards. Disarm them.'

It seemed little enough to ask in the circumstances. After they had relieved their fellow Germans of their weapons, the pitiable remnants of the Death's Head élite, bereft of food and water, were kept in a lonely Austrian valley for two nights, overlooked by American Sherman tanks. They were not needed; the rump of Totenkopf Division had no stomach to move anywhere.

On the third morning, American loudspeakers announced that the Totenkopf would be moved westward to Linz.

Westwards! With rising hopes, the filthy, starving SS strode confidently under the shadow of the American tanks.

Then it happened.

The Shermans turned on them, forcing them to move smartly back to the Russian lines. Half-crazed with fear, they faced Russian officers who spoke immaculate German and told them as one man: *'Keiner von euch kommt zurueck'*. ('None of you will ever return').

Those who would never return to Germany were not just the prisoners. Arrogant and merciless fighters of Totenkopf had already reaped the whirlwind of the horror they had themselves helped so much to create. Thousands had perished in liquid mud and freezing hell of steppe and tundra. Death had meant being barbecued in the petrol blaze of a burning tank or being reduced to pulp beneath the tracks.

But not always. Death for a Totenkopf man could also come before a dawn firing-squad in a lonely prison courtyard.

The fate of thousands — indeed, hundreds of thousands — remains unsure to this day. Sometimes, though, the Russians have allowed a single chink of light to pierce the darkness.

That happened in the case of Hellmuth Becker. In the early 1950s, he was sentenced with a clutch of his comrades to twenty-five years' hard labour; he had been a member of the hated Totenkopf and that in itself had been sufficient justification for such a sentence. He was put in charge of a construction gang rebuilding shattered Russian cities.

But he had enemies among his fellow prisoners. One denounced him to the Russians for deliberately cementing an unexploded grenade into the wall of a house.

There followed a quick trial before a military court. The sentence was death before a firing-squad.

The Russians, as was their way, took their time before announcing that the sentence had been carried out. It was not until the early 1960s that Becker's widow was informed of her husband's execution.

With Becker's death confirmed, some fifteen years after the war, the bloody saga of the Death's Head Division had at last reached its end.